Popularizing the Past

Historians, Publishers, and Readers in Postwar America

NICK WITHAM

The University of Chicago Press
Chicago and London

The University of Chicago Press, Chicago 60637
The University of Chicago Press, Ltd., London
© 2023 by The University of Chicago
Published 2023
Printed in the United States of America

32 31 30 29 28 27 26 25 24 23   1 2 3 4 5

ISBN-13: 978-0-226-82697-4 (cloth)
ISBN-13: 978-0-226-82699-8 (paper)
ISBN-13: 978-0-226-82698-1 (e-book)
DOI: https://doi.org/10.7208/chicago/9780226826981.001.0001

Library of Congress Cataloging-in-Publication Data

Names: Witham, Nick, author.
Title: Popularizing the past : historians, publishers, and readers in postwar America / Nick Witham.
Description: Chicago : The University of Chicago Press, 2023. | Includes bibliographical references and index.
Identifiers: LCCN 2022045680 | ISBN 9780226826974 (cloth) | ISBN 9780226826998 (paperback) | ISBN 9780226826981 (ebook)
Subjects: LCSH: Historiography—United States. | Popular culture—United States.
Classification: LCC E175 .W58 2023 | DDC 973.07202—dc23/eng/20220928
LC record available at https://lccn.loc.gov/2022045680

♾ This paper meets the requirements of ANSI/NISO Z39.48-1992 (Permanence of Paper).

Popularizing the Past

For Lydia

Contents

What's the Matter with History?
The Problem of Popularity in Postwar
American Historical Writing

"What's the matter with history?" asked Columbia University's Allan Nevins in February 1939. In the pages of the *Saturday Review of Literature*, a popular literary magazine, he bemoaned the lack of quality history books published the previous year, as well as the state of American historical writing more generally. Nevins blamed a school of writers he termed "pedants," who were based in high-ranking universities and had done "immeasurable damage to right concepts of historical writing" by emphasizing erudition and research without thinking to address audiences beyond the academy. At the same time, he criticized authors he called "popularizers" for being "so preoccupied with the literary values of their work—with interest and color—that they are careless or even contemptuous of precision and thoroughness." For Nevins, it was vital to find a middle ground. "It must be evident to all except the blindest doctrinaires," he argued, "that the health of history depends upon keeping the median group, the writers who try to reconcile fact and art, strong at the expense of the two extremes."[1]

Four decades later, another Columbia University historian, Eric Foner, struck a similar note, declaring history a "discipline in crisis." Writing in the *New York Times* in April 1980, he suggested that his peers had "abandoned non-academic audiences to television documentaries, historical novels, and gossipy biographies," resulting in a form of popularization that betrayed a "weakness for oversimplified explanations."[2] A year later, Foner's peer Herbert Gutman took to the pages of *The Nation* to lament the "seemingly endless affliction" that beset the historical profession: scholarly obscurantism. "We know more about the past as we enter the 1980s than we did when we entered the 1960s," he argued. "And yet the past is more inaccessible to non-historians than it was thirty or fifty years ago."[3] Foner and Gutman shared an explanation for the alarming decline in college enrollments for history majors and a concurrent crunch in the academic job market. In their arguments, the growth of a range of subfields—African American history, working-class history, women's history—had not resulted in writing that would render them intelligible to general readers. As scholars delved into these important areas of inquiry, Gutman argued, "*pattern* and *context* are often ignored. The new history has failed to produce a new synthesis. And that is why its potential audience is so small."[4]

A further four decades on, Harvard historian Jill Lepore gave voice to a similar set of arguments. In November 2018, she gave an interview to the *Chronicle of Higher Education* headlined "The Academy Is Largely Itself Responsible for Its Own Peril." Lamenting the historical profession's inability to engage with the reading public, Lepore argued that "the retreat of humanists from public life has had enormous consequences for the prestige of humanistic ways of knowing and understanding the world. . . . The resources of institutions of higher learning have gone to teaching students how to engineer problems rather than speak to people." The answer to this crisis was to write history in a manner that that avoided "abstruse prose" and emphasized "storybook clarity, even and especially if you're writing about something that's complicated or morally ambiguous."[5]

These complaints were written in different historical moments and responded to different sets of literary, social, and political contexts. But they each highlight a recurring complaint among professional historians, especially those who are prominent enough to write for, or be profiled in, national newspapers and literary magazines. In essay after essay and interview after interview about the latest "crisis" in the field, well-meaning and prominent scholars sketch narratives of declension. They tell their audiences that once upon a time, American historians were capable of writing for a general audience without succumbing to vulgarization. But now, they continue, this is no longer true: the profession has succumbed to specialization and, in doing so, has ceded ground to popularizers without academic credentials and the expertise that comes with them.

However, the real story of postwar American historical writing does not conform to these narratives of declension. Accordingly, this book starts from a different set of assumptions, asking what happens if, rather than gloomily assuming crisis and failure, we go looking for stories that illustrate and explain the experiences of postwar professional historians who *did* write books for non-academic audiences? In pursuing this question, it tells the stories of five scholars who, in the fifty years after Nevins first asked his

question, wrote history that was informed by both their professional expertise *and* their literary ambitions. Richard Hofstadter, Daniel Boorstin, John
Hope Franklin, Howard Zinn, and Gerda Lerner are well known as interpret-
ers of the American past. Less well known is their role in popularizing those
interpretations by packaging them for everyday readers between the covers of
books that sold hundreds of thousands—in some cases, millions—of copies.
In doing so, each of these historians self-consciously developed identities as
writers as well as academics. They wrestled with the question of how to make
their work "popular" without sacrificing the quality and professionalism of
their insights; how, in other words, to best fuse their literary and scholarly
identities.

Despite these shared experiences, the process of popularizing the past in
postwar America was not a singular or homogeneous one. The most prominent dividing line between the five historians, and the one around which this
book is organized, was the way they conceptualized their popular readers.
For postwar historians like Hofstadter and Boorstin, the key to writing for
non-academic audiences was crafting engaging narratives that would capture
readers' attention at the same time as they provided insights into the American past. They were writing for what they imagined to be "general" readers,
seeking a subtle blend of information and entertainment. However, historians such as Franklin, Zinn, and Lerner had less literary and more political
intentions: they wanted to produce narratives that tapped into the passions
ignited by a range of postwar social upheavals, and thus write versions of the
past that would be usable by those involved in, or at least sympathetic with,
the period's protest movements. These were "activist" readers.

The division I draw between these two readerships is, in part, an arti-
ficial one. Historians who cared deeply about the literary qualities of their
writing also had political intentions, and those with an avowedly partisan
approach to the past were not indifferent to the importance of high-quality
prose. Nonetheless, and as we shall see, these labels capture two competing
conceptions of what popular history should be, how it should be promoted,
and who it was for that cropped up again and again in the interactions between postwar historians, their publishers, and readers. In ways that have yet
to be fully recognized, the American historical profession was fundamentally
shaped by its postwar encounter with the marketplace of print, and in ways
that continue to shape its relationship to the reading public today.[6]

Hofstadter, Boorstin, Franklin, Zinn, and Lerner were all born in an eight-
year period between 1914 and 1922, and their early lives were shaped by the
Great Depression and World War II. Then, after 1945, they each emerged into

professional maturity under the influence of the Cold War. As we will see, Lerner—a woman and a political refugee from central Europe—experienced these events very differently from Hofstadter and Zinn, white men from New York State, or Boorstin and Franklin, a Jew and an African American, respectively, who both grew up in Oklahoma. Nonetheless, their shared generational perspective informed their literary and scholarly sensibilities in important and interlocking ways.

The five also shared a professional identity. During or after the war, each of them earned a PhD in history and/or gained employment in history departments at major American universities.[7] Subsequently, they each went on to forge identities as popular writers by authoring single-volume or multivolume histories that synthesized large bodies of scholarship and intervened in public discussions about American national identity. These books told sweeping stories about the history of the United States, from the nation's inception (whether defined as the moment of contact between European and Indigenous people, the start of the transatlantic slave trade, or the revolutionary era) through to the time of writing. In doing so, they created a genre of historical writing that was distinct from other widely read varieties, such as military history and presidential biography. I call this genre "popular national history."

In each of their books, the five historians engaged with the long arc of American political development. They did so from different places on the political spectrum: Boorstin shifted between liberalism and conservatism over the course of his career, Franklin and Hofstadter blended liberal politics with more radical critiques of the American system, while Zinn and Lerner were famous for their outspoken opposition to the status quo and firm associations with the American Left. The contemporary questions that animated these identities ranged from the outcomes of national elections and the development of the Cold War to America's long history of racism, the social upheavals of the 1960s, and the rise of the New Right. In some cases, the stories they told were optimistic and even celebratory, while, in others, their narratives were laced with irony and pessimism. For all five, though, writing was an opportunity to draw connections between the past and the present. History and politics were thus deeply connected.

For Hofstadter and Boorstin, this meant writing from within the mainstream of professional historical interpretation, but at the same time seeking to reorient the national story to suit their own intellectual and political motivations. For Franklin and Zinn, on the other hand, the point was to fundamentally rewrite the American past from the perspectives of those left out of conventional narratives, such as African Americans and the working class. For Lerner, the goal was similar, but with a twist: to focus on the history of women's oppression and opportunities for liberation, she took world history as her canvas, thus expanding beyond the conventional scope of popular national history. However, she kept her narratives rooted in the stories she could tell *American* audiences. All five were thus "citizen-historians," who used their work to link the historical profession and the public.[8]

The personal stories of Hofstadter, Boorstin, Franklin, Zinn, and Lerner are also important because they show that writing popular history was an intensely collaborative process, one that transcended the skill and talent of any single person. This culture required not only the work of authors, but also of publishers, editors, marketing professionals, reviewers, and, ultimately, readers, all of whom were involved—directly or indirectly, consciously or unconsciously—in a significant debate about what it meant for history to be "popular." They all wanted the same finished product: history that was at once intellectually credible, engagingly readable, and politically relevant. However, this raised any number of scholarly, commercial, political, and cultural problems. Some participants—like Nevins in the 1940s, Foner and Gutman in the 1980s, and Lepore in the 2010s—doubted the ability of academic historians to succeed in this task, citing the overwhelming trend toward professional specialization. However, other scholars, publishing professionals, and readers showed faith in the idea that, given the right support and guided by the right understanding of what made for popular history, the historical profession could produce work that would inspire everyday Americans to think differently about their nation's past.

As far back as the early nineteenth century, antiquarians and writers such as George Bancroft and Francis Parkman wrote about the emergence of the American republic and its conquest of the continental United States in ways that melded romantic storytelling with commitments to impartiality and detachment, to the extent these ideals were ever attainable.[9] Writing in a period when the lines between "history" and "fiction" were considerably more blurred than they are today, they stood alongside authors such as Nathaniel Hawthorne and James Fenimore Cooper, who crafted stories that helped Americans to imagine their young nation existing in historical time and space.[10] Later in the nineteenth century, the expansion of both literacy and national networks of door-to-door booksellers gave rise to cheap and entertaining accounts of American and world history by writers such as William Cullen Bryant and John Clark Ridpath, whose books were sold in large numbers to middle-class readers and significantly expanded the reach of popular history.[11]

Alongside these developments, the late nineteenth century witnessed the growing professionalization of history as an academic discipline. A key moment came in 1884, with the establishment of the American Historical Association (AHA) and, along with it, a distinct historical *profession* in the United States. Influenced by the thinking of German historian Leopold von Ranke, who came to epitomize a "scientific" approach to historical research, scholars such as Herbert Baxter Adams and Frederick Jackson Turner thoroughly professionalized the discipline, rooting its existence in university departments and scholarly associations, as well as developing a multifaceted "historical enterprise" that drew together professional historians, archivists, librarians, and history teachers.[12]

It was in this moment of professionalization, critics such as Nevins argued, that historians started to concentrate their research in ever more narrow subdisciplines and to imagine audiences of academic peers rather than less-specialized readers. In the 1920s and 1930s, this perception prompted historical writers without professional credentials—such as James Truslow Adams and Bernard DeVoto, as well as those more solidly rooted in the profession by training, such as Charles A. Beard and Henry Steele Commager—to imagine a new melding of "fact and art."[13] The Society of American Historians (SAH) was established in 1939, which aimed to blur the boundaries between the professional and the popular, and to make high-quality historical writing accessible to the general public.[14] Parallel to these developments, a range of writers demonstrated that the effort of popularizing American history in the early twentieth century was not the sole preserve of white men. Black historians such as Carter G. Woodson and Lorenzo Johnston Greene, and women such as Mary Ritter Beard and Angie Debo, for example, all found ways to engage non-academic audiences with their writing.[15] Collectively, these important precursors laid the foundations for the postwar generation of historians.

Popular historical writing aimed at audiences beyond the academy therefore existed in the United States well before the conclusion of World War II. Nonetheless, the post-1945 period provided a set of important contexts in which the link between historians and the public became a matter of unusually intense debate. One of these contexts was provided by changes in the publishing industry. During the 1930s and 1940s, the "paperback revolution" transformed the business of books in America. Paperbacks were cheaper to print and distribute than clothbound volumes and were sold in significantly larger numbers. They were more attractive to readers, who found pocket-sized books easier to transport. Indeed, as mass distribution became the norm, Americans also found books easier to purchase, and paperbacks became available not only via specialized booksellers and mail-order catalogs, but also in drugstores, train stations, and bus terminals.[16] The period saw the rise of new nationwide distribution networks such as the Book-of-the-Month

Club, the History Book Club, and others.[17] Paperback sales and profitability therefore expanded dramatically in the postwar period: in 1947 approximately 95 million paperbacks sold for $14 million, but by 1959 these figures had risen to 286 million and $67 million, respectively.[18] In this way, the so-called "middlebrow" of American literary life came into being, prompting authors and publishers to find ways of making specialized learning digestible for non-academic readers.[19] This process allowed writers and publishers to imagine a democratization of American culture, with so-called "great books" made available to wide audiences in order to combat cultural blandness and conformity.[20] It also prompted Americans to rethink their relationship to religion, as the parameters of faith were refashioned by popular literature.[21] In these ways, the paperback fundamentally reshaped American intellectual life and opened new vistas for popular scholarship in a range of disciplines, including history.

The postwar period also marked the moment that magazine publisher Henry Luce famously termed the "American Century."[22] Ideas about the superiority of US democratic institutions circulated the globe and were promoted as part of the cultural Cold War, a state-funded propaganda campaign that involved, whether knowingly or unknowingly, hundreds of intellectuals, academics, writers, and artists.[23] Popular history developed considerable salience in this context and circulated via the books, magazines, radio programs, films, and television shows that were part and parcel of postwar culture.[24] However, while the national past was regularly molded into a form of propaganda, the Cold War also provided an opportunity for historians to reframe American history to suit a range of dissenting political perspectives. As we will see, rather than telling simplistic stories that promoted the interests of the state, Hofstadter, Boorstin, Franklin, Zinn, and Lerner all found ways of questioning Cold War ideology at the same time as they benefited from its intellectual and literary cultures.

The post-1945 moment also witnessed significant changes in the landscape of American higher education. With the establishment of the 1944 Servicemen's Readjustment Act, or GI Bill, more Americans attended university than ever before. Many of these students subsequently become the voracious yet discriminating readers to whom the postwar melding of "fact and art" most appealed.[25] Then, in the 1960s and 1970s, a second wave of university expansion took place, and paperback nonfiction was increasingly used in college classrooms to educate diverse groups of students seeking to critically reinterpret the national past through the lenses of race, gender, and their opposition to the Vietnam War.[26] Throughout the period between the 1940s and the 1990s, trade publishers and ambitious university presses commissioned books by professional historians aimed at these new communities of readers, some of which went on to have a dramatic impact on the way that American history was understood in the nation at large.

This new form of popular history intersected with the development of American mass culture. The midcentury period was one in which American publishing became "mainstream" in its attempts to derive significant profit from book selling.[27] Books therefore arrived alongside jazz music, Hollywood films, and other forms of popular culture as part of the "folklore of industrial society."[28] This process was intensely personal, and paperbacks allowed ideas and emotions to circulate in unexpected ways. They were, in this sense, a powerful new technology that reshaped a range of literary genres and led to the emergence of "pulp" literature.[29] But they also reshaped popular historical writing. As best-selling Civil War historian Bruce Catton put it in 1967, the most accomplished authors in the genre were capable of "appealing to people down inside, of stirring emotions, of creating a new understanding."[30] Catton had in mind responses to military history, but as we will see, readers of popular national histories often reacted most intensely not to heart-wrenching battle scenes, but to sharply written analysis of politics and everyday life, as well as to depictions of social and economic injustice, all of which they were able to weave into their personal narratives of American history. In this way, popular national histories not only convinced readers with the clear and coherent presentation of facts and interpretations rooted in professional scholarship, but also elicited a range of affective responses that were at once personalized and political.

While Hofstadter, Boorstin, Franklin, Zinn, and Lerner all capitalized on their talents as popularizers who could appeal to readers on an emotional level, they remained highly trained academics. In attempting to reconcile "fact and art," these historians were not alone among postwar academics. For example, David Riesman's classic of sociology, *The Lonely Crowd* (1950), bridged the divide between academic and popular writing and sold hundreds of thousands of copies, as did the work of Lionel Trilling in literary criticism, Margaret Mead in anthropology, and Hans Morgenthau in international relations.[31] Furthermore, high-profile nonfiction books such as Rachel Carson's *Silent Spring* (1962) and Betty Friedan's *The Feminine Mystique* (1963) drew heavily on advances in academic knowledge to popularize their accounts of environmental and social ills.[32] This was a moment in which a range of academic disciplines were able to successfully disseminate ideas and knowledge derived from cutting-edge research, and one in which the American public was particularly attuned to the question of what experts—whether in the sciences, social sciences, or humanities—might be able to teach them about their everyday lives.[33]

✳

What, then, did it mean for historians to write for popular audiences during the second half of the twentieth century? How did they define their readership, and what impact did this have on the politics of their work? How did non-academic readers respond to such writing? The personal papers of Hofstadter, Boorstin, Franklin, Zinn, and Lerner, as well as the archives of their publishing houses, reveal the intellectual and cultural conditions that shaped these historians as they encountered non-academic audiences through their best-selling works of history. We can thus understand *whom* professional historians thought they were writing for beyond the academy, *how* this conceptualization shaped the history they wrote, and *what* popular audiences made of their books.[34] At the same time, we can better comprehend the role of the publishing professionals who supported them, many of whom, far from playing bit parts in the story of postwar popular history, were vitally important in shaping the books they worked with authors to produce.[35]

The notion of "popularity" was centrally important to Hofstadter, Boorstin, Franklin, Zinn, and Lerner, as well as their publishers and readers. However, as they wrote, each of them had different "popular" audiences in mind. Their experiences as authors were often shaped not only by their personal biographies, but also by their relationships with a profession, an industry, and a wider society that were deeply riven by conflicts rooted in race, gender, and political affiliation. Through careful attention to their editorial correspondence, draft manuscripts, publicity material, and other documents, we can reconstruct how historians, editors, and publishers went about navigating these experiences as they defined popular audiences through the writing, editing, designing, and marketing of individual works.

At the same time, the archival record provides rich resources to show how popular historical writing mattered not only to the historians who wrote it and to the publishers who helped to produce it, but also to everyday readers. These resources include reviews and features in publications ranging from broadsheet newspapers to high school newsletters, and written correspondence from readers as varied as prominent public figures, suburban mothers, and autodidact ex-servicemen. They show that historical writing is always socially embedded, which in turn shapes our understanding of the relationship between academic communities and public audiences. Ultimately, these audiences played an important role in the development of popular history: they were not passive receptors of knowledge, but instead reworked and reimagined the meaning of the popular history with which they engaged.

I argue that popular historians like Hofstadter, Boorstin, Franklin, Zinn, and Lerner are best thought of as intellectuals who created their own publics. In writing for non-academic audiences, they did not engage with a singular "mass" audience. Indeed, throughout the second half of the twentieth century, the "public" was not a stable entity.[36] Hofstadter and Boorstin, for example, assumed that the audiences for their popular histories would be made up of primarily white, well-educated, and middle-class Americans embedded in the postwar liberal consensus. These "general" readers are the subjects of part I. On the other hand, Franklin, Zinn, and Lerner self-consciously addressed popular audiences that were engaged with struggles for equality and political change. These "activist" readers are the subjects of part II. As we will see, there were multiple and competing publics for popular history, and, at least in part, they were created by historians as they wrote about historical problems that resonated with different groups of readers.

Of course, the five historians considered here were not the only writers in the period who might be described as "popular historians." The label just as easily encompasses Arthur Schlesinger Jr. and Eric F. Goldman, both of whom made names for themselves as professional historians and public intellectuals before playing integral roles in Democratic presidential administrations.[37] We might also think of popular writers who worked outside of academia, such as Bruce Catton and Barbara Tuchman, who fundamentally shaped public understandings of American history via best-selling works on the Civil War and World War I, respectively.[38] Furthermore, a deep tradition of popular historical writing emerged over the course of the twentieth century from the African American intellectual tradition, perhaps best exemplified by W. E. B. Du Bois and Lerone Bennett Jr., whose historical insights provided inspiration to generations of activists in the Black freedom struggle.[39] Nevertheless, the individual stories of Hofstadter, Boorstin, Franklin, Zinn, and Lerner range across issues of politics, culture, race, and gender, and open vantages onto key debates about American life and its political future.

In recent years, historians have come to see the postwar period as one in which the intellectual life of the United States underwent an "age of fracture," as the ideas and metaphors used to describe society shifted from those that stressed the consolidation of a single American civilization to those that emphasized multiple and competing claims on identity and selfhood.[40] Undoubtedly, this process both influenced and is evident in the work of Hofstadter, Boorstin, Franklin, Zinn and Lerner. As mainstream understandings of America's past expanded to include the history of difference along the axes of class, race, and gender, new readerships for such histories emerged. In the 1940s and 1950s, trade publishers could imagine a single "general" readership made up of white, middle-class readers embedded in the postwar "liberal consensus," and who consequently assumed that American economic prosperity would lead to ever more common ground between liberals and conservatives, Democrats and Republicans.[41] After the 1960s, however, authors and editors sought out readers influenced by a range of new social movements on both the left and right, which tended to emphasize political conflict rather than consensus. While this may have felt like a process of "fracturing" at the time, we can see it today as a *broadening* and *diversification* of the imagined audience for popular history. Examining the ways that historians' engagement with the marketplace of print shaped these changes also expands our understanding of the modern historical profession—specifically, how it is located not only in a nexus of specialist ideas and interpretations, but how these ideas and interpretations come to inform popular understandings of the national past.

The terms "popular history" and "popular historian" are not strict antonyms for "academic history" and "academic historian." While the genre and its practitioners have sometimes been theorized as existing in a separate realm from that of the university-bound historical profession, I argue that no hard-and-fast distinction between the "academic" and the "public" can, or indeed should, be drawn.[42] In describing Hofstadter, Boorstin, Franklin, Zinn, and Lerner as "popular historians," then, I blur the boundaries between the academic and non-academic, in terms of authorial identity, writing style, marketing and publicity, and, finally, reader engagement. Nonetheless, a distinction between the "popular" and the "academic" did exist in the minds of those working to write, publish, and consume historical writing in the second half of the twentieth century. Historians wrote to each other to praise or chastise a book because of its apparent "popularity." Editors pleaded with historians to rewrite sections of their manuscripts to make them more accessible for "non-academic" readers. Marketing professionals wrote copy for advertisements emphasizing historians' abilities to transcend the "stuffiness" of their university settings. Reviewers often praised successful books in very similar terms. Finally, readers themselves wrote to authors to explain that they had succeeded in grappling with their ideas, and thus felt empowered to view their nation's history anew. In doing so, all these participants in the process of popularizing the past were cognizant of the tension between the "popular" and the "academic." Yet, at the same time, they highlighted how the everyday acts of engaging with popular national histories complicated, blurred, and perhaps even rendered that tension meaningless.

To better understand the story of popular historical writing after 1945, then, we need to traverse the histories of historical writing, publishing, reading, education, intellectual culture, and social movements. As we do so, we will see how Hofstadter, Boorstin, Franklin, Zinn, and Lerner navigated the often-dizzying upheavals of life in the postwar United States to produce new perspectives on the nation's history for everyday audiences. We will also see them participating in a dialogue about how popular readers should best be characterized: as generalists seeking an engaging and entertaining past, or as activists seeking a politically charged usable past. The fruits of this dialogue were, in part, *objects*: books published between paper covers that circulated widely and proved highly influential. But they were also *ideas* that demonstrated not only the impact of the historical profession on the world beyond the university, but also the power of popular national histories—in all their manifold complexity—to shape and reshape the meaning of the past in the American imagination.

PART I

Popular History and General Readers

Richard Hofstadter: Popular History and the Contradictions of Consensus

Richard Hofstadter was thirty-two years old when, in April 1948, he received a letter from his former doctoral adviser, Merle Curti, about the impending publication of his second book, *The American Political Tradition and the Men Who Made It*. "You have done a skillful job—and a very hard one," Curti wrote, before adding, "I predict it will be accepted as popular history in the *best* sense."[1] This description suggested Hofstadter had written a book that would appeal to audiences outside of the American historical profession. But in describing the work as popular history at its "best," Curti also implied that Hofstadter had not pandered to common sentiment about the past. Rather, *The American Political Tradition*'s unusual arguments and acerbic prose style led him to anticipate that it would challenge the assumptions of its non-academic readers. In the weeks and months that followed the book's publication, Curti's prediction was upheld, and the phrase "popular history" was used repeatedly by reviewers, who celebrated the book's combination of literary and intellectual merit.

On the surface, *The American Political Tradition* was an orthodox work of scholarship, consisting of twelve biographical chapters on specific individuals or groups of individuals already prominent in the nation's historical imagination: from the Founding Fathers, Andrew Jackson, and Abraham Lincoln to William Jennings Bryan, Woodrow Wilson, and Franklin D. Roosevelt. However, Hofstadter's arguments were far from orthodox. His central conceit, as outlined in the book's introduction, was that American history was characterized by a "common climate of . . . opinion" among its major political figures, which was based on shared values that "accepted the economic virtues of capitalist culture as necessary qualities of man." In particular, these values consisted of property rights, economic individualism, and the spirit of competition, all of which had been prioritized by the politicians, business-men, and intellectuals Hofstadter analyzed, regardless of their party affilia-tions.[2] In the decades that followed, these arguments became the bedrock for the development of "consensus" historiography, and Hofstadter was catego-rized alongside other historians who, in one way or another, stressed deep-seated lines of continuity in American historical development.

However, *The American Political Tradition* was not only a contribution to professional historiography. As Curti so presciently forecasted, it was also a "popular" history, and it would remain in print for decades, sell over a mil-lion copies, and thus highlight the public contributions that could be made by historians writing for audiences beyond the academy. The book was commis-sioned by a trade press, Alfred A. Knopf, rather than the University of Penn-sylvania Press, which had published Hofstadter's first book, *Social Darwinism in American Thought* (1944). The historian was keenly aware of the expanded audience his new publisher provided. He worked with editorial and publicity staff at Knopf to develop his writing for what was commonly referred to as a "general" audience, which consisted of educated and intelligent American citizens from across the political spectrum who appreciated the opportunity to learn from experts.

Nonetheless, Hofstadter did not intend to write bland or nationalistic his-tory. Instead, he wanted to confront his readers with a critique of American democracy. *The American Political Tradition*'s position in the postwar literary marketplace therefore highlights an element of Hofstadter's persona in which he sought to shape himself as a literary and political intellectual. Centrally concerned with writerly style, he aimed his work at non-academic readers not to convince them of the virtues of postwar politics, but instead to criticize the foundations of American democracy from the vantage point of a radical-ism that owed much to his intellectual and political formation during the Depression years.

A detailed understanding of Hofstadter's early professional life—as well as the writing, marketing, and reception of *The American Political Tradition*—is therefore an important starting point from which to plot the entangled liter-ary and political significance of postwar popular history. This is because, in using the genre to educate the public about the politics of the present as well as the past, Hofstadter demonstrated the contradictions of midcentury ideas about consensus. One contradiction was professional, the other political. At the professional level, Hofstadter's ability to benefit from publishers' and read-ers' thirst for popular historical writing was rooted in his status as a creden-tialed historian associated with an elite institution like Columbia University. And yet, so much of his own identity as a popular writer was bound up with a rejection of what he perceived as the narrowness and specialism of most historians' writing about the past. This tendency, which at times bordered on snobbishness, meant that he struggled to reconcile his scholarly and literary identities, even as he succeeded in writing searching and sophisticated prose. At the political level, popular historical writing was shaped by the anticipation that, when packaged properly, it could appeal to readers from across the political spectrum. However, as a young man writing popular history for the first time, Hofstadter wanted to champion the political values of the Left and challenge what he saw as the centuries-long dominance of an unrestrained American capitalism. Ultimately, then, *The American Political Tradition* was a politicized history written for an audience that defied political categorization. Despite the book's tremendous success, these were professional and political contradictions that Hofstadter struggled to resolve.

The young man who wrote *The American Political Tradition* was formed in important ways by the radicalism of the 1930s New York Left. Born in Buffalo, New York, in 1916, he took a degree in philosophy and history at the University of Buffalo between 1933 and 1937, during which time he met his first wife, Felice Swados, whom he married in 1936. In 1937 the couple moved to New York City, where, after a short-lived attempt to train as a lawyer, Hofstadter joined the graduate program in history at Columbia University, from which he graduated with a PhD in 1942. He moved to his first teaching post at the University of Maryland in the same year, before leaving to return to Columbia in 1946, where he would remain until his death from leukemia in 1970 at the age of fifty-four.

Unsurprisingly, given this chronology, Hofstadter developed his ideas about politics and intellectual life in a context firmly shaped by the economic, political, and social instability of the Great Depression and, subsequently, World War II. As described by his close friend Alfred Kazin in the book *On Native Grounds* (1942), the 1930s were a period in which "something happened that was more than the sum of the sufferings inflicted, the billions lost, the institutions and people uprooted: it was an education by shock." Kazin went on to highlight the specific appeal of Marxism, which nourished a generation deeply disillusioned with American capitalism. "Bolshevism had iron in it, militancy, spirit, and a Program," he wrote, concluding that "to be a Marxist writer . . . was to give one's work a new dignity and ennobling seriousness." However, Kazin was also harshly critical of what he saw as the reductionist Marxism that circulated within the Communist Party of the United States (CPUSA), animated as it was by "a headlong zeal . . . which brought energy to mediocrity and fear."[3] In this view, if the experience of the 1930s meant that many of Hofstadter's generation developed a radical political consciousness, it also rapidly disabused them of the notion that party politics, especially that represented by the CPUSA, was the answer to the problems of American democracy.

Shortly after it was published, Hofstadter praised *On Native Grounds* as "one of the best things" he had read on "the mood of the thirties."[4] Unsurprisingly, then, his approach to politics during the decade mapped closely onto the coordinates Kazin had plotted. He spent only a brief period as a member of the CPUSA between 1937 and 1938, but was, for much of the decade, a committed fellow traveler. This phase in his life represented an "extended, intensive personal experience" with Marxism that fundamentally shaped his approach to historical writing.[5] Drawn into this world while an undergraduate in Buffalo, his commitment entered a new phase upon moving to New York, an urban location in which the influence of the Russian Revolution demanded concrete positions from everyone participating in the city's intellectual life.[6]

This was also a space and time characterized by discourses about the "crisis of man," in which a litany of international political emergencies gave intellectuals and writers a sense of impending catastrophe, thus drawing the very notions of civilization and human nature into question.[7] One element in concretizing Hofstadter's radicalism in this context was the Spanish Civil War (1936–39), which Kazin described as "the last great cause" of the American Left.[8] However, almost as soon as the conflict crystallized Hofstadter's opposition to European fascism and American complicity in its rise to power, revelations about the Moscow show trials (1936–38) and, finally, the Nazi-Soviet Pact (1939), drew him away from the orbit of the CPUSA. Through the twists and turns of Soviet foreign policy, the party relentlessly justified the actions of the USSR and refused to brook any criticism among its members. It was this intransigence that offended Hofstadter's sensibilities. "I hate capitalism and everything that goes with it," he wrote to his brother-in-law, the radical novelist Harvey Swados, in 1939,

> but I also hate the simpering dogmatic religious-minded Janizaries that make up the CP. I hate their regimented thinking. I rather doubt that I would be permitted to live under any system they could set up, and I am quite sure I wouldn't enjoy it.[9]

With this, Hofstadter demonstrated what would become a characteristic refusal to toe party lines.

However, his break from the CPUSA did not represent a break with Marxism, which continued to play a role in his political thinking throughout the 1940s. Soon after leaving the party, Hofstadter was spared military service in World War II on medical grounds and relocated to teach in Maryland. There, he and Felice befriended a group of like-minded left-wing intellectuals, including historians Frank Freidel and Kenneth Stampp and sociologist C. Wright Mills. Reflecting on this period in 1972, Elizabeth Earley, who was married to Freidel during the 1940s, said, "We were all left-wing. . . . The radicalism, the anti-establishmentarianism, was so general that it never occurred to me to question whether Dick was radical. I took it for granted."[10] The spirited discussions that took place among this group were important to Hofstadter's political thinking, and during this period he started work on *The American Political Tradition*. While he was removed from New York City by geography, he thus maintained a connection to the heated debates that characterized his experience of the late 1930s.

Nonetheless, Hofstadter missed the intellectual life of the metropolis and, after returning to Columbia, wrote to Stampp in 1947 to tell him that he had felt "homeless" during his period in Maryland and that back in New York, "for the first time I am settled again."[11] He had returned to a vastly altered political landscape. In the immediate postwar period, the debates that took place among New York leftists and liberals were less likely to revolve around the internal politics of the CPUSA than of the future of American democracy. The central tenets within mainstream left-liberal thinking in the immediate postwar period centered on the desire for a charismatic president in the mold of Franklin Roosevelt, a belief that Keynesian economic policies were the only way to avoid further depression and inflation, and a conviction that US cooperation with the USSR and active participation in the United Nations were essential to postwar global stability. On each of these scores, Roosevelt's successor in the White House, Harry S. Truman, was deemed a disappointment.[12] The continuing power of these assumptions, which had been forged by the politics of the Depression era, allowed for the existence of a "powerful forum for social democratic ideas" in late 1940s US political culture, one that only disappeared after the early 1950s, as the anti-communism provoked by the rapid escalation of the Cold War took hold.[13]

Many radical and liberal intellectuals therefore welcomed the establishment in 1948 of the Progressive Party by former vice president Henry A. Wallace, who advocated what amounted to a continuation of the radicalism of the 1930s and sought to draw together a coalition of left-wing groups around a platform of "democratic revolution" in opposition to the anti-communism of the Truman administration.[14] Hofstadter, however, "was not tempted by Wallace."[15] In the aftermath of Truman's victory in November 1948, he wrote to congratulate Stampp for leaving the Progressive Party's campaign before Election Day. Stampp had switched his support to the ticket of the Socialist

Workers Party, represented by the trade unionist Farrell Dobbs, whom Hofstadter praised, but he confided to Stampp that he had preferred "our tired old friend" Norman Thomas, the Socialist Party candidate and stalwart of the American Left since the early twentieth century.[16] While he was ambivalent about party politics, it is clear that Hofstadter remained a functioning constituent in postwar debates among leftists and liberals. Furthermore, his support for Thomas as an alternative to Wallace demonstrates that he retained the radical sensibilities forged during his years in the orbit of the CPUSA.

The American Political Tradition, which had been published only two months before the election, was an intervention in these political debates, particularly those relating to the strength of presidential leadership and the significance of Keynesian political economy. Indeed, Hofstadter confirmed this in 1967, when he reflected that although the book "appeared on the eve of the 1950s, it was to a very large extent an intellectual product of the experience of the 1930s."[17] In other words, its attempt to use national history to engage with questions of political economy and the role of the federal government was shaped by the radical politics of the Depression era, which retained vital currency in the postwar public sphere.

If New York life provided an important backdrop for the formation of Hofstadter's ideas about politics, the city also shaped his understanding of literary life and the role of the public intellectual. Hofstadter took the opportunity provided by *The American Political Tradition* to model himself after the "socially responsible intellectuals" of the Progressive Era whom he had written about in his first book on social Darwinism, most notably the pragmatist philosopher John Dewey.[18] Dewey's dedication to education as an agent of social change meant that he was a hero to Hofstadter.[19] As a Columbia professor, albeit one who had retired before the young historian had arrived in New York for graduate school, Dewey set an example as a scholar able to transcend the life of the university to impact public debate on a range of topics. This was an intellectual model that inspired Hofstadter to pursue his literary and political ambitions of making US history relevant to postwar society and, more specifically, elucidating what he saw as the pitfalls of American democracy. Indeed, he made this point directly in the final paragraph of the book's introduction:

> I have no desire to add to a literature of hero worship and national self-congratulation, which is already large. It seems to me less important to estimate how great our public men have been than to analyze their historical roles. A democratic society, in any case, can more safely be overcritical than overindulgent in its attitude toward public leadership.[20]

Hofstadter thus demonstrated his desire for a popular audience, but also for the opportunity to articulate an anti-nostalgic analysis of national history that would serve a political as well as a scholarly purpose.

As well as being influenced by Dewey, Hofstadter sought to emulate another high-profile New York intellectual: Edmund Wilson. Wilson made his reputation during the 1920s and 1930s as a literary critic who embraced both modernism and Marxism, and was viewed by his contemporaries as the archetypal "free man of letters," able to write urbane and penetrating literary criticism that "kept alive the general conversation of citizens."[21] Praising him in 1942, Kazin spoke for many in his generation when he suggested that Wilson's great strength derived from his "fluid, catholic, supple mind." "In an age of fanaticisms," Kazin continued, "Wilson stood out as the quiet arbiter, the private reader of patience and wisdom whose very skill gave him public importance."[22] It was this quality that Hofstadter alluded to when he suggested that during the 1940s, he considered himself to be "much more of an essayist than a historian," before admitting, "I read a good deal of literary criticism, and a lot of the cues I've taken for my own writing come from it. . . . I think people like Edmund Wilson had much more influence on my style than any historian."[23] This period marked the start of what would become a characteristic snobbishness about the ability of most professional historians to successfully write for audiences beyond the academy.

However, this influence was not simply a literary one. As well as being a highly regarded critic, Wilson was also a keen analyst of radical political thought, having published his important intellectual history of Marxism, *To the Finland Station*, in 1940. In a short essay in 1941, entitled "Marxism at the End of the Thirties," Wilson demonstrated some of the same concerns about dogmatic interpretations of dialectical materialism that Hofstadter had expressed upon leaving the CPUSA three years earlier. He criticized the addiction of the "liberal mind" to "shifting generalities," suggested that the overthrow of the state could "never guarantee the happiness of anybody but the dictators themselves," and argued against the interpretation of "Marxist creeds" as if they were "holy writ." Nonetheless, Wilson maintained that Marxism's "technique of analyzing political phenomena in social-economic terms" remained essential to any solid understanding of history and politics.[24]

This was another lesson that Hofstadter carried into his authorship of *The American Political Tradition*. It is particularly evident in the book's chapters on John C. Calhoun and Wendell Phillips, two political outsiders Hofstadter used to discuss the nature of American democracy. In his introduction, the historian argued that while the nation's political system demonstrated a

"strong bias in favor of equalitarian democracy," it was a "democracy in cupidity rather than a democracy of fraternity."[25] In making this case, he demonstrated an ability to take a cherished theme of American history, in this
case equalitarianism, and turn it on its head. To do so, he pursued an approach to history oriented toward socioeconomic explanations of continuity
and change.

The book's chapter on Calhoun explored this theme further, describing
the slave owner, South Carolina politician, and seventh vice president as "the
Marx of the Master Class." Calhoun earned this description because in his
defense of slavery, he retained a relentless focus on the functions of class and
materialism in American politics. Hofstadter argued that Calhoun shared a
worldview with Karl Marx, albeit one that the German philosopher "elaborated and refined" in later years. However, the key difference was that while
both figures predicted "social revolution," Marx welcomed it, while Calhoun
"proposed that no revolution should be allowed to take place."[26] His strategy for the avoidance of such upheaval was a strict constitutional balance
between the North and South, in which neither would have full control.[27]
In this mindset, the commitment to a "democracy of cupidity" that united
the dominant figures in American politics was also evident in the mindset of a southerner who was committed to the profit-making institution of
slavery. While this ultimately put him on a collision course with those in
the North who believed American capitalism would expand more effectively
in the absence of slave labor, he was, nonetheless, an archetype of the American tradition.

The Boston-based attorney and abolitionist Wendell Phillips was an outsider of a very different stripe. Hofstadter argued that rather than having a
grand "philosophy of history" like Calhoun's, Phillips was motivated by a "philosophy of agitation," in which the function of the agitator was not to "make
laws or determine policy," but to "influence the public mind in the interest of
some large social transformation." His anti-slavery activism during the 1840s
and 1850s meant that when emancipation became a national issue during the
Civil War, "although he never held office, [Phillips] became one of the most
influential Americans," helping as he did to shape the policies pursued by the
Lincoln administration. In making this case, and in suggesting that Phillips
was, throughout his career, "a thorn in the side of complacency," Hofstadter
demonstrated the historical significance not only of adherence to, but also
dissent from, the dominant political tradition.[28] To be a radical, even in the
face of incredulity, was therefore an honorable pursuit, and one that was vital
to the healthy functioning of a democracy with ambitions to extend beyond
its roots in avarice.

In his analysis of Calhoun, Hofstadter established his debts to Marxist theory, while in his discussion of Phillips, he demonstrated a commitment to the idea that social action, at a remove from the traditional sphere of politics, could change the course of history. These observations had contemporary as well as historical relevance. For example, Hofstadter argued that Calhoun helped to explain the twentieth-century connections between "Northern conservatives and Southern reactionaries" better than any other historical figure, because he highlighted the power of "caste prejudice" when it was conjoined with conservative politics. It was this combination that had stunted political reform in the South, making the region a "major stronghold of American capitalism." Phillips, on the other hand, demonstrated that "the agitator is necessary to a republican commonwealth" to the extent that he highlighted the "ideas of the masses," which were more important in a "democratic age" than those of elites.[29] Indeed, Hofstadter's editor, Harold Strauss, saw the connections between the example set by Phillips in the nineteenth century and contemporary politics, and argued in the summer of 1947 that "the chapter constantly suggests a comparison between Phillips and Henry Wallace."[30] Although Hofstadter was no supporter of Wallace when he ran for the presidency in 1948, his praise for Phillips as an agitator, alongside his critique of Calhoun as a racial capitalist, demonstrates the clear and immediate political relevance of his prose.

Hofstadter's conceptualization of himself as a literary and political intellectual influenced by New York radicalism thus took on two interconnected valences. First, it stood for integrating a radical—and, where appropriate, Marxist—political viewpoint into its retelling of the nation's past. Second, it meant introducing the literary tropes of irony and tragedy as key themes in *The American Political Tradition*, to stress the persistent gap between the rhetoric of liberty and justice advanced by key historical actors and the turbulent realities of American inequality. Hofstadter reinforced this perspective toward the end of his career, when he suggested that good historical writing necessitated an awareness of "defeat and failure: it tends to deny that high sense of expectation, that hope of ultimate triumph that sustains good combatants."[31] By integrating these themes into the series of biographical sketches that make up *The American Political Tradition*, and by focusing on canonical figures with which most readers would already be familiar, Hofstadter forged a version of popular history that maintained a critical stance toward the past while addressing an audience whose ideas he sought to fundamentally disrupt.

In December 1945, Stanley Pargellis, the head of the Newberry Library in Chicago, took to the pages of the city's *Sun* newspaper to lament the state of contemporary historical writing:

> For fifty years university specialists have been writing for one another, vaguely
> hoping that their books will be read outside the narrow family circle, but de-
> riving their real satisfaction from the thought that if 20 men in the country
> know enough . . . to understand a weighty book on a subject, its author has
> done his duty and has justified the 10 years of work and study he put on it. . . .
> The men who can write American history fit to match the achievements of the
> American people can be counted on one's two hands.[32]

Pargellis's anxiety about academics turning their backs on the reading public
by writing for one another, and consequently doing an injustice to the subject
matter of US history, was a widespread one. Arthur Schlesinger Jr., for example, who was a peer of Hofstadter's in the generation of historians coming
of age at midcentury, had written to his editor at Little, Brown & Co. five years
earlier: "The two essentials of good history . . . are sound interpretation and
writing colorful enough to reproduce a sense of the emotions and feelings
of the period. Ordinarily you get one without the other."[33] Schlesinger was
writing to pitch the book that would become the Pulitzer Prize–winning *The
Age of Jackson* (1945) and was playing up to the prejudice that the majority of
"academic" historians were bad at writing, while the majority of "popular"
historians simply rehashed national myths to no intellectual avail. In doing
so, he implied that there was a niche in the market for histories that ably combined both popularity and complexity.

This was a strain of thinking that Hofstadter was keenly aware of as he
wrote *The American Political Tradition*. In reviewing Schlesinger's book for
the *New Republic*, for example, he argued that a considerable proportion of
"widely praised and widely read" historical writing was actually "second-rate
or downright shoddy," and that it was therefore "a pleasure to report on a book
like this and find oneself part of a general chorus of approval."[34] Indeed, Hofstadter's desire to write for publications such as the *New Republic* was part
of an active mission to shape his New York literary persona and to develop
a more popular style of writing. This is demonstrated in a letter he wrote to
Kazin soon after the review was published, in which he suggested: "I am very
much concerned to develop a popular medium. I am tired of academic writing
and thinking. (Hence the essential lightness and even triviality of my current
project.)"[35] The "current project" was *The American Political Tradition*, which
had been in gestation since early 1944, and it is particularly illuminating that,
at such an early stage, Hofstadter conceived of the book as an opportunity to
widen the scope of his readership beyond the confines of the academy.

The primary financial impetus for this effort came from a fellowship
awarded to the historian by Knopf in 1945. The purpose of the award was to
encourage exactly the type of projects in history, biography, and science that

staff at the house thought the literary world lacked. As the advertisement for the award in 1945 made clear, "It is the nature of the fellowships . . . made available as they are by a general publisher, that they can be awarded only to projects containing the promise of trustworthy scholarship combined with literary distinction of the kind that means some breadth of appeal."[36] In line with these expectations, Hofstadter's application to complete his work on the manuscript was described by an anonymous referee as "the outstanding submission for our history fellowship."[37] However, he was forced to split the $5,000 award with another scholar, primarily because their benefactors could not be convinced that the collection of biographical sketches for which Hofstadter had applied for funding would prove a best seller. The award of the fellowship was the first indication of the potential of the manuscript, but the project's initial reception by its readers at Knopf also highlighted that he had much writing to do to make it a work of history that would resonate beyond the academy.

As Hofstadter's draft chapters arrived at the publishing house, excitement grew about the text's potential. However, the manuscript still did not have the coherence Hofstadter's editor, Harold Strauss, demanded. He therefore suggested that the historian write an introduction to tie the chapters together. In an internal memo, the editor explained his thinking: "H. must ask himself 'what in brief am I trying to say'—and then re-examine his own material in light of whether it advances or detracts from the central point he is trying to make."[38] It was this type of coherence, Strauss felt, which would aid the book's sales by providing a sense of narrative.[39] Hofstadter agreed and described the introduction as "a kind of public relations exercise which will arouse interest and be of some use when promoting the book."[40] Even if the introduction to *The American Political Tradition* was "only an afterthought," then, a few months before publication, editor and author were in accord: it was vitally important, both as a means of reaching out to a readership beyond the Ivory Tower and of highlighting the book's status as both a popular and sophisticated contribution to US historical writing.[41]

Perhaps because of the totemic significance placed on the book's introduction by all involved, Hofstadter found it very difficult to compose. He complained to Stampp in the summer of 1947 that he had been forced to write at least four drafts, all of which had met with disapproval from the team at Knopf.[42] At least one of Strauss's objections was that Hofstadter had reverted from the bracing prose style of the book's constituent chapters and was churning out "methodological statements that are of no interest to anyone save your fellow scholars."[43] This was a damning indictment for a historian who desperately wanted to avoid being tarnished by negative comparison to his professional peers, and Hofstadter committed himself to ruthless editing. Nonetheless, there are some revealing passages in the drafts rejected by Strauss that help to flesh out how Hofstadter conceived of the main goals of the book. "In each of these essays I have concentrated on a few dominant ideas . . . mindful that brief studies must be done with few strokes," he wrote, before continuing:

> My method has less in common with the glossy, painstaking portraiture in official commissioned portraits than with caricature, but I have tried to re-member that the successful caricaturist stresses traits that are conspicuous in the subject and that good caricature is always instantly recognizable.[44]

The idea of Hofstadter as a "caricaturist" goes some way to bridging the gap between his scholarly and literary identities. He was invested in the process of using academic understanding drawn from a synthesis of extant histori-cal scholarship and combining it with caustic, sometimes humorous insight drawn from popular literary criticism and journalism. This combination ex-plains the praise heaped on *The American Political Tradition*'s prose style after it was published. It also shows the importance of Hofstadter's idea of him-self as a writer centrally focused on blurring the literary boundaries between scholarly and popular writing.

Hofstadter's approach to his subject matter was particularly evident in *The American Political Tradition*'s chapter on Abraham Lincoln. The histo-rian suggested that the most accurate way to view the nation's sixteenth presi-dent, whose reputation had become shrouded in myth in the years since his assassination in 1865, was through the lens of the widely held American ideol-ogy of "self-help." Hofstadter's chapter charted the Illinois politician's route to political power during the 1840s and 1850s, and argued that Lincoln's desire to "make something of himself through his own honest efforts" demonstrated that he was driven by intense personal ambition and was, therefore, "typically American." Even by the time he was presiding over the Union in the Civil War, Lincoln was dedicated to using the power of the government to develop a "system of social life that gave the common man a chance." This meant that while he was "politically on the radical or 'popular' side of the fight," he was ultimately "historically conservative" because he aimed to "preserve a long-established order that had well served the common man in the past." Lincoln's signature of the Emancipation Proclamation in 1863 made this es-pecially apparent. Its text, from Hofstadter's perspective in the late 1940s, had "a wretched tone," because it emphasized freeing enslaved people not because of their humanity, but because it made political and military sense to do so.[45] Rather than being a semi-mythical "Great Emancipator," then, Lincoln stood as an ordinary, if very successful, politician.

In presenting these arguments, Hofstadter wove a narrative of Lincoln's career that, on the one hand, highlighted the "high tragedy" of American politics but, on the other, also demonstrated the inherently conservative nature of the president's approach to politics.[46] Lincoln's tragedy was thus rooted in the fact that his relentless ambition to succeed went unfulfilled. Even in the aftermath of the Union's victory in the Civil War,

> he could see the truth of what he had long dimly known and perhaps hopefully suppressed—that for a man of sensitivity and compassion to exercise great powers in a time of crisis is a grim and agonizing thing. Instead of glory, he once said, he had found only "ashes and blood."[47]

This passage demonstrates Hofstadter's powerful prose style, as well as his eye for historical irony. The Lincoln presented in *The American Political Tradition* was a tragic figure who deserved his place in the pantheon of American history, but whose actions could not go without criticism, and whose mythology needed to be dismantled. In the mold of the caricaturist, then, Hofstadter had drawn on familiar elements of the president's legacy but subordinated them to his critical interpretation of the ideological homogeneity at the heart of US democracy.

Hofstadter worked hard to develop the prose style on display in *The American Political Tradition*. He reflected on this in a letter to Alfred Kazin:

> One thing that's very important: don't class me with the *genus historicus*. I suppose you're right that they look down their noses at *genus literarius*, but I am really a suppressed litterateur who couldn't make the grade just writing good prose and had to go into history. Unlike my brethren I look up to writers, and I'm fearfully afraid of them, all of them, from competent journalists to literary critics.[48]

As this quotation suggests, Hofstadter thought literary style was the key dividing line between a successful popular historian and the *"genus historicus."* Indeed, he developed the theme further three years after the publication of *The American Political Tradition* in an essay written for *The Progressive* magazine, in which he reflected on the fiction of F. Scott Fitzgerald. It is evident how much Hofstadter admired the novelist's elegant writing:

> He could see, because he felt it so keenly, what was human and wistful beneath the surface of competitive snobbery and extravagance; and when his lustrous prose caught some shimmering event in a shimmering phrase, one could see themes and characters that ordinarily do not rise above claptrap being endowed with a sweeping symbolic importance.[49]

The ideas expressed here about the difference between surface and depth, as well as of restoring symbolic importance to already familiar characters, chime with Hofstadter's self-conscious attempts to hone his style in *The American Political Tradition*. What he saw in Fitzgerald was exactly what he wanted to achieve in his own writing. This observation needs to be understood alongside the debates about the public function of historical writing in which *The American Political Tradition* intervened, the way the book was commissioned by Knopf, and Hofstadter's attempt to complicate the historical reputation of well-known figures such as Abraham Lincoln. Taken together, these elements of the book's authorship demonstrate how, in both its conception and execution, Hofstadter fruitfully used the idea of "popular" writing not to appeal to what he viewed as the lowest common denominator in contemporary culture, but to emulate his literary heroes while educating the American public.

Midcentury debates about the way academics should reach out to audiences beyond the university were by no means confined to the historical profession. The literary critic Lionel Trilling, for example, was also serious about making complex ideas accessible to general readers. *The Liberal Imagination* (1950) exemplifies this aspect of Trilling's criticism: published two years after *The American Political Tradition*, it collected a series of essays that had originally appeared in niche periodicals during the 1940s, all of which criticized the relationship that developed between American literary criticism and radical politics before and during World War II. Trilling described the job of the critic as "to recall liberalism to its first essential imagination of variousness and possibility, which implies the awareness of complexity and difficulty."[50] This message, he wrote to his editor in 1949, was intended for "the general reader, not for the literature student alone," with the goal of "addressing a crisis in our culture which requires bold and careful thought about our cultural beliefs."[51] Trilling's goal was therefore aligned with Hofstadter's, albeit with different subject matter: he wanted to replace in the public mind what he saw as simplistic interpretations of American literature with those of more complexity and nuance.

To this extent, he was very successful, with the book quickly selling over 100,000 copies.[52] However, Trilling ultimately succeeded in using *The Liberal Imagination* to announce himself as a public intellectual not only because of its impressive range and felicitous prose style, but also because of the way the book emerged into the literary market place as "one of the first serious paperbacks" aimed at "cultivated middle-class" audiences who "enjoyed as well as respected intellect."[53] Marketing, publicity, and the emergence of the paperback therefore played a key role in the success of Trilling's book.

A similar context shaped the publication of *The American Political Tradition*. Hofstadter and his publishers shared a common conception of the type of people who made up a general audience, and the book's ability to appeal to them was the topic of much discussion. For example, after the New York University scholar Thomas C. Cochran had read a draft of the chapter on Andrew Jackson, which he praised, he also offered the opinion that Hofstadter was wasting his "first rate talent" writing for the "intelligent lay reader," and by packaging his ideas in "the never-failing human-interest form."[54] While Cochran was skeptical of the value of engaging with non-academic audiences, the journalist Matthew Josephson proved more encouraging. Describing the book as "fresh and realistic," he told Hofstadter that his writing was "imbued with the critical spirit of an educated adult, which is ever so rare in this field."[55] Josephson and Cochran thus positioned the "general" reader as one benefiting from both intelligence and education. These ill-defined but important concepts implied that the audiences for popular history were firmly rooted in the middlebrow of American culture.

For his part, Hofstadter agreed. In a letter to Howard K. Beale, he told the University of Wisconsin historian that his readers were most likely to occupy the space "somewhere in between . . . the common American . . . and sober historians." He went on to mention that his arguments about Theodore Roosevelt were aimed at "liberal readers" who might doubt the twenty-sixth president's sincerity in his opposition to plutocracy while in the White House.[56] In this commentary, Hofstadter reinforced the idea propagated by so many other mid-century historians that "general" readers were interested in nonfiction that sat somewhere between vulgarity and scholarship. However, his mention of a "liberal" readership also imbued this imagined audience with a political identity: it was his goal, much like that of Lionel Trilling, to speak truth to the liberal mind.

The staff at Knopf also knew that it was important to harness Hofstadter's politicized understanding of his authorial role for it to work productively. For example, the anonymous reviewer of Hofstadter's application to the Knopf Fellowship warned that his arguments were unorthodox and that they had the potential to "outrage many people."[57] A similar opinion led Roger Shugg, an editor in the company's College Department, to criticize Hofstadter's "jaundiced" view of American politics, which he worried could "alienate many readers." In this interpretation, it was not so much the book's content that needed to be amended, but its tone: "The author should review and perhaps reconsider the severity of his strictures. . . . And throughout [he] must be less the arm-chair general in criticizing the inevitable compromises of political battles."[58] Establishing balance between criticism and praise of his venerable subjects was essential if Hofstadter's book was to appeal to readers who—in spite of being educated, intelligent, and political—were not ready to have their assumptions about American democracy upended all at once.

These discussions of "general" readers clarify an important point about the developing idiom of postwar popular history. Historians and publishers converged on an understanding of their ideal non-academic reader that assumed intelligence and political engagement. Although it was never explicitly mentioned, these readers were clearly coded as white, affluent, and educated. Hofstadter and his publishers were thus part of the intellectual and cultural elite formed by scholars, journalists, and publishers who developed a "shared language of consensus" during the period between the 1930s and 1950s. In trying to reach out to readers defined by their nonpolitical status as constituents of a "general" audience, they helped to develop a style that reached across the ideological divide between Left and Right, and, in doing so, masked fundamental political disagreements.[59] In one sense, Hofstadter accepted this definition of who his readers were. However, his radicalism meant that he chafed against it. Ultimately, Hofstadter wanted to appeal to audiences beyond the academy, but in a way that made them feel uncomfortable about the political realities that surrounded them.

This became even more clear in the months leading up to *The American Political Tradition*'s August 1948 release, as attention at Knopf turned to its promotion and how it could best be marketed. The first major question centered on the manuscript's title. Hofstadter had originally proposed "Men and Ideas in American Politics." However, Strauss felt that to have extensive salability, the book needed to tap into a public attitude of "very considerable nostalgia."[60] This led him to propose "Eminent Americans and the Growth of Political Traditions," which met resistance from the author:

> I have a very serious objection to the subtitle *and the growth of political traditions*. My book does not demonstrate any particular growth—indeed, if anything it suggests a relative absence of real growth in the American Political Tradition. Changes, permutations, combinations, yes—but almost no growth to speak of. Shrinkage would be more to the point.[61]

The response of the publishing house to Hofstadter's objections is represented in an outline table of contents prepared several months later, which gave the book the title "Eminent Americans and the Shape of Political Traditions: Great Men and Great Ideas in the American Past."[62] Nonetheless, the author remained displeased by his editor's attempt to aggrandize the book's contents, objecting to the repeated use of the word "great," which he described as "a violation of the spirit of the book."[63] In making these points, Hofstadter demonstrated that he had no interest in compromising the complexity of his historical message by having his book publicized as a contribution to national mythology.

The American Political Tradition's final title was reached by Strauss and Hofstadter over lunch in late March 1948, several months after the debate had started.[64] If, from a publicity standpoint, it is possible to understand the editor's attempts to use the title to magnify the book's status, it is also easy to sympathize with the author's reluctance to allow commercial interests to overstate the claims being made for his scholarship. However, what these dogged attempts by Strauss to get Hofstadter to reconsider the book's title also highlight is how its precise position within the literary marketplace would impact its status as popular history. While the historian seemed to be more concerned with the ideas contained *within* the pages of the manuscript, his editor recognized that its title would structure the meaning and importance of the text in the minds of its readers.

After *The American Political Tradition* was published, Hofstadter demonstrated that he was well attuned to this important literary process. The book received some positive early reviews, and the author was keen to make sure that they were used as publicity. Going over his editor's head by writing to Alfred A. Knopf himself, Hofstadter criticized the publicity strategy followed by the house:

> What concerns me is that nothing has been done in the way of advertising to acquaint the potential audience of the book with the composite estimate of its critics. . . . You do not hit the front page of the *Times* every other week, especially with a non-fiction item, nor do you often get quite such reviews from responsible critics.[65]

Hofstadter's negative analysis of the publisher's publicity strategy once again demonstrates his desire to reach an audience beyond the historical profession. In another letter to Knopf, the historian made this point even more explicitly, by citing the example of a review in the *Cleveland News*, which he thought might be of "special value" because it described the book as "clearly and simply for the enjoyment of the general reader."[66] Hofstadter therefore estimated that his corner of the literary market was located firmly in the space between a specialized academic audience and a mass readership.

In line with this estimation, *The American Political Tradition* was selected as a dividend by the History Book Club (HBC).[67] Established in 1947 by the writer and journalist Bernard DeVoto, the club brought a group of prominent historians together to select books for its members that would prove entertaining, but that would also link the past directly to the present. Arthur Schlesinger Jr. was one of the professional scholars brought on board by DeVoto, and the pair shared the belief that historical writing should be as accessible as possible.[68] The HBC therefore tapped into, and attempted to address, the widespread anxiety among intellectuals of the period about the function of American historical writing and its accessibility to a wide range of audiences. Again, though, the HBC was not interested in publicizing history that was merely popular: all the key figures involved shared a commitment to liberal politics and were only interested in the type of books that would confront "growing corporate power and the resurgence of conservatism" in postwar America.[69]

Sales networks of this type worked to delineate the parameters of popular taste, defining the "general reader" as a "rejection and critique of some other reader, presumably a reader not general but focused, professional, technical and specialized."[70] *The American Political Tradition*'s place within this literary nexus was cemented when, in 1954, it was one of the first books issued as a part of Knopf's nonfiction paperback imprint, Vintage Books. Vintage did not aim at a "mass" readership: instead, it was a literary institution dedicated to mediating between popularity and complexity. As Jason Epstein, the founder of Anchor Books, an outgrowth of Doubleday and a direct competitor to Vintage, suggested in 1974, "When Anchor Books and Vintage began they tried to occupy some ground which was free at the time; that is, they . . . were trying to reach a much smaller and more specific audience, mainly academic, literary—specialized in these and other ways."[71] As a consequence, the books published by Anchor and Vintage became known as "egghead paperbacks."[72]

A 1954 article in *Newsweek* noted the prominence of this literary phenomenon, arguing that the books' popularity derived from "the lightening spread of popular education, and with it the striking rise in public tastes. Drugstore book racks, once the undisputed home of Mickey Spillane, now also shelter the paper-bound works of Plato, Shakespeare, Freud, and St. Augustine."[73] Within this context, *The American Political Tradition* was an ideal candidate for a Vintage edition, and its publication as a paperback dramatically increased its sales.[74] In 1969 Hofstadter was able to write to his then-editor at Knopf, Ashbel Green, that "after fifteen years of paperback publication, *The American Political Tradition* is within striking range of its 1,000,000th copy."[75] Two years after the historian's death, Green wrote to his widow, Beatrice Hofstadter, to report the annual sales figures for all of his books published by Knopf. *The American Political Tradition* had outstripped his other titles by a significant magnitude, selling 49,259 copies in 1971 and 46,116 in 1972.[76] The public impact of Hofstadter's book, along with its status as popular history, is therefore unimaginable without the opportunities provided by the paperback revolution, and the position of Vintage Books within it.

In his 1960 essay "Masscult and Midcult," New York intellectual Dwight Macdonald criticized what he viewed as the increasing commoditization of American culture in the postwar period. In his view, publishers had adopted "a new subjective approach in which the question is not how good the work is but how popular it will be." Accordingly, he argued, books were treated as commodities and judged purely on "audience-response."[77] Macdonald believed this process of commoditization (present in music, film, and art as well as literature) had created not only a form of "masscult" that actively parodied high culture, but also a more pernicious form of "midcult," which sought to make difficult ideas and concepts salable to as wide an audience as possible. Ultimately, for Macdonald, this created the "agreeable ooze of the Midcult swamp," in which readers were never challenged by popular authors.[78]

Hofstadter and his publishers credited middlebrow readers with more intelligence than Macdonald, and therefore developed an alternative version of engagement with a large public audience. *The American Political Tradition* was a constituent part of the cultural process identified in "Masscult and Midcult," and the book was actively promoted as a work of popular history, offered as a dividend by a national book club, and continued to sell tens of thousands of paperback copies years after its publication date. However, in popularizing his scholarship, Hofstadter did not pander to nationalistic sentiment about America's past. Instead, he insisted that the critical tone of his writing be emphasized in Knopf's publicity for the book. Hofstadter also insisted that the middlebrow audiences at which he aimed his work be taken seriously. They were intelligent, responsible, and ready for a nuanced approach to the American past. *The American Political Tradition* therefore undercuts the idea that middlebrow nonfiction was unable to articulate complex and critical analyses of US society. The book was at once a part of, and resistant to, the midcentury consensus highlighted by Hofstadter and his publisher's preoccupation with courting a "general" readership.

Where Hofstadter did mimic Macdonald's condescension, however, was in the way he set himself fundamentally apart from the historical profession. In arguing that he represented the *"genus literarius"* rather than the *"genus historicus,"* he created an intellectual identity for himself that centered on his supposed superiority as a writer and thinker when compared to his peers in the academy. At the same time as he demonstrated the ability of historians to appeal to trade audiences, then, he also discredited his fellow scholars in a manner that reinforced the arguments of those, such as Allan Nevins, who had been suggesting since the late 1930s that writers who blurred the boundary between the academic and the popular were somehow exceptional, and not representative of any broader potential for the discipline to shape popular ideas about the past.

The intellectuals, journalists, and scholars who reviewed *The American Political Tradition* upon its publication in August 1948 also played a significant role in defining its place within the postwar popular historical imagination. Several reviewers were impressed by the way *The American Political Tradition* fused credible scholarship with writerly panache and were at pains to emphasize its accessibility. The *New York Times*, for example, "heartily recommended" it as required reading in a presidential election year, praising Hofstadter's fusion of erudition and readability.[79] The *Newark News* told its readers that "Hofstadter's tour of American history is one of the most amusing and instructive ever made."[80] The *Cleveland News* concurred, reporting that the book was "written clearly and simply for the enjoyment of the general reader and with many a well-turned phrase," while the reviewer for the *Los Angeles Examiner* described it as "a literary flight into the political stratosphere that anyone can take without an oxygen mask."[81] All of these outlets were at pains to stress to their readers that while Hofstadter dealt with complex political ideas and concepts, he did so in a way that would draw the engaged reader into the fold, rather than overload them with abstraction.

What is more, and in a way that must have delighted staff at Knopf, multiple readers emphasized not only the accessibility of *The American Political Tradition*, but also its uniqueness as a popular history. In the political magazine *Commentary*, Oscar Handlin described the book as "popular history at its best."[82] Daniel Aaron, reviewing it for the academic journal *American Quarterly*, concurred: "*The American Political Tradition* is a good example of popular writing in the best sense—learned and readable, dispassionate and critical."[83] These repeated invocations of Hofstadter's work as the "best" form of popular history echoed Merle Curti's prediction earlier in 1947 and implied that the young historian's book was *better* than a range of other, albeit unnamed, popular historical works. Indeed, this was a sentiment that had been foreshadowed in a letter written by Matthew Josephson to Hofstadter after reading the manuscript in May 1948: "It is literally years since I've read anything this 'grownup' on the subject of our political traditions. . . . Everywhere I see only James Truslow Adamses all around me."[84] Adams was a writer best known for popularizing the concept of the "American Dream" in his 1931 book *The Epic of America*, and, in making this comparison, Josephson suggested that Hofstadter had avoided such a disavowal of historical complexity.

Reviewers for the literary periodicals the *Yale Review* and the *Antioch Review* also grappled with the intellectual and political implications of the book's position within the genre of popular history. For example, Fred V. Cahill wrote:

> Whether one believes in celebrating the past or seeks to disprove an accepted belief in its relevance, it is clearly a function of scholarship to make the traditions of a society available to those ultimately responsible for its welfare. In a society based upon popular choice, as we like to suppose ours to be, this imposes certain obligations upon historical writing and has resulted in the increasingly recurrent phenomenon of the "popular history." Mr. Hofstadter's book is an excellent example. It deserves and will undoubtedly achieve a wide audience.[85]

Cahill thereby set the genre of popular history within the contexts of both American democracy and the politics of capitalist consumption: if the nation's politicians were to be held to account by its citizenry, historians would have a significant role to play by offering their readers, who were also consumers, the opportunity to purchase their work and therefore engage with the nation's political traditions.

Louis Filler made a similar connection by comparing Hofstadter's work to Schlesinger's *The Age of Jackson*, which, he suggested, had benefited from literary institutions such as the Book Find Club and had therefore received "a striking amount of popular appreciation." The critic went on to suggest that the prime source of the reputation of Schlesinger's book was the manner in which he had "read a kind of Franklin D. Roosevelt into Andrew Jackson, and in so doing warmed the cockles of many a liberal heart." Filler clearly preferred Hofstadter's more cynical portrait of the seventh president as "a representative of 'liberal capitalist' tendencies, rather than a thinker or humanitarian."[86] In making this point, he argued that a debunking spirit was vital to the manner in which *The American Political Tradition* used the popular historical form to make a political intervention. This was also the case with his portrait of Abraham Lincoln:

> Apparently, he feels that too intense a concern with the "great" Lincoln, as opposed to the Lincoln whom his contemporaries knew, would result in losing the real Lincoln—a Lincoln who could be recognized by reasonable people and studied for light on our own times as well as his.[87]

In making this point, Filler drew his readers' attention to the public significance of popular history: the book would help them to understand their nation's past, and therefore to make informed decisions about contemporary political issues.

Contemporaneous reviews of *The American Political Tradition* were also sensitive to the critical tone of its account of national history. The conservative *New York Herald Tribune*, for example, suggested that rather than providing readers with "an easy chair at the national pageant," Hofstadter took them "firmly by the hand . . . down the long trail to active investigation."[88] Similarly, but from a radically different position on the political spectrum, the CPUSA's newspaper, *The Daily Worker*, drew a comparison between Hofstadter's analysis and its Stalinist worldview:

> Neither a naïve believer in, nor a cynical peddler of, the hokum which passes conventionally as American history, the author of *The American Political Tradition* has kept his eye—and his pen—on the basic social and economic issues which agitated the U.S. on the road to its present status as the world's great capitalist power.[89]

This view was backed up by Hofstadter's academic peers. In the *Mississippi Valley Historical Review*, for example, C. Vann Woodward suggested that in certain hands, arguments for unity of purpose among American politicians could have contributed to "the literature of nationalism and complacency." However, Hofstadter's book was "severe, analytical, and unsparing," a tone with which Woodward was quite comfortable.[90] In each of these reviews, Hofstadter's historical arguments were understood by midcentury readers to have avoided celebrations of the American political tradition and to have offered a rendering of the nation's past in complex yet readable terms.

This is even clearer when we consider the relationship between *The American Political Tradition* and the 1948 election. The politics of the Depression era and their significance in the immediate postwar period loomed large in *The American Political Tradition*'s account of American historical development. The final two chapters of the book covered the competing social and political visions of Herbert Hoover and Franklin D. Roosevelt, connecting them to the individualist tradition that Hofstadter argued was so central to American political life. In this analysis, "the things Hoover believed in—efficiency, enterprise, opportunity, individualism, substantial laissez faire, personal success, material welfare—were all in the dominant American tradition." However, while "in the language of Jefferson and Lincoln, these ideas had been both fresh and invigorating; in the language of Hoover they seemed stale and oppressive." Hoover's failure in the face of the economic crisis brought on by the crash of 1929 therefore signaled the bankruptcy of the American political tradition Hofstadter had so carefully and iconoclastically traced: it was unable to win popular support because "the people had no ear for spokesmen of the old faith."[91]

Roosevelt was spared such a withering treatment, but Hofstadter was nonetheless keen to highlight the contradictions of his presidential administrations. He was, at heart, a patrician who had been reared on "a social and economic philosophy rather similar to Hoover's."[92] By implementing the New

Deal, he demonstrated that he was able to transcend the temperament of his upper-class background in order to become "an individual sounding-board for the grievances and remedies of the nation," which he tried to weave into a program that would correct the problems caused by an unwavering faith in laissez-faire capitalism. However, in Hofstadter's analysis, Roosevelt's policies were by no means coherent, and he wavered between prioritizing the interests of big business and implementing an approach that would emphasize channeling the fruits of future prosperity into a program of "distributive justice."[93] As such, if Hoover functioned as the villain of Hofstadter's narrative, Roosevelt was by no means its hero:

> There are ample texts in his writings for men of good will to feed upon; but it would be fatal to rest content with his belief in personal benevolence, personal arrangements, the sufficiency of good intentions and month-to-month improvisation, without trying to achieve a more inclusive and systematic conception of what is happening in the world.[94]

Hofstadter's suggestion that the Depression led the American electorate to become tired of Hoover's stale rhetoric, and his argument that Roosevelt's view of American capitalism, while in some dimensions progressive, was not "systematic" enough, both demonstrate the influence of the ideas of postwar radicalism in his work. This was recognized and amplified by reviewers and critics of the book. Writing in *The Nation*, Perry Miller suggested that *The American Political Tradition* was "an index of its times," in that it found contemporary American liberalism "rudderless and demoralized" and was therefore an implicit rejection of the Democratic Party and its presidential candidate Harry Truman.[95] This sense of political relevance was not restricted to reviews written in the buildup to the 1948 election. Soon after Truman's inauguration, the *William and Mary Quarterly*'s reviewer Arthur Mann suggested that the book "decries the 'national nostalgia' and urges that we adopt a new ideology of centralized planning for modern corporate America."[96] In these readings, *The American Political Tradition* represented a radical attempt to shake the kaleidoscope of modern American history and, in so doing, rethink the tradition of left-wing political thinking in the nation.

The position of an "egghead" intellectual such as Hofstadter within postwar American culture was a paradoxical one. Eggheads were celebrated for their intellectual superiority, but at the same time deemed "repellent" and "transgressive" because of the ways their arguments and identities chipped away at established political, racial, and gender norms.[97] In light of this observation, what is most revealing about the reception of *The American Political Tradition* is that it was celebrated precisely *because* of its transgression of national historical pieties. The book was understood as a critical intervention from the left of the political spectrum, and by no means a celebration of American values. The numerous positive reviews it received therefore highlight how it functioned in its late 1940s context as a critique of individualism, charting the intellectual lineage of this idea in the political thinking of influential historical figures, as well as the downturn of its popular fortunes during the 1930s.

In this sense, *The American Political Tradition* very effectively used historical writing as a form of political critique. The response to the book's version of popular history in the national and local press, as well as in academic journals and literary periodicals, also highlights the continuing relevance of questions concerning political economy and the limitations of contemporary capitalism in postwar American historical writing. Hofstadter's style may have appeared to his readers as clear, provocative, and inherently "popular," then, but he was also centrally concerned with the development of American democracy in the aftermath of World War II and keen to press for a more radical view of politics than that provided by the contemporary Democratic Party.

In the decades that followed the publication of *The American Political Tradition*, one intellectual who continued to interpret the book in this way was the radical historian Howard Zinn. Although roughly the same age as Hofstadter, Zinn was firmly embedded in the generational sensibilities of the 1960s. Shaped by the Black freedom struggle and the anti–Vietnam War movement, he articulated a highly partisan, left-wing version of popular American history. In doing so, he took significant inspiration from Hofstadter's book. Writing in 1970, Zinn contrasted its bracing style with what he described as the "monstrous irrelevancy" of most historical writing, arguing that its author's "deflation of liberal heroes" had a clear public and political relevance not only for audiences in the late 1940s, but also for the New Left as they battled against a "liberal consensus" in the historical profession that did not allow individual scholars to write seriously about themes such as protest and dissent.[98]

Zinn's praise of Hofstadter continued in his landmark 1980 book *A People's History of the United States*, a synthetic account of the nation's past written from "the bottom up." In the first edition of the book, for example, Zinn positively cited *The American Political Tradition*'s essays on Abraham Lincoln and Woodrow Wilson, among others.[99] Then, in the second edition, published in 1995, Zinn used Hofstadter's arguments to frame his brand-new discussion of American politics during the Carter, Reagan, and Bush presidencies:

> Halfway through the twentieth century, the historian Richard Hofstadter, in his book *The American Political Tradition*, examined our important national lead-

ers, from Jefferson and Jackson to Herbert Hoover and the two Roosevelts—
Republicans and Democrats, liberals and conservatives. . . . Coming to the end
of the twentieth century, observing its last twenty-five years, we have seen exactly that limited vision Hofstadter talked about—a capitalistic encouragement
of enormous fortunes alongside desperate poverty, a nationalistic acceptance of
war and preparations for war. Governmental power swung from Republicans
to Democrats and back again, but neither party showed itself capable of going
beyond that vision.[100]

In Zinn's hands, Hofstadter's arguments about the existence of ideological
homogeneity in American politics retained their relevance five decades after
their first appearance and provided a way of framing a critical understanding of the nation's past in a manner that would be digestible for a popular
audience.

Despite this, during the 1960s and 1970s, Hofstadter was not without his
critics in the New Left, many of whom grouped him together with a range of
other "consensus" historians whose arguments for fundamental unity at the
heart of American history were offered in the spirit of celebration rather than
criticism. John Higham initiated this attack in two widely cited essays. The
first, written for *Commentary* magazine in 1959, used Hofstadter to exemplify a "strikingly conservative" vein in contemporary historical writing that
rendered the nation's past "placid" and "unexciting."[101] Following up in the
American Historical Review in 1962, Higham cited Hofstadter—along with
Daniel Boorstin, Louis Hartz, and David Potter—when he voiced further
objection to the work of consensus historians: in searching for "uniformity,"
"stability" and an all-encompassing "national character" in American history,
he argued, they evidenced a trend of historical explanation that was wedded
to the goals of the Cold War state, in that it sought to demonstrate the superiority of the American system of government to that of the Soviet Union.[102]

This was a critique that was shared by other young left-wing historians. In
1960 Norman Pollack cited *The American Political Tradition* when he described
consensus history as being "established on an *ahistorical* basis."[103] Writing for
the New Left journal *Studies on the Left* in 1965, Aileen Kraditor used Hofstadter's chapter on Phillips, along with writing on the abolitionists by David
Donald and Arthur Schlesinger Jr., to argue that these historians all demonstrated "contempt for reform movements in general."[104] Furthermore, in his
collection *Towards a New Past*, which attempted to bring together the views of
a range of New Left historians, Barton Bernstein argued that his generation's
most fundamental target was the type of "narrow framework" offered by Hofstadter, "in which even the dissenters usually accepted the fundamental tenets

of the liberal tradition."[105] This new generation of dissenting historians took a dim view of Hofstadter and *The American Political Tradition*.

The reasons were multivalent. At the political level, by the late 1960s Hofstadter had made himself an enemy of the New Left, having opposed the widely reported protests that took place on the Columbia campus in 1968, and then playing a key role in defeating the 1970 attempt to elect an anti-war candidate to the presidency of the AHA.[106] But at the intellectual level, the situation was more complex. The New Left historians wanted to read and write history that explained their experiences of protest. Unsurprisingly, they framed their opposition to Hofstadter in these terms. Pollack rejected the "equilibrium framework" proposed by the consensus historians because it could not explain the existence of protest.[107] Kraditor, similarly, yearned for historical studies that provided insight into the "efficacy" of the tactics adopted by protest movements, while Bernstein denied what he saw as the consensus historians' view of dissent as rooted in "irrationality." Overall, Hofstadter's scholarship "reflected the needs and values of the fifties" to the extent that it rejected radical political change to appeal to a broad, nonpartisan readership.[108] This critique rejected the idea that *The American Political Tradition* was a radical attempt to disrupt popular understandings of the national past. Indeed, it has shaped a common and persistent understanding of Hofstadter as an archetypal "consensus" historian. This has meant that the most prominent debate in the scholarly literature on Hofstadter has revolved around the accuracy of describing him in such a way.[109]

The entwined literary and political problematics addressed by *The American Political Tradition* have therefore gone overlooked: first, Hofstadter's self-conscious attempt to author popular history, reach out to audiences beyond the academy, and engage with what has come to be understood as the "middlebrow" of American culture; second, his desire to criticize the predominant climate of nostalgia regarding the national past and to replace this with a more complex rendering of its key political figures that would speak to the specific debates taking place between American radicals and liberals in the late 1940s. Hofstadter *was* a consensus historian, but *The American Political Tradition* demonstrates that he was no cheerleader for the political culture of individualism and laissez-faire that he described. As he reflected in 1968, to suggest that consensus history was intrinsically celebratory was to "assume that the consensus idea is . . . a *prescriptive* one which commits us to this or that particular arrangement."[110] In Hofstadter's mind, at least, this was decidedly not the case. Instead, his ideas about the ideological consensus at the heart of American history were shaped by an instinctive political radicalism that he had developed since his youth, one that drew him to critique rather than celebrate ideological conformity.

When he died in 1970, Richard Hofstadter was hard at work on a three-volume "political history of the American people" aimed at a "general readership." Knopf's faith in the project was such that the historian was paid an advance of $270,000, with the first volume appearing posthumously in 1971 as *America at 1750: A Social Portrait*.[111] In the final years of his life, the desire to write a synthesis of American history accessible to those outside of the academy was once again central to Hofstadter's understanding of his scholarly vocation. Furthermore, three decades after he had first written for a popular audience, Hofstadter maintained the definition of a "general" readership that he had developed in the 1940s: it was made up of "the educated public that reads and makes intellectual use of sophisticated history."[112]

This commitment to writing for an elite, educated audience was a theme picked up by Alfred Kazin in an obituary published in the *American Scholar*, in which the historian's friend wrote lyrically about their shared passion for literature:

> The special pleasure I always took in reading Dick was in his polemics, his gift for criticism, his intellectual irony, his passion for giveaway quotations, his marshalling of historical argument as a form of literature. He cared as much about literature as any writer I have known, knew it intimately and lovingly, and he responded to other people's writing with the same feeling for literary effect that he sought in his own.[113]

In making this case, Kazin argued that Hofstadter had contributed to American intellectual life not only through his capacity as a historian, but also through his capacity as a writer. In this understanding, "popular" writing was not something he did in his spare time, or that was divorced from his professional ambitions. It was, instead, the very essence of his intellectual persona, and one that he felt set him apart from other historians.

Three strands tie together the overall significance of *The American Political Tradition*, not only in the development of Hofstadter's understanding of the public function of his work, but also in the broader history of postwar popular historical writing. The first is his self-conscious location within the New York world of literary intellectuals writing for nonprofessional audiences. He modeled himself on scholars such as John Dewey, critics such as Edmund Wilson, and novelists such as F. Scott Fitzgerald. However, the process of learning to write in a stylish, popular idiom was a fundamentally collaborative one, in which Hofstadter's friends and mentors played a vital role. Even more important was the role played by his publisher. Indeed, the book would not have been as accessible and lucid as it was without the material support and editorial guidance provided by staff at Knopf.

The second strand is the context provided by the emergence of the American "middlebrow," which transformed both the world of publishing and the consumption habits of readers. It was this culture that provided Hofstadter, as well as a range of other professional scholars working at midcentury, with an audience outside of colleges and universities. Access to these readers was amplified by significant coverage of intelligent nonfiction in national and local newspapers, as well as widely read literary periodicals. Furthermore, the rise of the paperback, and the subsequent publication of *The American Political Tradition* under the auspices of Knopf's Vintage imprint, meant that the book was accessible to an even wider range of audiences. Ultimately, this context catapulted the book, as well as its author, into the literary spotlight.

The third strand centers on Hofstadter's connections with the radical politics of his generation. Throughout the period in which he was writing *The American Political Tradition*, the historian was strongly influenced by Marxism. This meant that Hofstadter harnessed popular historical writing not to celebrate the most prominent figures in the nation's history, but to criticize their unrelenting commitment to the furtherance of capitalism. He courted controversy by skewering Abraham Lincoln, by arguing that Herbert Hoover and Franklin D. Roosevelt shared a common ideology, and by using the examples of John C. Calhoun and Wendell Phillips to understand modern racism and political activism. In doing all of this, he demonstrated his desire to use popular historical writing to intervene in contemporary political debates on behalf of radical social change.

In writing *The American Political Tradition*, Richard Hofstadter therefore found himself caught in the contradictions of consensus imposed on him by both his position in the literary marketplace and his highly charged political ideas. He participated in, and was shaped by, the process in which postwar writers and publishers imagined a "general" audience to exist among readers whose education and intelligence rendered their political differences inconsequential. But, at the same time, he wanted to amplify these political differences, and to prioritize the values of the Left at the expense of those of the Right. That he is more often remembered as an archetype of the midcentury consensus, rather than a relentless critic of it, demonstrates the challenges he faced in writing history that was at once popular and radical.

Not all postwar historians found these contradictions so difficult to navigate. If the stories they wanted to tell general readers about the nation's past

were celebratory and less laced with irony and paradox, then the genre of popular national history was more easily adaptable to their goals. They could meld
their ideas and values with those most predominant in the Cold War public
sphere by highlighting the dynamism of American capitalism, the industrial
and technological achievements engendered by continental expansion, and the
uniqueness of the nation's democratic system, all the while downplaying questions of conquest, violence, and inequality. If they so wished, they could even
integrate these themes into a decidedly conservative perspective on the past,
one that would intersect with the growing postwar intellectual movement on
the right and, eventually, the political resurgence of the Republican Party. The
most prominent of these historians was Daniel Boorstin, and in framing his
ideas for popular audiences, he saw Hofstadter's example not as one to emulate,
but as one to reject.

Daniel Boorstin: Popular History between Liberalism and Conservatism

On December 29, 1960, the University of Chicago historian Daniel J. Boorstin addressed the annual meeting of the American Historical Association (AHA) in the Grand Ballroom of the Statler Hilton Hotel, New York City. Speaking on a panel entitled "Where Is American Historiography Going?" he criticized his colleagues' postwar turn toward the social sciences, which, he argued, had "nearly incapacitated many of our professional historians from helping to relieve our historical malaise."[1] To illustrate the point, Boorstin offered the example of Richard Hofstadter and his 1955 Pulitzer Prize–winning book *The Age of Reform*:

> [Hofstadter's] past is less a stage than a laboratory. There he tests images. Although his account is not entirely lacking in dramatic interest, the focus of his interest is on—and whatever suspense there is in his story comes from—the recurrence of the fixed and credible images concocted by social scientists.[2]

This was an intervention in a debate about the entanglement of cutting-edge scholarship and literary style. In evoking concepts such as "dramatic interest" and "suspense," Boorstin contended that many of his peers, including Hofstadter, had sacrificed readability for a jargon-laden rigor that could never appeal to nonspecialist audiences.

Hofstadter left his reply until 1968, when, in the final chapter of his book *The Progressive Historians*, he chose to emphasize the differences between his interpretation of American history and Boorstin's. By this point, the two historians shared comparable public profiles rooted in their attempts to engage audiences beyond the academy. What is more, they were often lumped together as part of the so-called "consensus school." However, Hofstadter wanted any comparison to end there. While endorsing Boorstin's "exceptional gift for discerning . . . a distinctive American style," he expressed anxiety about his peer's "entertaining" prose, which, he felt, offered nothing in the way of substantive arguments about American political development.[3] In private, Hofstadter was more scathing, telling the British historian Jack Pole, "I can't stand Boorstin's smug nationalism and his anti-intellectualism."[4] In framing the disagreement in these terms, Hofstadter was *not* claiming that all popular history was intellectually untrustworthy. As we have seen, his professional identity was instead bound up with his ambition to be a "litterateur" who could speak directly and engagingly to nonprofessional readers. Instead, Hofstadter's disagreement with Boorstin was based on a critique of a particular type of popular history, one that he felt emphasized entertainment over ideas, simplicity over complexity.

In contrast, Boorstin embraced the idea of the historian as entertainer. This conviction was rooted in what he described in the first part of his popular three-volume trilogy, *The Americans* (1958–73), as the core identity of "American men of letters" in the eighteenth century. These men were not "literati." Instead, they were "clergymen, physicians, printers, lawyers, farmers." This made for a "peculiarly American emphasis on relevance, utility, 'reader-interest,' and catholicity of appeal." Ultimately, the archetypal American writer was "not the artist but the publicist."[5] This account of practical, entertaining prose devoid of literary pretensions was one he had in mind as he crafted his own identity as a writer working against the grain of his discipline. While Hofstadter and Boorstin were both remarkably popular historians, then, they were at odds about what made for high-quality popular history.

Unlike Hofstadter's *The American Political Tradition*, all three volumes of Boorstin's *The Americans* were framed as celebrations of the national past, rather than critiques of it. The books were strongly influenced by Boorstin's postwar political thought, in which he moved between the politics of liberalism and conservatism, gradually shifting from left to right on the political spectrum as the decades went by, but never quite encapsulating either label in a pure or simple way. At the same time, his ideas intersected both the relationship between Depression-era communism and Cold War anti-communism, as well as debates about Jewish identity and its place in American life. He pioneered the study of the nation's social and technological achievements, while ironing out, or simply ignoring, much of the conflict and violence that had characterized its past. This, along with the books' focus on stories that would entertain middle-class Americans, made them ideal fare for suburban audiences.

Boorstin was thus a more conservative political thinker than Hofstadter. Indeed, his vision of national exceptionalism proved popular not only with non-academic readers, but also with right-wing intellectuals in the latter decades of the twentieth century, who saw in it a historical framing for their

opposition to American liberalism. For Boorstin, there were fewer contradictions than there were for Hofstadter between the form and the politics
of popular history. In his view, entertaining "general" readers went together
with informing them, and thus creating a robust political culture that could
withstand the pressures placed on it by the postwar expansion of the liberal
state and the social upheavals of the 1960s, developments in national life that
Boorstin looked on with anxiety. Such a culture emphasized rugged individualism, the "go-getting spirit," and what Boorstin called "a new democratic
world." This was democracy defined not in terms of political participation,
as Hofstadter had done, but in terms of economic consumption. In the "new
democracy of consumers" that emerged in America after the Civil War, he explained, "it was assumed that any man might be a buyer."[6]

In successfully making this case to hundreds of thousands of readers,
Boorstin wove his books into the fabric of postwar mass culture. They existed
alongside, at the same time as they helped to explain, phenomena as diverse
as new highways, suburban settlements, shopping centers, advertising, and
the rise of television.[7] By writing popular history against this cultural and
commercial backdrop, Boorstin inspired conservative readers, who put his
ideas to use as they went in search of a "usable past" that would suit their
views of modern politics in an increasingly polarized climate.

If the political and literary contexts that informed Hofstadter's popular historical writing were firmly rooted in a single city—New York—Boorstin's
were more peripatetic. Born in 1914 in Atlanta, Georgia, shortly before his family moved to Tulsa, Oklahoma, where he grew up, Boorstin was an academic
prodigy. At sixteen years old, he commenced undergraduate studies at Harvard University, where he majored in history and literature, served as an editor of the university's student newspaper the *Crimson*, and graduated in 1934.
He subsequently won a Rhodes Scholarship to study law in England, before
returning to the United States in 1938 to complete a JSD at Yale University,
graduating in 1940.

Boorstin's experience of World War II and the immediate postwar years
was a restless one. He married Ruth Frankel in 1941, before qualifying for the
Massachusetts bar and serving briefly as an attorney in the Lend-Lease administration. Despite his preparation for a career in law, Boorstin harbored
an ambition to be an academic: during his time studying law at Yale, he had
also served as an instructor in history and literature at Harvard. This ambition was satisfied in 1942, when he was hired by Swarthmore College to teach
history and then, two years later, to undertake the same role at the University
of Chicago. There he remained for twenty-five years, until he was appointed

director of the National Museum of History and Technology at the Smithsonian Institution in Washington, DC, in 1969. After six years at the Smithsonian, Boorstin's career culminated in 1975 with his nomination by the administration of President Gerald Ford to serve as Librarian of Congress, a role he undertook until his retirement in 1987.[8]

As well as traversing geographical space—ranging from the South to the Great Plains, New England to the Midwest, and ending in the nation's capital— Boorstin also blurred several professional boundaries over the course of his life. While his doctorate and vocational qualifications were in law rather than history, he nonetheless established himself as a prominent historian in one of the nation's leading university departments. However, by the time he was appointed Librarian of Congress, a moment that highlighted his newfound status as a prominent administrator and political appointee, he still regarded himself as an "amateur" historian, a profile he reveled in.[9] Indeed, throughout his career, Boorstin happily pushed back against what he saw as the historical profession's conventions and norms, thus prizing his identity as a popular author who used his expertise to communicate with "general" readers. In 1975 he drew specific attention to this status in the lengthy US Senate hearings that preceded his appointment to the Library of Congress. Asked by the Senate Committee on Rules and Administration whether he would stop publishing books to focus exclusively on the role, he answered, "I will not say I will give up writing. . . . All my life I have been a writer and I would not ever want to set myself the objective of giving that up."[10]

If Boorstin self-identified as any one thing throughout his career, then, it was not as a lawyer, a historian, or an administrator, but as a *writer*. This impacted his understanding of what it meant to be a popular historian, which, in turn, shaped his relationship with the publishing professionals who supported him in that endeavor, and the readers who encountered and engaged with his prose. To better understand this identity, we need to turn to three overlapping contexts that framed Boorstin's popular histories against the backdrop of Cold War American life: the politics of anti-communism, the specter of comparison between the United States and Europe, and the historian's Jewish identity. Each of these contexts demonstrates why, although they both identified primarily as writers rather than professional historians, Boorstin and Hofstadter differed so fundamentally in the historical and political perspectives they offered their readers.

Like Hofstadter, Boorstin spent a short period in the late 1930s as a member of the CPUSA. While studying in England in 1936 and 1937, he participated in a Marxist study group and, at the same time, had minor involvement in Labour Party electoral campaigns. Then, upon his return to America, he joined the CPUSA while serving as an instructor at Harvard. This association lasted less than twelve months, and in September 1939, along with many other Jewish radicals, he severed ties with the party and renounced his communist identity in response to the Nazi-Soviet Pact.[11] However, unlike Hofstadter, Boorstin spoke very publicly about his experiences in the party and, in doing so, embraced the politics of Cold War anti-communism. In February 1953, at the height of the early Cold War red scare, he testified to the House Un-American Activities Committee (HUAC) about his left-wing youth. In the context of the Cold War, he explained that he now helped further the goals of HUAC in two ways: first, via "affirmative participation in religious activities," which he saw as a "bulwark against communism," and second, via his "teaching and writing," in which, he claimed, he upheld "the unique virtues of American democracy."[12]

However, as it was expressed in his writings during the 1950s, Boorstin's anti-communist thought was more complex than this account implies, and his friendly testimony should not be read as wholehearted endorsement of the repressive politics of the red scare. In the same year that he appeared before the committee, he also published a short book entitled *The Genius of American Politics*. It offered an overview of American history, arguing that the idea of "givenness" was rooted in the nation's status as an "exemplar of the continuity of history and of the fruits which have come from cultivating institutions suited to a time and place, in continuity with the past." For Boorstin, history showed that American politics was therefore non-ideological: the nation simply had "no philosophy" that could be exported to the rest of the world.[13]

This was an account of the past rooted in the political exigencies of anti-communism, but it also contained a veiled criticism of McCarthyism. In the book's final chapter, which attempted to diagnose the nation's "cultural hypochondria," Boorstin argued against what he termed "modern abolitionists" who fought the Cold War using aggressive and confrontational rhetoric:

> Soviet communism provides them the sense of "givenness," of obviousness in their objective. For them, Communists embody the spirit of Satan as vividly as the American Indians did for the first Puritans, or as the southern slaveowners did for fire-eaters like Phillips and Garrison. Some of them would seem almost as willing as Garrison to burn the Constitution in order to attain their admirable objective. There are others who take a more Lincolnian view. Like Lincoln, these people hate slavery anywhere, but they doubt their capacity to make a perfect world. Their main concern is to preserve and improve free institutions where they now exist.[14]

This reversed the judgment of Hofstadter's *The American Political Tradition*, which had skewered the popular memory of Lincoln as the "Great Emancipator," at the same time as it argued that an outsider like Wendell Phillips deserved admiration. Instead, Boorstin highlighted Lincoln's status as an archetypal American pragmatist, while critiquing the ideology of abolitionism. In making this point alongside his HUAC testimony, he demonstrated that while he used American history to inform his interpretation of anti-communism, he was no simple advocate of political repression.

One explanation of this complexity is rooted in Boorstin's anxieties about American liberalism. It is important to remember that the anti-communist political culture of the 1940s and 1950s was more "liberal" than it was "conservative," to the extent that it was liberals within the Democratic Party, trade unions, and other political organizations that had most to gain from the marginalization of communists in national life.[15] Understood in this context, Boorstin's opposition to "abolitionist" anti-communism is best conceptualized as a critique of a particular strain of "crusading liberalism" that would remain consistent throughout his career.[16] As he argued in an essay published in 1956: "To tell ourselves that perpetual peace would be in sight if 'communism' were only conquered . . . expresses and reinforces an oversimplified antithesis." These liberal ideas were based on a dramatic "misconception" that needed to be rooted out from discourses of American power, both at home and abroad.[17]

In making this case, Boorstin owed a considerable debt to the Christian theologian and public intellectual Reinhold Niebuhr, who was a key reference point in his 1950s writings. Boorstin was influenced by Niebuhr's Cold War critique not only of Soviet communism and its international offshoots, but also of those American liberals who, he argued, denied the doctrine of original sin by trying to rationalize and perfect the economic and political life of the nation. This was an abiding theme of Niebuhr's postwar thought, powerfully expressed in books such as *The Children of Light and the Children of Darkness* (1944) and *The Irony of American History* (1952). In the latter, Niebuhr attacked the approach of America's so-called "wise men," who, he argued, could not come to terms with "the limits of all human striving, the fragmentariness of all human wisdom, the precariousness of all human configurations of power, and the mixture of good and evil in all human virtue."[18] It was exactly this ambivalence about the limits of human perfectibility that Boorstin channeled in the final words of *The Genius of American Politics*: "We must refuse to become crusaders for liberalism, in order to remain liberals. . . . We must refuse to become crusaders for conservatism, in order to conserve the institutions and the genius which have made America great."[19] In positioning himself between liberal and conservative thought in such a way, Boorstin evidenced a mistrust of political ideology that was shaped by his early Cold War experiences and would remain an important theme in his historical thinking.

Another factor in Boorstin's thought was the specter of comparison between European and American history. Molded by numerous visits to Europe, this was a hallmark that shaped his sense of America as a fundamentally postcolonial nation-state.[20] Boorstin's first book written for a trade press, *The Lost World of Thomas Jefferson* (1948), framed the "Jeffersonian tradition" as the nation's "principal check on the demands of irresponsible power."[21] In this argument, everything that was laudable in Jefferson's thought was rooted in its distinctive Americanness, which led Boorstin to frame the contemporary relevance of his arguments for readers more familiar with the Cold War than the early national period:

> Leon Trotsky has observed that Russian history was decisively affected by the fact that Russia skipped over the "stages" of Protestantism and capitalist democracy. . . . But America was the scene of a still more remarkable abbreviation: settlers on this continent transplanted the institutions and techniques of modern Europe to a landscape that had never even experienced the Middle Ages. The American mind, outdoing Russian precocity, skipped at least two thousand years of the calendar of western social geography.[22]

In this argument, the key to understanding American history lay in its distinctiveness, which needed to be understood before comparisons to Europe were dispensed with.

This was a theme Boorstin returned to in a 1955 review of Louis Hartz's book *The Liberal Tradition in America*, an important touchstone of so-called "consensus" thinking about the national past. He used the essay, published in *Commentary* magazine, to return to the idea that systematic comparison between European and American traditions of thought was not a productive lens through which to view national history. Boorstin accused Hartz of "confining his thinking about America in a prison of European comparisons," before concluding that "this is all like describing a horse by saying it is an animal that lacks the trunk of the elephant, has not the neck of the giraffe, and also cannot jump like a kangaroo." This was a tongue-in-cheek critique of Hartz's writing style: because of his comparative framework, Boorstin argued, the book was "a monument of hyper-intellectualism," its author representing "the current 'liberal' tradition, which seems unable to avert its gaze from the library long enough to discover the characteristic processes and virtues of American life."[23]

Understood against this backdrop, volume 1 of *The Americans*, which Boorstin was working on as he wrote the review, is best understood as an attempt to provide both an intellectual and a literary alternative to Hartz. The book sought to show how "dreams made in Europe . . . were dissipated or transformed by the American reality" in the seventeenth and eighteenth centuries, a process that rendered the lives of those living in the "New World" as an entirely "new civilization."[24] Boorstin explained this most clearly in the book's chapter on the development of American thought, in which he argued that practical knowledge was more important than abstract theory in the process by which everyday settlers developed a "popular epistemology" rooted in the "philosophy of the unexpected." This, he argued, "was not a system of a few great American Thinkers, but the mood of Americans thinking."[25]

In "looking up from the library" for long enough to engage popular readers in a way that he thought would keep their attention, Boorstin told them that one of the key lessons of the colonial period was the nation's practicality, once again framed as an entirely different spirit to that which characterized European history. This argument was a kind of propaganda seeking to "define democracy" in the United States in the manner that was characteristic of the radio shows, films, and publications circulated by American intelligence agencies during the early Cold War.[26] Indeed, Boorstin skillfully tapped into this broader culture, and it shaped the book's success in the literary marketplace.

Nonetheless, the historian's writing was not pure propaganda. In 1954, for example, he had contributed to a series called "Democracy and Its Discontents" published in the Cold War magazine *Encounter*. The piece proposed a "pluralist" point of view on the relationship between America and Europe and, in doing so, again cited Niebuhr as a key exemplar of this new perspective, along with other midcentury public intellectuals such as Walter Lippmann and George Kennan. These thinkers, Boorstin argued, were "less uniform and less dogmatic" than their counterparts:

> They start neither with a rigid demand to preserve a particular set of economic arrangements, nor with any predilection for the methods of European domestic politics. They are not alarmed by new expedients, nor do they automatically prefer them. They simply warn us against being obsessed either by our uniqueness or by the perils to it. The great enemy of nations, they say, is illusion. Satisfied by moderate objectives, they unashamedly plead for defense of the national interest.[27]

In this view, exceptionalism was a form of knowledge that would help Americans "understand ourselves," rather than one that would underpin a crusading form of policymaking in the name of the Cold War.

These arguments help us to understand Boorstin's motivations as he started to write popular history in the mid- to late 1950s. That they appeared

in *Encounter*, a transatlantic magazine, highlights their author's cosmopoli-
tanism, as well as his links to the cultural Cold War. But they also show the
complexity of his intellectual context and the way it blurred the boundaries
between liberal and conservative political ideas. Intellectuals like Boorstin
were disaffected from radicalism after their movement away from communism, but this did not mean that they unequivocally supported the Cold War.[28]
Again, then, Boorstin's ambivalence toward contemporary American politics
was intertwined with his confidence that the nation's past had instructive,
affirmative lessons to teach his readers. But at this stage in his career, it was
not clear whether these lessons would be primarily liberal or conservative in
their political tone.

This intellectual and political liminality is even better illuminated when
viewed through the lens of Boorstin's Jewishness. His rise to prominence as a
public intellectual and popular historian took place against the backdrop of the
de-Christianization of American life.[29] A significant factor in this process was
the rise to prominence of "free-thinking" Jewish social scientists such as Daniel
Bell and David Riesman, whose popular works allowed them to speak authori-
tatively to educated Americans. These thinkers were not Jewish parochialists.
Instead, their ethnic and religious identities were shaped by their public status
against the backdrop of the ethnic transformation of American universities.[30]
This was also a period defined by a set of debates about the significance of
"Judeo-Christian culture," in which intellectuals of various faiths raised questions of religious pluralism and secularization and debated their significance
for American life and politics.[31] By the middle of the twentieth century, then,
Jews were a fundamental part of the nation's intellectual scene, but in a way that
left much about their specific contributions to political debate unsettled.

Boorstin was fundamentally shaped by these developments. Reflecting on
his biography in a 1957 letter, for example, he told an enthusiastic reader of
The Genius of American Politics, "I am, of course, Jewish. . . . But my own
Jewish education has been meagre." His grandparents had been Orthodox
Jews and immigrants to the United States from Poland in the 1890s, and his
parents were Reformed Jews who were proud members of their local syna-
gogue and Anti-Defamation League, but who did not regularly participate in
the activities of these institutions. Nonetheless, by 1957 he had "become more
interested in all things Jewish" and had even taken up the study of Hebrew.[32]

Boorstin's self-conscious identity as a free-thinking Jew thus shaped his
intellectual trajectory in the years before he published *The Americans*. In the
mid-1940s, the historian was involved in a joint project with other University of Chicago academics, in which they debated what the historian came
to characterize as "the moral mission of the intellectual Jew." This mission

was based on the lessons that had been learned by left-wing Jewish thinkers before and during World War II, as they "abandoned the Marxism of the
1930s" and, swiftly after that, "discovered that liberalism did not yet provide a
self-sustaining philosophy." In rejecting both political traditions, "the young
Jewish intellectual discovered the saving fact that he was Jewish."[33] While this
essay was never published, it fed into Boorstin's observations two years later,
in an essay for *Commentary*, that Jewish thinkers like himself experienced a
kind of double identity in relation to American life:

> Some of the differences between the American and the Jewish historical ex-
> periences are general distinctions between secular and religious cultures. But
> if this is true the Jew living in America is all the better qualified to throw
> into sharp relief another striking feature of American life—its insistent secu-
> larity. . . . This is, of course, not to say that American Jews are any the less
> American because they are Jews, but that if they would accept their double
> inheritance, they must also accept the burden of an inner tension. In America
> of all places, they cannot refuse to be Double-men.[34]

These arguments, which echoed W. E. B. Du Bois's 1903 articulation of African
American "double consciousness,"[35] demonstrated how significantly Boorstin's
persona as a public intellectual was shaped by a conscious set of ideas about
the relationship between his identities as an American and as a Jew.

Similar ideas shaped his interpretation of American history. Again, this
was partly rooted in the circumstances of his biography. Shortly after Boorstin's birth, his family was forced to leave Atlanta and move to Tulsa because
of the participation of his father, who was a lawyer, in the criminal defense of
Leo Frank, a young Jewish man convicted in 1913 of the murder of thirteen-
year-old Mary Phagan and lynched two years later after having his death sentence commuted. The Frank case was a major controversy in Atlanta because
of the way it raised questions about the city's racial and sexual hierarchies.
A bastion of the industrial and economic dynamism of the early twentieth-
century "New South," Atlanta proved a popular destination for many upwardly mobile Jews, who perceived it as an urban space in which they were
more likely to benefit from the privileges of whiteness than in the North.[36]

This assumption of Jewish whiteness was exploded by the Frank case,
which unleashed a wave of "reactionary populism" rooted in a range of sexual
and racial anxieties, including deep-seated anti-Semitism.[37] All of the lawyers
who served on Frank's defense team received death threats, and in the aftermath of his lynching, the threat of violence proved too much for the Boorstin
family. Young Daniel therefore grew up not as a "Southern Jew," but as an
"Oklahoma Jew." Indeed, although the Tulsa of his youth was characterized

by segregation, racial violence, and the rise of the second Ku Klux Klan, his recollection that these social forces "were not visible or prominent" demonstrates the ways in which the family's relocation allowed them to benefit once again from the assumption of whiteness. Boorstin's father went on to become a prominent figure in Tulsa, as well as a booster for the city that his son later described as "the Optimism Capital of the World."[38] This story—which combined migration, hard work, assimilation, and economic success, along with an indifference to entrenched racial inequalities—was precisely the type of story he would later come to tell about the American past in his role as a popular historian.

Once again, as well as being a product of his biography, this understanding of history was developed and nuanced in the midcentury writing that laid the foundations for *The Americans*. For example, in 1957 the sociologist Nathan Glazer wrote a short book entitled *American Judaism* as part of the Chicago History of American Civilization series, for which Boorstin served as the academic editor. In his preface to the book, the historian explained:

> In telling the story of a people with a vivid tradition who have had to come to terms with the New World, Mr. Glazer is retelling the story of all Americans. He helps us understand how many ancient, iridescent threads have been woven into the complex fabric of American culture, producing a still more remarkable iridescence.[39]

In making this case, Boorstin positioned himself as part of a generation of intellectuals who saw the story of Jewish integration as the story of America.[40] If scholars such as Glazer were using their writing about American Judaism as a way of writing about American history, the reverse might therefore be said of Boorstin: in writing about American history, he was making sense of, and coming to terms with, his own Jewish identity.

This argument is most clear in *The Genius of American Politics*. In the book's fifth chapter, entitled "The Mingling of Political and Religious Thought," Boorstin argued that "religions are unimportant in American life; but Religion is of enormous importance." He suggested that this situation was rooted in "a kind of generalized American religion, and the tendency to talk a great deal about what we believe without feeling the obligation to sharpen our definitions," both of which highlighted "a unity in American life."[41] The basis for Boorstin's view of the "consensus" in American history therefore lay in the overlapping contexts provided by the de-Christianization that led out of European immigration, and the consequent integration of the Catholic and Jewish faiths into the discourse of a mainline Judeo-Christian tradition, or what he called the "generalized American religion."[42]

In making this case, Boorstin was not embarking on an idiosyncratic in-tellectual mission. As well as writing against the backdrop of the rise of anti-communism, arguments about the links between European and American political ideas, and the shifting contexts of American understandings of re-ligion, he was also intervening in a culture in which Jewish Americans were experiencing upward mobility, relocating to the suburbs, and thus grappling with a newfound "middle-class" identity that did not map neatly onto prevail-ing assumptions about their sociopolitical status.[43] The navigation of these experiences was central to Boorstin's narration of national history in *The Americans*. He would go on to use the trilogy to universalize and popularize the social experiences that were becoming widespread for considerable seg-ments of the American population, at least those who could lay claim to the mantles of economic and cultural privilege that he had achieved during his youth and early career.

As he embarked upon the project that would become *The Americans*, Boorstin repeatedly articulated his desire to write for "general" readers. Like Hofstadter, he was keen to embrace the emergence of so-called "middlebrow" audiences for popular history that had been created by the paperback revolution and the attendant transformations it wrought on the publishing industry. Furthermore, Boorstin took these audiences just as seriously as Hofstadter did: rather than denigrating their status like some midcentury critics, he conceptualized his ideal audience as intelligent, educated, and politically engaged.

However, there were also differences in the historians' opinions of their imagined publics. Unlike Hofstadter, Boorstin only rarely challenged patri-otic assumptions about the American past; instead, he wanted to buttress them by providing readers with an understanding of how their everyday lives fit into the national pageant of economic and cultural progress. Furthermore, because he wrote the three volumes over a period of two decades, Boor-stin's understanding of popular history and his status as a public intellectual evolved as he navigated developments in the publishing industry that pushed authors and publishers away from a singularized idea of who a "general" reader might be, and toward a more variegated definition of the book-buying public as segmented into a range of "general readerships," each with its own tastes and ideas about what made for high-quality historical writing.

Before he started work on *The Americans*, Boorstin had pitched his ear-lier book *The Genius of American Politics* to several trade publishers. For ex-ample, in 1953 he wrote to an editor at Harper & Brothers, suggesting that "this book, far more than anything I've written before, is directed to a general audience. I am eager to reach as many readers as possible."[44] In rejecting the manuscript, the editor told Boorstin that it was simply "too abstract," and that it would make "more interesting reading" if he "used more frequent examples and specific illustrations; many readers find it difficult to sustain attention on an abstract and theoretical plane for very long at a stretch."[45] The book was eventually published by the University of Chicago Press and garnered significant attention in literary and political periodicals. Nonetheless, this type of rejection showed Boorstin that he needed to find a more engaging literary style if he was to truly expand his readership.

This was reflected in a proposal the historian wrote to the Relm Foundation in 1955, who awarded him $10,000 to pursue *The Americans*, which was then under contract with Random House. In pitching the trilogy to the foundation, Boorstin explained that "to be successful my work must be rich in the aroma of life at particular times and places in our past, yet broad enough in geographic and chronological perspective to encompass the manifold variety of American life." He would achieve this by employing "an illustrative technique" that would give the books a "literary quality . . . that might commend them to the general reader."[46] This conception of the relationship between form, style, and marketability demonstrated an evolution in his ideas about how to reach non-academic audiences.

Boorstin's editors at Random House were Jess Stein and Hiram Haydn, both of whom were employed in the company's College Department in the 1950s. However, their ambitions as publishing professionals meant that they looked beyond the horizon of the textbook market and regularly sought ways to blur the boundary between "educational" and "general" readerships. In early correspondence with Boorstin, for example, Stein argued that he saw potential in volume 1 as "both as a textbook and as a general trade book," with the historian reiterating that he hoped for "the widest possible audience" that would extend beyond his fellow historians and their students to embrace "the literate public" as a whole.[47] To achieve this, the book needed to be positioned as a prestigious literary product. This point was summed up by Stein:

> Since we feel that your book will have a highly individual quality to it, it seems difficult to visualize a book competing with it. . . . The point I'm getting at is that we see your manuscript as highly unique and individually distinguished, to the extent that it is in a class by itself and simply not open to competition. I cannot imagine our undertaking another large project of this kind in the same area, but neither can I imagine how another book might really compete with yours.[48]

There was an element of flattery in this statement. But in making it, Stein also argued that Boorstin would be on strong commercial ground only if he successfully combined popularity with literary quality.

Another factor in discussions about the intended audience for *The Americans* was the question of timeliness. This was particularly the case with volume 1, *The Colonial Experience*, which focused on the periods of history most firmly removed from the 1950s. Reflecting on his reading of an early draft of the manuscript, the writer and television broadcaster Keith Berwick commented that it was at its strongest when drawing analogies to the twentieth century. In his view, future drafts needed to "emphasize timeliness; point up continuities, analogies, precedents." The book was the "first of a three-volume text for the times, which draws its illustrations from the colonial period," he went on, before telling author and publisher: "I think you should underscore its character as a contemporary commentary."[49]

In this argument, popular history was timely history, and Boorstin made significant efforts to oblige. For example, in the opening pages of volume 1, he engaged in an extended comparison between Puritan intellectual culture and that of postwar America:

> American Puritans were hardly more distracted from their practical tasks by theology and metaphysics than we are today. . . . Had they spent as much of their energy in debating with each other as did their English contemporaries, they might have lacked the singlemindedness needed to overcome the dark, unpredictable perils of a wilderness. They might have merited praise as precursors of modern liberalism, but they might never have helped found a nation.[50]

Volume 1 was replete with this type of analysis, and it highlighted one of the key literary techniques Boorstin used to address the non-academic readers he imagined as the audience for his popular history. It also demonstrated that, like Hofstadter, his writing was shaped by a set of interactions with publishing professionals that assumed the "general" reader to be firmly embedded in the mass culture of the period.

However, when volume 1 crossed the desk of the tastemakers at the Book-of-the-Month Club, they did not feel that Boorstin had succeeded in his attempt to write for such an audience. One of the club's critics called the book "an excellent, readable survey," while another stated that the historian's style was "pleasantly lacking in ponderosity."[51] But both readers concurred that it should not be a monthly selection. As one of them summarized: "This is an excellent example of a class of books which have become common in recent years: a work of indisputable scholarship which is purposefully miscellaneous in content. . . . Its appeal will be to the specialized rather than the general reader."[52] In this assessment, Boorstin and his editors had not yet succeeded in producing a book that transcended its origins in Random House's College

Department: too heavily rooted in its author's professional expertise, it would not succeed in entertaining non-academic readers.

Boorstin's approach to popular history changed markedly as he researched and wrote volumes 2 and 3 of *The Americans, The National Experience* and *The Democratic Experience*, respectively. Most specifically, he moved away from the relatively conventional history of the "American mind" that characterized volume 1 and toward an innovative type of social history that emphasized the entanglements between economic and technological development and the everyday experiences of middle-class Americans. The books focused on the contributions made to the nation's development by lawyers, doctors, and other professional groups. These were the social ranks from which it was assumed many of Boorstin's readers would be drawn. The books also focused on the rise of businesses such as insurance and consumer credit, which all middle-class Americans interacted with, either as managers, employees, or consumers. These groups were, as Boorstin put it in volume 3, the cornerstones of "American enterprise" that had been inspired by "the energy and rhetoric of American Go-Getters," and could only have emerged in "the first large-scale democratic nation."[53]

This sense of American dynamism was underscored by Boorstin's entertaining stories about the historical roots of everyday experience. Volume 2 opened with a discussion of Frederic Tudor, the so-called "Ice King" of the early nineteenth century, whose "adventuring energies" to pioneer ice as a consumer good led directly to the development of the "Ice Age of the American diet—with its emphasis on sanitation, nutrition, and refreshment, on the health of the body rather than the pleasures of the palate."[54] Similarly, the early pages of volume 3 framed economic expansion after the Civil War via the history of beef farming's westward expansion.[55] Contemporary Americans' connection to the ice in their drinks and the food on their plate, Boorstin argued, had a direct connection to their predecessors' economic dynamism.

Boorstin also sought to familiarize his historical writing by locating the roots of consumer institutions such as the hotel and the department store in the longer history of American democracy. Hotels, he explained in volume 2, "were among the earliest facilities that bound the nation together," allowing Americans to develop the habit of "gathering from all corners of the nation for mixed public-private, business-pleasure purposes." In making this case, he argued for the hotel as a site where middle-class notions of national belonging were formed across geographical and ethnic boundaries: "What was a hotel, or a republic, if it was not a place where citizens 'tolerably well dressed and well behaved' could rub elbows at a public table?"[56] Boorstin picked this thread up again in volume 3, where he wrote that the twentieth-century department

store, like the nineteenth-century hotel that preceded it, "gave dignity, importance, and publicity to the acts of shopping and buying—new communal acts
in a new America."[57] Once again, the historian's focus was the overlap between
national identity and class identity:

> Now a flowing, indiscriminate public wandered freely among attractive, open
> displays of goods of all kinds and qualities. One needed no longer be a "person
> of quality" to view goods of quality. . . . In this new democracy of consumers
> it was assumed that any man might be a buyer.[58]

These historical experiences thus defined who had the privilege to belong in
the "consumption communities" that made up modern American life.

Boorstin's depiction of American historical development was a primarily but not uniformly positive one. Volume 3, for example, which focused on
the period from the 1860s to the 1960s, expressed some anxiety about recent
changes in American life. In the book's sixth part, titled "Mass-Producing the
Moment," Boorstin asked his readers to pause and imagine the life of a suburban housewife named Rebecca, whose relationship with her television set
represented a broader American malaise:

> Just as Rebecca no longer needed to go to the village well to gather her water
> (and her gossip), so now, too, in her eighth-floor kitchenette, she received
> the current of hot and cold running images. By 1970, more than 95 percent of
> American households had television sets. Now the normal way to enjoy com-
> munity experience was at home in your living room. . . . While she watched
> her TV, the lonely Rebecca was thrust back on herself. She could exclaim or
> applaud or hiss, but nobody heard her except for the children in the kitchen
> or the family in the living room, who probably already knew her sentiments
> too well.[59]

This portrait adopted Boorstin's earlier observations about television in his
book *The Image* (1961) and fused them with a gloss on the arguments made
by Betty Friedan in her 1963 best seller *The Feminine Mystique* about the
"problem that has no name" and its impact on women's mental health.[60] It
thus represented the historian's eclectic use of political references to mount a
conservative critique of contemporary culture. But, at the same time, it also
demonstrated the centrality of the suburban citizen-consumer to Boorstin's
perception of who the readers for his popular histories were: upwardly mobile, middle-class Americans, perhaps recently assimilated, but now part of
the democracy of consumption that his trilogy celebrated. They wanted to
be informed about the historical roots of their everyday lives, as well as entertained by witty stories that zeroed in on their preoccupations as well as, in
certain instances, their anxieties.

These assumptions were reflected in the way the books were sold in the literary marketplace. A 1958 advertisement for volume 1, for example, posed a set of questions to curious readers that the book promised to answer, including: "Why do we produce so many inventors but very few theoretical scientists?" and "Why do women have an exceptionally prominent place in American life?"[61] Furthermore, both volumes 2 and 3 were successfully sold to the History Book Club, which, a staffer in the Random House Rights Department told Boorstin in 1965, provided "the ideal market" and would "help spread word of the book among those people who will like it best."[62] This was buttressed by the write-up volume 3 received in the club's newsletter in 1975, which described the historian's "inclusion of colorful incident along with concrete detail" as a key selling point, before telling potential readers that the book's "grand theme is informative, knowledgeable, and beautifully crafted."[63] It represented, in short, the perfect combination of entertainment and intellectual invigoration.

Boorstin's books were therefore sold in a manner that highlighted both their literary and scholarly qualities, a combination that remained highly valued in the market for popular history throughout the period from the late 1950s through the early 1970s. This was underscored when the Quality Paperback Book Service included a three-volume set of *The Americans* alongside books by Albert Camus, Sigmund Freud, Sylvia Plath, and J. R. R. Tolkien in a 1975 *New York Times* advertisement:

> What makes a paperback a Quality Paperback? Pick one up and see. Feel the rich finish of the paper. The heft of the book itself. Hold a page up to the light. See how crisp and clear the type is . . . and how the printing on the other side doesn't show through. Open and close the book a few times, then thumb through the pages and listen for the distinctive "snap." You'll quickly understand why the books Quality Paperback Book Service offers to members compare favorably with the finest hardcover editions . . . and why you'll be proud to display them in your home library. . . . The books we offer members are chosen for their aesthetic appeal as well as their literary merit.[64]

As well as narrating a celebratory history of American mass consumption, the books had thus become cherished objects of that very culture, the ownership of which bestowed status on middle-class readers.

A vein of continuity therefore linked the ideas about popular history and its audiences that existed in the 1940s, when Hofstadter published *The American Political Tradition*, and the 1970s, when Boorstin published the third and final volume of *The Americans*. But this was not the whole story. After the publication of volume 2 in 1965, Boorstin received a letter from Edward Bernays, the Austrian American pioneer in the field of public relations. He told the historian, "I can't help but think of the promotional aspects [the book] has inherent in it. I can see a tremendous market outside of the ordinary book channels and institutional markets." This perspective led Bernays to recommend "a segmental approach for selling the volume in larger quantities," which would involve "finding those groups who would be particularly interested in the new insights and facts that you have discovered about them."[65]

In making this point, Bernays argued that the new approach to "market segmentation" that had emerged in American consumer culture since the 1950s was directly relevant to Boorstin's popular history. This replaced the idea of a singular "mass" consumer base for goods as widespread as cigarettes and refrigerators with a new axiom that sought to create a vast heterogeneity of markets across the United States.[66] This was an approach that Random House took up directly in marketing volume 3 in 1973. For example, a press release targeted at "Texas Newspapers" played up Boorstin's focus on the history of beef farming:

> In his new book, *The Americans: The Democratic Experience*, just published by Random House, Dr. Daniel Boorstin . . . credits the Longhorn with transforming life in the West, and, indirectly, shaping some of the habits and myths of the rest of the country. . . . The cast of characters of the cattleman's heyday—the cowboy, the cattle baron, the rustler, the Marshall and the desperado—gradually disappeared with the rise of barbed-wire fences and the disappearance of the range. But, Dr. Boorstin indicates, they, like the Texas Longhorn, had all put their brand on the history of America.[67]

Similarly, a release aimed at the "Women's Press" promoted the book's relevance for suburban housewives, by highlighting its status as a guide to the history behind the "thousands of brand name cans, jars, boxes and bags in today's supermarket," a deeper understanding of which would reveal to its readers "the very special history of America."[68] These sales tactics showed that while Boorstin and his publishers continued to pay lip service to the idealized "general" reader, those most directly involved with marketing his popular histories recognized that such an ideal, if it had ever existed at all, was becoming less and less relevant as the publishing industry, and the broader consumer culture of which it was a part, underwent significant changes.

Boorstin himself expressed anxiety about these changes. This was primarily because his relationship with Jess Stein changed over the two decades that it took him to write *The Americans*. While in the 1950s Stein had been an attentive editor in the company's College Department, by the mid-1960s he had risen rapidly to become a senior executive at Random House in the wake of its

acquisition of Alfred A. Knopf in 1960 and Pantheon in 1961—two of a wave
of mergers and acquisitions that would transform the face of the American
publishing industry in the thirty years that followed. Stein's professional success caused Boorstin some chagrin, and the historian repeatedly complained
that he was not receiving enough attention from his editor. This led Boorstin
to threaten to leave his contract with Random House in 1963 after receiving
an offer to publish volumes 2 and 3 with Atheneum, a smaller house recently
established by Hiram Haydn, who had worked with Boorstin and Stein on
volume 1. In one letter, he complained that Stein's "vast new administrative
responsibilities" meant that their communication was "very intermittent, subject to great delays, and not entirely relaxed."[69] In another, he zeroed in on the
process by which he felt Random House had started to "treat books as pure
merchandise and authors as mere producers of merchandise."[70] A key element
in the dispute was the historian's perception that he was being disadvantaged
by the broader process of commercialization that was taking place at Random
and the industry at large.

Viewed with the benefit of hindsight, these complaints appear as a storm
in a teacup: Boorstin did not follow through on his threat and, indeed, enjoyed a long and fruitful relationship with his publisher during the remainder
of his career. But located in the specific historical moment when the "business of books" was shifting to mean that, in the words of Pantheon publisher
André Schiffrin, commercial publishers had to fit into one of two molds—
"purveyors of entertainment or of hard information"—they are revealing
about Boorstin's conceptualization of himself as a public intellectual.[71] Ultimately, he worried that the specific type of literary prestige bestowed on books
published by companies such as Random House was declining, and that this
would impact his ability to function as a popular historian who was able to
maintain the tricky balance between popularity and intellectual seriousness.

Boorstin's anxieties about popularization arose again in the 1970s, when
he worked with MGM on a TV documentary based on one of the key themes
of *The Americans*: "Getting There First." As he explained in volume 2, this
idea was rooted in a specific understanding of westward expansion in the
nineteenth century as "the American determination to get there first, to build
quickly and cheaply, and to travel fast," which, he argued, helped to explain
"many of the peculiar virtues then already visible in American technology."
His characteristic gloss on the importance of this idea involved comparison
with the history of Great Britain: "The British confidence in the future, and in
its resemblance to the past, made it hard for Britishers even to imagine obsolescence. But belief in obsolescence became an article of American faith. . . . A
rough equality was the product of [American] experience."[72] "Getting There

First" was thus a key concept in Boorstin's framing of a unique and dynamic course for US history.

In 1970 Boorstin was approached to produce a film based on these ideas and, a year later, agreed to terms for a television release in 1972 with the title *Getting There First: The American Experience*. The original sales presentation for the show explicitly engaged with the challenges of adaptation by quoting at length from Boorstin's recently published book *The Decline of Radicalism* (1969):

> Is it possible to produce television programs that will sell but which do not capitalize on or catalyze dissent and dissension, the feeling of apartness from the community? Is it possible for our media, without becoming pollyannas or chauvinists or super patriots or good humor salesman, to find new ways of expressing and affirming, dramatizing, and illuminating what people agree upon? The future of American society may depend on whether and how these questions are answered.[73]

As well as expressing the conservative political values with which Boorstin was quickly becoming associated in the late 1960s and early 1970s, this statement set the scene for the historian's anxious engagement with the television adaptation of his work. Desperately keen for a "much larger audience" for his ideas, he was also concerned by the challenge posed by his attempt to affirm, dramatize, and illuminate the American past without being labeled either a "super patriot" or "good humor salesman," which would imply that he had simplified his ideas to get them broadcast.[74]

This concern is also represented in Boorstin's reaction to the final script for the show in 1972. He worried that the producers' decision to focus attention on his boyhood home state of Oklahoma risked being perceived as "a cliché" and mounted the same criticism at a key line in the script: "*Because* it involves risks, not despite them, getting there first has become an American synonym for adventure."[75] He was also opposed on political grounds to the characterization of both the countercultural "Back to the Land" movement and Black Power activism, which had presumably been included to appeal to the youth market, as contemporary examples of "getting there first." Indeed, in the margins of the script that Boorstin annotated, he exclaimed, "No! No!" in response to both inclusions.[76]

In spite of this opposition, the show was broadcast as scripted, with its executive producer at MGM, Nicolas Noxon, writing to Boorstin to tell him that "it is clear to everyone involved that you have strong reservations about the latest script and the right to disassociate yourself from the film."[77] While Boorstin did participate in its promotion by writing an article in *Life* magazine, even this piece highlighted his ambivalence about the process by which his ideas had ended up on-screen. It recycled the historian's material from volume 3 by picturing a housewife sitting in loneliness in front of her television set, before he argued:

> Here is a great, rich, literate, equalitarian nation suddenly fragmented into mysterious, anonymous island audiences, newly separated from one another, newly isolated from their entertainers and their educators and their political representatives, suddenly enshrouded in a fog of new ambiguities. . . . Many admirable features of American life today—the new points of our conscience, the wondrous universalizing of our experience, the sharing of the exotic, the remote, the unexpected—come from television. But they will come to little unless we find ways to overcome the new provincialism, the new isolation, the new frustrations and the new confusion which come from our new segregation.[78]

As much as he embraced the idea of popular history, Boorstin simply could not escape such fretfulness.

The problems the historian perceived in the 1960s and 1970s were fundamentally rooted in his relationship to mass culture. Market segmentation, the beginnings of conglomeration, and the decentered nature of TV scriptwriting all made him feel uneasy about his role as a popularizer. Like Hofstadter, he was most comfortable envisioning well-educated "general" readers as a homogeneous group residing within the postwar political consensus. In this imagined market, there was much less contradiction between the form and the content of popular history. However, Boorstin's own experiences suggested that the reality was more complex. In response, the historian's ideas became more conservative, thus providing fertile ground for their adoption by a range of right-wing intellectuals seeking historical ballast for their opposition to American liberalism.

Boorstin's increasingly conservative mood was evident as early as 1959, the year he received the Bancroft Prize for volume 1 of *The Americans*. The speech he delivered at Columbia University to accept the award focused on the contemporary problems of American culture:

> Never before, perhaps, has a culture been so fragmented into groups, each full of its own virtues, each annoyed and irritated at others. The sure and familiar formula for a successful non-fiction book, for a novel, for a movie, or for a TV show, is to expose the vices of some occupation, some section, or some class. We are ashamed of our hucksters, our hidden persuaders, our exurbanites, our men in grey flannel suits, our occupiers of executive suites and their wives, our organization men, our labor racketeers, our anti-intellectual, TV watching,

comic book reading populace, and our ineffectual egghead professors. Adults are horrified by our beatnik youth, and our beatnik youth are horrified by the squares who are us. Northern pulpits respond with outrage at the inhumanity of their fellow Americans in the South, and Southerners are astonished at the anarchistic love of violence of the NAACP and their Northern supporters including the Supreme Court.[79]

This was a literary complaint about the demise of a coherent "general" audience. But it was also a conservative political statement about the type of popular history Boorstin wanted to write. In focusing on the everyday lives of middle-class citizens seemingly going about their business in an ever-changing America, he was writing history for what Richard Nixon would later term the "silent majority" of Americans. This political constituency was rooted in the politics of middle-class, color-blind respectability that emerged in the late 1960s and early 1970s. It fused opposition to specific issues, such as enforced school desegregation, with broader concerns about the postwar expansion of the liberal state and the protest movements of the period, thus creating a powerful and innovative new brand of American conservatism.[80] The emergence of this "New Right" was thus an important backdrop for the reception of Boorstin's popular history, as well as the mutations of his political thought as he engaged in a dialogue with a range of right-wing thinkers.

Boorstin's visibility was amplified by the postwar American conservative movement, which developed when three disparate trends of transatlantic thinking—libertarianism, traditionalism, and anti-communism—were "fused" in the 1950s and 1960s by conservative thinkers intent on gaining mainstream acceptance for their ideas.[81] Led by William F. Buckley and his flagship journal *National Review*, they sought to legitimize opposition to the dominance of liberalism in the United States, at the same time as they articulated a fundamental skepticism about the effective functioning of mass democracy.[82] This was the "reactionary mind" of modern conservatism: a tradition of thinking that responded passionately to the various perceived challenges to the traditional American social order posed by the New Deal, Supreme Court decisions such as *Brown v. Board of Education* (1954), and, later, the struggles for Black freedom, student power, women's equal rights, and gay liberation.[83]

These broader intellectual currents were given particular focus in the work of conservative thinkers such as Russell Kirk, Robert Weaver, and Peter Viereck, all of whom wrote books and articles during the 1950s and 1960s that sought to create a "usable past" by focusing on traditions of American resistance to the "tyranny of the majority" and "national consolidation."[84] Conservative ideas penetrated academic culture via the work of historian

Rowland Berthoff, who, in 1960, called for a "broad conservative synthesis" of the American past rooted in the study of social history.[85] This led, a decade later, to the publication of his landmark *An Unsettled People* (1971), which was written from a perspective that rejected "the liberal individualism that pervades most of the American past and writing about it."[86] Berthoff argued that attempts to "subvert or abandon the values embodied in a well-ordered institutional structure" led to "great peril" for the nation:

> Social institutions may be good or abusively or neglectfully bad, but at times when Americans have simply flung institutional constraints aside, even in the honored name of pioneer individualism, free enterprise, and opportunity for all, they have found the consequences unacceptable.[87]

Boorstin was an elemental part of this conservative historical culture. While some of his ideas differed from those of Kirk, Weaver, Viereck, and Berthoff, like them he used the American past to highlight conservative values as a route to defending abstract ideas such as morality and community.[88]

Against this backdrop, the popularity of *The Americans* was rooted in readers' attraction not only to Boorstin's entertaining prose style, but also to his rapidly evolving and outspoken intellectual conservatism. This became particularly clear after the publication of volume 3. Describing Boorstin as a "conservative consensus historian," the *St. Louis Post Dispatch* told its readers that the power of the book lay in its author's ability to "rhapsodize about America's past greatness while decrying those trends which threaten American virtues and values."[89] In the *Philadelphia Bulletin*, the book was written up as "an underground history of American civilization" because of its focus on ordinary Americans, with the paper's reviewer telling readers, "Never a man to hedge his bets, [Boorstin] has ... ruthlessly put down the political process. . . . But the fundamental thrust of his argument is clear: Americans achieved what they did by pragmatic techniques, not by cosmological insights."[90] Reviews such as these showed that Boorstin's status as an opponent of liberal opinion gained him traction as a popular historian. In that process, he became an important spokesperson for a conservative vision of the American past.

The fundamental opposition of Boorstin's popular writing to mainstream liberal ideology was highlighted by his critics as well as his advocates. One example is the political scientist Sheldon Wolin, who penned a synoptic review of all three volumes of *The Americans* for the *New York Review of Books* in 1974. Writing amid the Watergate scandal, Wolin decried Boorstin's "hollowing out of the political content of 'democracy' and 'community' and their reduction to consumerism," which he described as "crucial to the larger strategy of eliminating politics from remembered experience."[91] This was dangerous, he argued, precisely because Watergate served as a timely reminder of the centrality of political corruption in the nation's development:

> Our present crisis is, in the most fundamental sense, political: it concerns con-
> stitutional power, the political virtues of our public men, and the civic virtue
> of citizens. By blanking out our political past, we invite solutions that are dan-
> gerous because ignorant of all but the marketplace understanding of politics.[92]

For Wolin, Boorstin had missed one of the central processes in American history: the wielding of political power, something which the historian's focus on everyday experience almost completely ignored.

The significance of Boorstin's conservatism is also evident in correspondence between the historian and his readers. In some cases, they simply emphasized the sense of national pride that *The Americans* instilled, with one writing in 1975 to tell Boorstin simply, "You've helped me to love this incredible country."[93] On another level, readers reported that his approach to American history was refreshingly devoid of what they perceived to be liberal bias, with one particularly high-profile correspondent, former president Dwight Eisenhower, exemplifying this trend when he told the historian in 1965, "In these days, when some historians have become mere propagandists for particular political and economic theories, your book stands out as the product of a real and sympathetic scholar."[94]

As well as praising Boorstin's patriotic boosterism and his deviation from the liberal norm, readers also engaged with the more complex side of the historian's thinking. One wrote to him after reading volume 3 to say that the book made her feel like a "typical American, if there is such a thing." She went on, "The distillation of your work that my mind has performed somewhere in its depths has been crucially important. . . . I hope other readers will feel this way. It has to do with the very complex and confusing state we are in as a society."[95] For readers such as this, the anxieties and confusions prompted by modern life were uppermost in their minds as they read *The Americans*, and the books helped them navigate such unsettling topics as continuing racial inequality, the growing liberal state, and the rapid and high-profile emergence of political unrest.

Boorstin's arguments in *The Americans* appealed not only to these types of readers, but also to intellectuals working within the conservative intellectual movement. One reason was the historian's appeals throughout the trilogy to the pragmatism of Edmund Burke, a set of ideas with great traction on the postwar right. Burke was an Irish politician and political theorist most famous for his *Reflections on the Revolution in France* (1790), which criticized the ideological zeal of the Jacobins from a perspective that emphasized the importance of stability in political society. Boorstin frequently used American history to highlight the power of such observations. For example, in volume 1, he made much of colonial New England as "a noble experiment in applied theology." He argued that the Puritans were not the religious zealots of the popular imagination. Instead, they were a group whose ideas were rooted in "a practical common-law orthodoxy," which preferred "programs of action and schemes of confederation" to theological dogma, and thus "foreshadowed American political life for centuries to come."[96] In volume 2, he continued this theme, arguing that antebellum New England's intellectual versatility was vital to the development of pragmatism as a school of American thinking with which Boorstin expressed intellectual sympathy. This new body of thought was, in the historian's formulation, a "substitute for philosophy" because it emphasized the slow evolution of societal norms from below, rather than their dictation from on high.[97]

In volume 3, however, Boorstin burnished his conservative credentials by pivoting to a critique of pragmatism as it had come to be exemplified by a bogeyman of the American Right (and a hero of Hofstadter's): John Dewey.[98] The historian argued that the philosopher's attempt to create a modernizing educational system was uniquely problematic:

> [Dewey] spoke for the future, an America where old landmarks were to be dissolved, so that men would be more free, though perhaps more lost, than ever before. He pushed the American promise to its extreme fault. He made an America of the mind. And he brought men new promise, New Hope, and a new bewilderment.[99]

For Boorstin, then, it was Burke's version of pragmatism, and not Dewey's, that Americans should heed. Much earlier in his career, in *The Genius of American Politics*, the historian had argued that the Irish philosopher's significance lay in his emphasis on political freedom as "an inheritance," an observation that, he suggested, "leads us away from extravagant and presumptuous speculations."[100]

In making this case and then using all three volumes of *The Americans* to outline its historical validity, Boorstin placed himself firmly alongside a range of other Cold War conservatives who used Burke's philosophy as a means of arguing that liberalism was a form of ideological fanaticism.[101] Another exponent of this approach was Russell Kirk. A traditionalist conservative who made his name with *The Conservative Mind: From Burke to Santayana* (1953), Kirk consistently argued that Americans were, by instinct, "pragmatists" rather than "fanatics," who thus rejected the type of political ideology that had resulted in the French and Russian Revolutions.[102] Kirk was also a long-time friend of Boorstin's, and even went as far as describing himself in correspondence with the historian as a "Boorstinite, that is, a devotee of prudence, an anti-universalist, and an enemy of ideology."[103]

The intellectual debt Kirk owed Boorstin was best exemplified in a 1985 essay he wrote for the conservative journal *Modern Age*, in which he praised both *The Genius of American Politics* and *The Americans*:

> The attainment of America's independence, Boorstin makes clear in his writings, was not the work of what Burke called "theoretic dogma." What most moved the Americans of that time was their own colonial experience: they were defending their right to go on living in the future much as they had lived in the past; they were not marching to Zion.[104]

For Kirk, such an observation had contemporary as well as historical resonance: citing recent events in Ethiopia, Chad, Cambodia, and Timor, he argued that "the crying need of our age is to avert revolutions, not to multiply them," before continuing, "What we call the American Revolution had fortunate consequences because, in some sense, it was a revolution not made but prevented."[105] In making this case, Kirk showed how Boorstin's popular history could be utilized to create a usable past for the conservative movement.

If, by the 1980s, Boorstin had become a lodestar for conservative intellectuals such as Kirk, praise for *The Americans* was by no means universal on the right. One conservative critic of his overwhelmingly positive account of eighteenth- and nineteenth-century American history was the journalist and public intellectual Irving Kristol. Writing in 1969 to question the centrality of "the democratic ideal" in American history, he singled Boorstin out for a mixture of praise and admonition. Kristol concurred with what he described as the historian's "consensus" view of the past, as well as his Burkean take on the nation's lack of "excessive curiosity" about political ideology.[106] However, he went on to question the positive account of American democratic life provided by *The Americans*:

> Reading Boorstin . . . one comes away with the strong impression that America has been a very lucky country. I do not doubt this for a moment. But unless one is willing to claim that this luck is a sign of enduing Divine benevolence— unless one believes that Americans are indeed Sons of the Covenant, a Chosen People—it is very difficult to argue from the fact of luck to the notion that democracy in America is a *good* form of government.[107]

Boorstin was thus a vital interlocuter as Kristol developed his argument that the realities of the nation's politics should not attract immediate devotion from conservatives: "I do not see that the condition of American democracy is such as automatically to call forth my love and honor, although I respect it enough to offer it my obedience."[108]

In volume 3, Boorstin shifted his arguments, thus drawing his position closer to critics like Kristol and cementing his transition from liberalism to conservatism. He did this by developing the opposition to liberalism that had its origins early in his career into a critique of the dilemmas of twentieth-century modernity. While the final installment of *The Americans* remained broadly celebratory in its discussion of the nation's economic and techno-logical dynamism, it was also written from a position of discomfort when discussing mass culture and politics. Boorstin's praise for "consumption com-munities," for example, was undercut by his concern that Americans were no longer held together by the "iron bonds" of religion and social custom, but instead by "gossamer webs" of consumerism that could not deliver profound spiritual meaning.[109]

Boorstin also used volume 3 to attack liberal attempts to combat racial and economic inequality. For example, he described African Americans as "indelible immigrants," who were "condemned by slavery to remain outside the mainstream of American opportunity." Nonetheless, this historical injus-tice was only furthered by "efforts to compensate . . . by quotas, reverse dis-crimination, and other devices," which were problematic because of the way they created "a new suspiciousness and resentment" among white Americans, and thus sowed a fundamental and problematic division.[110] In making this ar-gument, Boorstin channeled his historical pessimism into a critique of liberal attempts at racial justice that was typical of the conservative backlash against affirmative action in the late 1960s and early 1970s.[111] His response also typi-fied those of many conservative Jewish intellectuals as they turned away from the civil rights movement in response to the rise of Black nationalism. Once sympathetic to a universalist vision of racial equality, these thinkers were now hostile to a form of cultural particularism they viewed as a threat to the suc-cess story of Jewish assimilation.[112]

These arguments were connected to another aspect of Boorstin's political thinking: his staunch opposition to the student New Left.[113] In 1969 he had described student activism, along with that of the Black Power movement, as an atavistic "New Barbarianism," which posed a threat to the nation because its advocates were "diffuse, wild, and disorganized."[114] The historian toned down this line of argument in *The Americans*, but did not miss multiple op-portunities to criticize the New Left. For example, the book's discussion of the politics of poverty described student activists as "romantic and conscience-ridden" because of what Boorstin perceived as their attempts to radicalize the Community Action Programs established by Lyndon Johnson's Great Society.

This, he argued, was representative of the New Left's fundamental secession from the "dominant motif of American civilization," which he characterized as poverty reduction via economic expansion and individualism, rather than government initiatives.[115]

In the final pages of volume 3, Boorstin pulled these arguments together to express his fundamental anxieties about the development of American society in the twentieth century:

> The sense of momentum . . . burdened the ordinary citizen. The pace of research and development, of advertising, of ingenious, pervasive, and inescapable new ways for making and marketing nearly everything to nearly everybody, made it seem that the future of American civilization and the shape of everyday life could not fail to be determined by the mass and velocity of the enterprises already in being. . . . This new climate of negative decision, this new unfreedom of omnipotence was confirmed by forces outside the industrial machinery. . . . Not legislation or the wisdom of statesman but something else determined the future. And of all things on earth the growth of knowledge remained still the most spontaneous and unpredictable.[116]

The "democratic experience" of the book's subtitle was therefore not an altogether positive one, and in striking another Niebuhrian note in his criticism of "the wisdom of statesmen," Boorstin highlighted his belief that this was a problem not only of student radicalism, but also of overreach on the part of elected officials.

As he made this case, Boorstin chimed in with the postwar Right's fundamental skepticism about the state of American democracy, a theme that brought him to the attention of another influential conservative: the journalist George Will. In 1979 and 1980, Will used volume 3 as a touchstone for several of his regular *Newsweek* columns, in which he represented the experience of modernity as a threat to the authentic communities of an earlier American way of life.[117] Citing the book's discussion of the rise of the American suburb, he argued that the idea of a golden age of consumerism was a misleading fiction. In the coming years, Will predicted, this would become ever more apparent to Americans, as they became accustomed to politics being centered on "the allocation of scarcity."[118] Less than a month later, he provided his readers with another riff on Boorstin in an article entitled "The Virtues of Boldness," which argued that the key message of recent American history was that "doubt itself has become a dogma."[119] For Will, like Boorstin, this was a sign of the inherent limitations of American liberalism.

These brief references to *The Americans* were supplemented in Will's book *Statecraft as Soulcraft* (1983), which used Boorstin's trilogy to underpin its author's argument that "portraits of America as the confident, unworried 'happy Republic' have never been entirely accurate. . . . Pessimism is as American as apple pie."[120] Expanding on this theme, he echoed Boorstin's mistrust of modernity:

> Conservatism is about the cultivation and conservation of certain values, or it is nothing. But industrialism has been a thorough solvent of traditional values, a revolutionary force for change. It is unreasonably *a priori* to assume that the unregulated consequences of unfettered industrialism—whatever they may be—are compatible with, let alone identifiable with, conservative aspirations.[121]

Once again, this argument demonstrated how Boorstin's ideas became a touchstone for right-wing thinkers in the 1970s and 1980s as they mounted a critique of postwar American politics.

By the early 1970s, Boorstin was using his position as director of the National Museum of History and Technology to play a significant role in the political life of the nation's capital. The historian walked the corridors of power and took regular meetings with conservative politicians and advisers such as Nelson Rockefeller, Spiro Agnew, and Henry Kissinger. Indeed, after one meeting with Boorstin, Kissinger reported to President Richard Nixon in glowing terms: "He isn't so good on foreign policy. . . . But about the American image of itself, what America's role in the world should be, he's one of the most brilliant people around. Exceptionally thoughtful and basically on our side."[122]

The synergy between Boorstin's ideas and those of the Republican Party was highlighted in 1972, when the historian delivered a statement to the party's national platform committee at its annual convention in Miami, Florida. Arguing that the nation was suffering from "a crisis of memory and understanding," he chose to focus his remarks on the history of race and racism. Boorstin told his audience that "the direction of our history was never to give *power* to minorities. The aim, rather, was to break down barriers, and so to allow each of these groups—Negroes, women, young persons, aged persons, or any others—to take their rightful place in the ranks of all Americans."[123] In opposition to such a culture, he offered a conservative vision of "a nation with fewer barriers" between its citizens. "A more open America" he argued, would be

> not a nation of proud, chauvinistic, self-seeking "minorities." We must not allow ourselves to become the Quota States of America. By reminding us of our common hopes and common destiny, your Republican platform committee can help redeem us from our crisis of memory, can help give us the courage of our history. The Party of Lincoln must seek ways not to divide but to unite, and so to build the community of all Americans.[124]

Boorstin was now feeding his historical ideas directly into the national political conversation. This demonstrated that popular history of the type that had made him famous could be used not only to entertain so-called "general" readers, but also to shape the intellectual agenda of the American conservative movement.

In 2004 *The Economist* published an obituary of Boorstin, who had died in February of that year, aged eighty-nine. In outlining the historian's contributions to American life, the article emphasized his belief that "mankind . . . had never produced a technical feat to match the book." With this idea in mind, he committed himself to a career as an intellectual: "Writing was his life, and he could not possibly stop." These efforts resulted in what the British magazine praised as a "unique" perspective on the past, which brought to the fore a politicized vision of everyday Americans' flexibility and pragmatism as they conquered "a wild continent." The article ultimately framed Boorstin's life as a continuous effort to "put twentieth-century Americans back in touch with literature and learning, and to unlock the possibilities of progress and creation latent in their minds."[125]

The Americans was a central part of that project. On one level, the trilogy was a high-profile stepping-stone to a career in the administration of large public institutions such as the Smithsonian and the Library of Congress, as well as to high-profile contributions to the political culture of the Republican Party. But its three volumes were not only this. They were also important interventions in the postwar culture of popular historical writing. They evidenced how ideas about politics, audience, and literary style shaped not only Boorstin's career, but also the conservative intellectual movement he so confidently and successfully intervened in. The books were thus important examples of the power that resided in popular history's navigation of the intertwined contexts provided by American liberalism and conservatism.

As we have seen, Richard Hofstadter turned away from the CPUSA as he wrote *The American Political Tradition*. But he did not turn away from the radicalism that had so influenced him in early life. He thus wrote popular history that skewered national mythology from the left of the political spectrum. Boorstin, on the other hand, forged an actively anti-communist and anti-radical popular history, one that originated in a liberal engagement with the politics of the Cold War, but grew increasingly conservative as it navigated developments in modern American life. Hofstadter aimed for a highly literary style of writing that emphasized complexity and contradiction, while Boorstin aimed more explicitly to entertain his audiences and convince them of their nation's greatness, even as, in volume 3, he turned his

mind to criticism of recent developments in American history. The two historians shared a commitment to popular history, then, but differed in how it
should be written. They also shared a conception of their readership that was
rooted in the American "middlebrow": their ideal audiences were middle-
class, white, educated, and politically engaged. However, while for Hofstadter
this conception remained relatively static after the publication of his second
book in 1948, Boorstin was more clearly influenced by concurrent changes
in the publishing industry, mass marketing, and political culture. While he
was perturbed by the fragmentation of the readership he had imagined in the
1950s, by the 1960s and 1970s he was catering for it by shaping his work not
only as a social history of bourgeois America, but also as a contribution to the
conservative intellectual movement.

Hofstadter's and Boorstin's attempts to write for "general" readers thus
highlighted the power and significance of popular history, as well as the significant intellectual and literary variety of so-called "consensus" historiography. Just as importantly, they demonstrated how postwar historians reframed
their approach to historical writing as they encountered the era's marketplace
of print, which provided them with expanded audiences and new opportunities to experiment with literary style and political argumentation. In this
way, the paperback revolution wrought its first set of transformations on the
American historical profession.

However, this was not the only model of postwar popular historical writing. Another approach was taken by historians who actively sought audiences
from outside the intellectual and political folds of the American "middlebrow." Targeted at Black readers, young radicals, and feminists, the popular
histories written by John Hope Franklin, Howard Zinn, and Gerda Lerner
help us to understand the emergence of alternative audiences for popular history: those made up of "activist" readers.

PART II

Popular History and Activist Readers

3

John Hope Franklin: The Racial Politics
of Popular History

In a December 1948 book review in *The Crisis*, Hugh H. Smythe, a sociologist and employee of the National Association for the Advancement of Colored People (NAACP), criticized the publication earlier that year by Charles Scribner's Sons of Roi Ottley's *Black Odyssey: The Story of the Negro in America*. A journalist, Ottley had written a self-described "reporter's job" of African American history from 1619 to 1945, intended for a mass readership.[1] Smythe's review listed numerous factual errors in the book, before concluding:

> It is time that publishers realize that any book on the theme of the Negro is not going to prove a bonanza. We are approaching the 1950s, and the lush days of the "Negro Renaissance" of the 1920s, when almost everything by and about the Negro was acclaimed by naïve publishers and a gullible public, are passé. The sooner publishers come to understand that a book about Negroes must measure up to acceptable standards, and will not sell unless it does this, the better.[2]

In launching this scathing attack on Ottley's book, Smythe echoed the sentiments of postwar historians and publishers by emphasizing that successful postwar historical writing aimed at popular audiences had to combine rigorous scholarship with a popular writing style. However, there was also a specificity to Smythe's intervention: he emphasized the significance of the color line and suggested that white publishers should not take readers, especially Black readers, for granted when publishing African American history.

As an alternative to Ottley's "half-baked writing job that has no reason for being," Smythe suggested that readers seek out John Hope Franklin's *From Slavery to Freedom: A History of American Negroes*. The book had been published by Alfred A. Knopf in 1947. Along with another Knopf title, Arna Bontemps's children's book *Story of the Negro* (1948), it stood, in Smythe's opinion, as one of "several creditable histories" of Black America aimed at popular audiences.[3] *From Slavery to Freedom* sat within a list that had a rich tradition of dealing with racial issues: since the 1920s, Knopf had published early editions of the poetry and fiction of Langston Hughes and Nella Larsen, as well as writings on the Harlem Renaissance by Carl Van Vechten and nonfiction treatments of race in the Americas by, among others, anthropologist Melville Herskovits, sociologist Frank Tannenbaum, and historian Gilberto Freyre.[4] Franklin's book presented a chronological survey of Black experience from the "cradle of civilization" in Egypt and Ethiopia, up to African American service in World War II. Its aim, as the historian summarized in its preface, was not to "recite achievements" of Black Americans, "but to tell the story of the process by which the Negro has sought to cast his lot with an evolving American civilization."[5]

A critical and commercial success, the book signaled Franklin's arrival as an important force not only within the American historical profession, but also on the national literary scene. He was greeted as a young African American scholar ready and able to speak to popular audiences across the color line and was embraced by Knopf, a publishing house committed to the tenets of the racial liberalism that were embraced by many white intellectuals during the 1940s and 1950s. However, a newfound popularity among students and activists participating in the Black freedom struggle during the 1960s and 1970s breathed new life into the book's fortunes as it was used to frame new ideas about the politics of Black cultural nationalism. Then, as the book was revised for several new editions during the 1980s and 1990s, Franklin entered dialogue with editors, peer reviewers, and, from 1985, his coauthor, Alfred A. Moss. In doing so, he modified and expanded the book's contents, as well as subtly altering its title, in ways that were shaped by both the Black history and African American studies movements.

From the outset, Franklin and his publishers assumed that *From Slavery to Freedom* was a book for an activist audience, made up of readers who would use it not only to understand but also to challenge the status quo in American "race relations." This was a public whose ideas were shaped against the backdrop of segregation: they consumed Black writing with a view to confronting Jim Crow.[6] However, as the agendas of Black and white activists shifted following the Civil Rights and Voting Rights Acts in the mid-1960s, so did the reception of the book's rendering of popular national history. *From Slavery to Freedom*'s six-decade career as the highest-profile history of Black Americans therefore offers an opportunity to chart the changing demands of popular audiences for African American history, audiences who persistently viewed their engagement with Franklin's work through the lens of racial politics.

★

Born in 1915 in Rentiesville, Oklahoma, John Hope Franklin attended Fisk University as an undergraduate student before undertaking doctoral study in history at Harvard University. He completed his dissertation in 1941 and started a teaching career at the North Carolina College for Negroes (now North Carolina Central University). During the period of his education and the initial years of his professional life, Franklin was shaped by three important intellectual contexts, each of which was vital to the development of *From Slavery to Freedom*. The first of these was his training in the approaches of the elite "New History" that had developed since the start of the twentieth century, and which molded his identity as a historian. The second was the rich tradition of subaltern historical writing by African Americans, which shaped the political interventions he would go on to make. The third was the emergence during the 1930s and 1940s of broad popular interest in African American history, in particular the development of Negro History Week, which provided a rich context for the reception of Franklin's ideas among the non-academic reading public.

The first of these contexts was provided by Franklin's graduate education at interwar Harvard, where he was influenced by the development of "progressive" or New History, which he subsequently expanded so that it encompassed the study of the Black past. Since the early 1900s, the profession had been shaped by scholars such as Frederick Jackson Turner, James Harvey Robinson, Charles Beard, and Carl Becker, each of whom argued that historians needed to expand their horizons beyond narrow studies of the state and policymaking to embrace the methods of economic, social, cultural, and intellectual history. This involved incorporating the insights of social scientists and setting an intellectual agenda that focused on quantifiable generalizations about the structures and forces that generated change in modern life. There was a political as well as a methodological thrust to these innovations. The dislocations of urban life and technological modernity at the beginning of the twentieth century drove historians and social scientists to conceptualize the historian's task as one of social engagement with the period's reform movements.[7] In doing so, the New Historians were not rejecting scholarly impartiality. Instead, they saw the incorporation of new perspectives as a way of expanding the objectivity of the discipline, allowing historical research influenced by social science to provide a more accurate and detailed understanding of American life that would speak to contemporary political concerns.[8]

When Franklin arrived at Harvard in 1935, he entered a doctoral program heavily influenced by these developments. He took a class on social and intellectual history with Arthur Schlesinger Sr., one of the leading inheritors of the progressive tradition, whose book *New Viewpoints in American History* (1922) stood as a widely read manifesto for an approach to the nation's past shaped by the social sciences.[9] Schlesinger's class helped to frame Franklin's interest in the connections between African American and broader national history, and drew him toward his dissertation subject: the study of free Blacks in antebellum North Carolina, which he went on to pursue under the supervision of another Harvard historian working in the New History tradition, Paul H. Buck.[10] The bibliographical essay Franklin included at the end of the first edition of *From Slavery to Freedom* foregrounded key scholarship from this school of thought, citing books by Beard, Schlesinger, and the younger historian Merle Curti as the "most valuable general works in American history."[11] This lineage was not lost on reviewers of the book, one of whom commented that in integrating "the social and cultural history of American colored people," Franklin was working firmly in a line of historians running back as far as Turner and thereby contributing to an important widening of perspective in the field.[12]

Furthermore, the New History's injunction to use social scientific theories to frame historical questions was one Franklin took seriously. He listed a string of important social scientific work by both white and Black scholars as vital to any historical understanding of the "condition of the Negro," including work by sociologists Gunnar Myrdal and E. Franklin Frazier, the anthropologist Melville J. Herskovits, and the economist Abram Harris Jr.[13] He was thus influenced by a series of important debates taking place among these social scientists about questions such as the persistence of African cultural practices in Black communities, the relationship between race and class in social inequality, and the question of whether or not the Black population was shaped by a destructive cycle of pathology that could only be escaped via thoroughgoing assimilation into the white mainstream.[14] In integrating these perspectives into American historiography, Franklin fit the mold of the New History perfectly.

However, just as important in Franklin's intellectual development was the African American historical writing that predated his own. In the late nineteenth and early twentieth centuries, this rich tradition developed separately from the mainstream of the American historical profession, primarily because Black scholars, who made up the vast majority of those doing such writing during the period, were excluded from teaching and research positions at white institutions. Looking back on his early career in a 1986 essay, Franklin argued that there were two generations of Black historical writing that had shaped his thinking. The first of these—which spanned the period between the publication of George Washington Williams's *History of the Negro Race* in 1882 and Booker T. Washington's *Story of the Negro* in 1909—was concerned with the "adjustment, adaption, and compatibility" of African Americans as they responded to "the white world in which they were compelled to live."[15] These historians paid considerable attention to the roots of Black culture in Africa, with the primary goal of resisting the widely held contemporary notion that the descendants of Africans were only fit for subjugation.[16] The second generation spanned the years 1915 to 1935 and was dominated by the figure of Carter G. Woodson, the founder of both the Association for the Study of Negro Life and History (ASNLH) in 1915 and the *Journal of Negro History* in 1916. As Franklin understood Woodson and his contemporaries, their aims were twofold. First, they developed institutions that would safeguard historical records pertaining to African Americans, which the mainstream historical profession did not see as valuable enough for preservation. Second, they pursued a celebratory agenda by highlighting the achievements of notable Black people.[17] As Woodson put it in the preface to his 1922 book *The Negro in Our History*, his key goal in studying "all phases of Negro life and history" was "to emphasize what the Negro has contributed to civilization."[18]

Again, Franklin's outlook was clearly shaped by those African American historians who came before him. *From Slavery to Freedom*'s bibliographical essay drew its readers' attention to the fact that it was "not widely known that a large and curious assortment of general histories of the Negro have appeared in the past century." It went on to foreground the scholarship of Williams and Washington as having considerable value, before cautiously describing Woodson's *The Negro in Our History* as "the most satisfactory general treatment" of the topic.[19] In the sections of the essay on the history of slavery, he also went on to highlight his debt to a generation of more radical Black historians—such as W. E. B. Du Bois, C. L. R. James, and Eric Williams— whose arguments fundamentally shaped his understanding of transatlantic slavery and its impact on African American history.[20] As well as fitting the mold of a Harvard-trained New Historian, then, Franklin was also significantly indebted to the tradition of professionalized African American historiography that had developed in parallel to the white historical profession during the first half of the twentieth century.

However, because of the impact of racial discrimination and professional segregation on Black intellectual life, organizations such as the ASNLH made interventions in the political as well as academic culture of early twentieth-century America, with historians such as Woodson and Lorenzo Greene playing the role of scholar-activists. They approached history through the lens of a "service ethic" and drew connections between the values of professional scholarship and the interests of schoolteachers, workers, and African American youths.[21] The best example of this is the creation of Negro History Week in 1926. The first systematic attempt to popularize the study of African American history, the ASNLH established the celebration as a way of introducing Black history into school and college curricula.[22] By the early 1940s, Negro History Week's remit had extended beyond this purely educational goal, with the African American newspaper the *Chicago Defender* encouraging its readers to hold "Quiz Parties on Negro History" that would emphasize the deep roots of this history not only in the United States, but throughout the world.[23] The ASNLH's *Negro History Bulletin* highlighted its interracial aims when it suggested that Negro History Week programs could "not only inspire the Negro but . . . convince and change the white man," and therefore effect "social revolution."[24] As the socialist magazine the *New Masses* put it in 1947, "There is nothing academic about Negro History Week. . . . Here is history brought forward as an urgently needed weapon. Here the lessons of the past become alive and fuse with the tactics for today—and the strategy for tomorrow."[25]

In the first edition of *From Slavery to Freedom*, Franklin described Negro History Week as one of a number of efforts during the interwar years that "stimulated the pride of race of many Negroes."[26] Ultimately, this was a public initiative that drew African American history out of the classroom and into everyday life, thereby creating new audiences for popular approaches to the past that *From Slavery to Freedom* would capitalize on. As well as being shaped by the professional contexts provided by the New History and African American historiography, Franklin's appreciation of the need to write for a popular audience was also molded by this expanding interest among the public—Black and white—in his chosen field.

Writing in 1957, Franklin drew these three contexts together to provide an incisive account of his reasons for writing African American history. Ten years after the publication of *From Slavery to Freedom*, he suggested that the book had placed him as part of a generation of historians working in the tradition of what he called the "new Negro history," all of whom sought to address the "remarkable growth of interest in the history of the Negro" among non-academic audiences. Their approach was "new" in methodological terms because it eschewed previous generations' efforts both to measure African American culture against the dominant white culture and to celebrate the achievements of acclaimed members of the race. Instead, Franklin and his peers recognized that African American history was embedded in national history to the extent that the two could not be disentangled. "Negro history is more than the overt actions of Negroes," he argued, "it is also America's treatment of the Negro. It is the impact of forces and events affecting the lives of Negroes in countless ways."[27] To understand Black history, it was vital to supplement traditional material with that which had not been produced by African Americans but had significantly impacted their status within the United States. In a scholarly sense, this was the only way to write full and accurate history, not only of the Black experience, but of the nation itself.

However, this was more than simply a methodological call to arms. Just as the New Historians saw their scholarship as embedded in movements for reform, Franklin's understanding of his generation's distinctiveness was also archly political:

> The new Negro history says to America that its rich heritage is the result of the struggles of all its peoples, playing the roles that conditions and circumstances have permitted them to play. These roles cannot be evaluated in terms of race. Rather, they must be judged in terms of their effect on the realization of the great American dream.... The new Negro history ... will provide *all America* with a lesson in the wastefulness, nay, the wickedness of human exploitation and injustice that have characterized too much of this nation's past. This is a lesson that must be learned if we are to survive and if we are to win the respect and admiration of the other peoples of the world.[28]

In Franklin's iteration of the historian's task, the goal was not simply to render the story of African American history accurately and objectively, but also to use it as a tool in the fight for racial equality. Franklin's political agenda was an integrationist one, in which "the great American dream" would prove accessible to all Americans, regardless of their racial identity. By integrating African American history into national history, "new Negro historians" could play a role in integrating African Americans into the civic life of the nation.

From Slavery to Freedom started life as "A History of the Negro," a manuscript commissioned in 1944 when Roger Shugg was an editor in Knopf's College Department. He had originally contracted the historian Charles H. Wesley to write the book, a more established figure than Franklin who was then serving as president of Wilberforce University. However, Shugg and his colleagues were unimpressed with the manuscript Wesley produced and, in early 1946, offered the young historian the opportunity to join him as a coauthor so that the book could be "compressed, rewritten and prepared for publication as soon as possible."[29] When Wesley pulled out of this relationship a month later, Shugg offered Franklin a contract to write his own book, noting "an urgent and widespread need" for a good survey of African American history.[30]

Over the course of eighteen months, Franklin put all other work on hold and rushed to produce the book that would define his career. From the outset, he planned a volume that would "set the history of the Negro in the general framework of American history," in order to emphasize the point that this history "did not take place in a vacuum but affected and was affected by almost everything else that was going on."[31] This was the first of Franklin's interventions: to demonstrate the deep entanglement of white and Black racial experience throughout American history. The second was his insistence that as well as being an account of national history, the book would also treat the Black experience as a transnational one, and he told Shugg that "three or four chapters" were required "on Africa," along with "several on the Caribbean and South America."[32] In this sense, the first edition's eventual subtitle, *A History of American Negroes*, was significant: Franklin was keen to place the history of African Americans within a broader story of the Black diaspora.

From Shugg's perspective, it was vital to encourage Franklin, who was less obviously interested in literary flair than historians such as Hofstadter and Boorstin, to write engagingly. In May 1946, for example, the editor praised an early draft, but encouraged the author to improve the quality of his prose by using "colorful detail and illustrative episodes wherever possible . . . even if it means occasionally inserting a paragraph or two for nothing but story value."[33] Franklin heeded this advice, and in an internal memo discussing another draft of the book, Shugg was able to tell his colleagues that the author's writing was "exceptionally lucid," and that while it had been commissioned by the College Department, the manuscript "should look like a trade book rather than a text book."[34] For Shugg, this meant that *From Slavery to Freedom* would "appeal to the interested general public as well as to the colleges."[35]

However, in discussions with his colleagues, Shugg also highlighted another aspect of the company's acquisition strategy when he suggested that an additional strength of Franklin's manuscript derived from the historian's "impeccable" scholarship. For Shugg, the book was "free of all racial chauvinism. According to scholars in a position to know, it should be an authentic and interesting work for many years to come."[36] Indeed, this assessment was reinforced shortly after the publication of *From Slavery to Freedom* in a letter written by the southern historian C. Vann Woodward in support of an application made by Franklin to the Guggenheim Foundation:

> In Mr. Franklin I believe we have a Negro historian of the type we have been hoping to see. It is true that his published work so far has been primarily in the history of the Negro. But it is freer of race-consciousness and propaganda than preceding works of the kind.[37]

Franklin's scholarship was valued because he wrote well, but also because, in the minds of his promoters, he was not an "advocate" for his race. Unlike his predecessors Woodson or Du Bois, Franklin was viewed as a fully professionalized historian engaged in the admirable process of making scholarly ideas accessible to non-academic audiences. In this assessment, his racial identity played a vital role. Whereas Hofstadter's and Boorstin's professional neutrality and objectivity were never seriously considered by their publishers, Franklin needed to demonstrate a solid veneer of impartiality to earn an opportunity to work with trade house such as Knopf.

The context in which Franklin wrote *From Slavery to Freedom* was therefore shaped by its publisher's commitment to the contradictory tenets of mid-century racial liberalism. In the aftermath of African American contributions to the American effort in World War II, as well as the publication of Gunnar Myrdal's *An American Dilemma* (1944), white liberals were on the lookout for Black intellectuals who could demonstrate the nation's potential for racial equality through the quality of their thought.[38] Franklin fulfilled this function effectively, and this was one of the reasons he was valued by Knopf, influenced as it was by a broader constellation of "race thinking" that placed overt discrimination rooted in the maladjusted psychology of white Americans as the core element of racism.[39] Indeed, in discussions of the book's title, Shugg had vetoed Franklin's suggestion of "Freedom's People" because of "some doubt about how it would affect the sale of the book in the Deep South."[40] In doing so, the editor demonstrated a faith in the ability of popular history, aimed at a broad audience, to shape the nation's conversation on race, as long as it was pitched in such a way as not to offend the sensibilities of southern readers.

Knopf's promotion of *From Slavery to Freedom* clearly chimed with the company's espousal of a racial liberalism. They sought to underscore Franklin's impartiality by highlighting Arthur Schlesinger's opinion of the book on its dust jacket:

> Franklin, I am pleased to say, writes without a chip on his shoulder. A reading of the book will give Negroes a new pride in their race, and it will cause white people to reassess the role of the Negro in American history to the latter's great advantage.[41]

Not only was Franklin deemed "without a chip on his shoulder" by the white establishment, but the publication of *From Slavery to Freedom* was promoted as the type of nonfiction that could challenge racial discrimination. Upon publication, then, it was viewed as a bastion of racial liberalism.

When the book was reviewed in the popular press, many critics picked up on these cues and praised Franklin's balance and neutrality. At the same time, though, they also highlighted the way *From Slavery to Freedom* intervened in debates about postwar racism and America's place in the world. For example, some situated the book as evidence of the expanding opportunities for African American citizenship. "Despite present disadvantages," a reviewer for the *Atlanta Journal* wrote, "the Negro today is on the road to becoming a full-fledged American citizen, regardless of race, rank, or previous condition of servitude. Such an achievement as *From Slavery to Freedom* is compelling evidence."[42] The *Christian Science Monitor*'s reviewer provided a similarly sanguine review:

> Grim as much of the story is, one cannot run through the book's 622 pages without gaining a feeling that he has followed an ascent from the abyss. That the turmoil and the tenseness of today reflect not just reaction, but also greater awareness by the Negro of his capacities and his rights, and an awakened conscience and a new perspective on the part of the American white man. One suspects that Dr. Franklin feels this too.[43]

These were fundamentally optimistic readings, that not only gave wholehearted praise to Franklin's achievement as a scholar, but also indicated that his book's very existence, especially when combined with the opportunities given to an African American historian by a major publisher such as Knopf, highlighted the possibilities for racial progress.

However, other reviewers used the opportunity provided by *From Slavery to Freedom* to be more critical about the postwar world. Writing for the *New York Herald Tribune*, Youra Qualls opined:

> One is reminded of Gunnar Myrdal's memorable account of the Negro as the gadfly of the American conscience. For *From Slavery to Freedom* shows that the Negro has continuously raised the urgent question of the way of functioning of American democracy toward him and against him.[44]

Furthermore, several commentators used Franklin's discussion of African American service in the US military to highlight how the experience "left the race disappointed for war's failure to make democracy really work."[45] Comparing the manner in which the majority of popular history written about traditional subjects such as the Founding Fathers would leave white readers "thrilling to our attainment of national freedom," the *New Haven Register* asked:

> What of our black brothers? Valiantly they have fought for this country in 1914 to 1918 and again 1941 to 1945, but have they anything like freedom? After years of slavery came years of fighting for the most primary rights of man. After Mr. Franklin traces the long and checkered history of his people, he cannot, unfortunately, end his history on an optimistic note.[46]

Wartime rhetoric of freedom and democracy consequently shaped contemporary understandings of *From Slavery to Freedom* and placed the book in a larger dialogue about race and citizenship in postwar America. As Alain Locke noted in his review for the *Saturday Review of Literature*, Franklin's presentation of national history placed African Americans at "the crux" of a range of political struggles: "of human rights and freedom, of truly universal suffrage, of the federal control and guarantee of civil rights, of the extension of economic democracy and labor union democratization, and finally of the nation's external reputation."[47] It seemed that there was hardly a contemporary political issue that Franklin's history did not speak to.

For midcentury liberals, education was also a vital element in the fight against racism, and the idea of "changing white minds" about African Americans was of paramount importance to the period's culture of racial individualism.[48] Again, elements of this ideology were evident in early reviews of the book. *From Slavery to Freedom* "should be compulsory reading for champions of white supremacy," wrote the *Christian Register's* reviewer, before dismissively adding, "If indeed they are able to read with comprehension its superb English prose."[49] This educational line was also taken by more radical reviewers. Writing for the Trotskyist *New International*, Ernest Rice McKinney compared Franklin to Du Bois, a favorite of postwar leftists:

> He has done what no other contemporary Negro historian has done, with the exception of Du Bois in parts of *Black Reconstruction*: he has recognized that the history of the Negro is part and parcel of the total history of the country, an integral part of the political, social and economic growth of the nation. His book should be read by everyone who thinks he knows something about the Negro.[50]

Furthermore, a reviewer for the *Bookshopper*—an in-house publication of the Washington Cooperative Bookshop, a communist-leaning bookstore in midcentury Washington, DC—suggested that the book would "find its way into homes, schools and libraries," and would help to combat the "convention, suppression, bigotry, pseudo-history and all of the other machinery which has served to keep the truth from Negroes and whites alike."[51]

Taken together, these reviews demonstrate the powerful formula that Franklin and Knopf had drawn together. By combining the language of scholarly objectivity with subject matter that had an obvious contemporary relevance, the book's readers thought it had the potential to serve as an educational text not only in school and university classrooms, but also for members of the public who needed to learn about the cruel ironies of Black Americans' place in the nation's history. The early success of the book was therefore inherently bound up with its relationship to the culture of midcentury racial liberalism, a context that saw popular history as a means of pushing back against the racist ideas that shaped American society.

✳

Despite its evident popularity among white readers, Franklin wanted *From Slavery to Freedom* to be more than a contribution to liberal hand-wringing about postwar racism. He voiced this concern most clearly in a letter to Shugg in which he complained about a negative review of *From Slavery to Freedom* written by Roi Ottley for the *New York Times*.[52] To Shugg and many other observers, the review was an ad hominem attack on Franklin's work by the author of a competing text, even more unfortunate because it had appeared in such a high-profile venue. What angered Franklin most, though, was that Ottley's review suggested that he had written "another 'Negro Problem' book on which any student of the problem, which includes everybody, can speak or write."[53] Franklin wanted it to be known that his qualifications as a professional historian set him apart from journalists such as Ottley. But he also wanted Knopf to acknowledge that there was the potential for a wide readership among Black Americans. Essentially, he sought a popular audience across the color line.

As early as 1946, Franklin had signaled to staff at Knopf that "the Negro market is fairly easily reached through the Negro press and national service organizations."[54] After publication, he fought with increasing frustration to highlight the value of "getting the book before the Negro public" via Black newspapers and magazines such as the *Pittsburgh Courier* and *Ebony*, as well as via Black colleges and schools.[55] Eventually, the publisher responded, sending letters to dozens of college presidents suggesting not only that they purchase the book for their libraries, but also that they use the opportunity it presented to offer "a full course in the history of American Negroes."[56] Along with the letter, Knopf sent a flyer laying out the strengths of the book, which echoed Franklin's response to Ottley when it argued, "Dr. Franklin has not written a 'Jim Crow' book. He does not regard the Negro apart from the current of American life but presents him as a moving force in the making of American civilization."[57] However, this effort amounted to the total of Knopf's efforts to promote *From Slavery to Freedom* among Black audiences.

Unsurprisingly, Franklin took matters into his own hands. For example, in August 1947 he wrote to Walter White, the executive secretary of the NAACP, to request access to the organization's mailing list. Telling White that he was "very anxious to reach as large a reading public as possible," he suggested that the organization's members "would be particularly interested in the book" because of the way it "undertakes to describe the revolution of the Negro in American life."[58] White responded enthusiastically, agreeing to circulate flyers for the book to local branches, youth councils, and college chapters. Franklin celebrated this progress, suggesting to Shugg that the influence wielded by the

NAACP "could be of great benefit to us."[59] Indeed, these connections, along with the early success of *From Slavery to Freedom*, paved the way for Franklin's association with Thurgood Marshall. In the late 1940s and early 1950s, Marshall was the executive director of the NAACP's Legal Defense Fund, which employed the historian as an expert witness in two important cases: *Lyman Johnson v. Board of Trustees of University of Kentucky* (1949), which challenged segregated college admissions, and the more famous *Brown v. Board of Education of Topeka* (1954), which outlawed segregation in public schooling.[60] Franklin's strategy of using the book to reach out to Black readers was not only a way of developing extra sales, then, but also developed his status as a scholar who fused research and advocacy to develop influence among activist communities.

Despite these efforts, *From Slavery to Freedom*'s fortunes were not radically transformed until the 1960s and 1970s, when the book's reception was reshaped by the politics of the civil rights movement, the emergence of Black Power, and, more specifically, the rise of Black cultural nationalism. This was a context in which massively increased attention and sales gave *From Slavery to Freedom* new relevance. For example, the publication of the third edition of the book in 1967 led to a significant spike in sales, with six-month totals rising from roughly 1,000 in 1967 to a peak of 50,000 in 1969, then leveling off at around 10,000 in the early 1980s.[61] These figures demonstrate a significant increase in sales of Franklin's book during the period in which the agendas of civil rights and Black Power became national talking points.

The most significant factor in this transformation of the book's fortunes was the publication of the first paperback edition of the book in 1969. *From Slavery to Freedom* benefited from the "paperback revolution" in the same way as Hofstadter's and Boorstin's popular histories, but only after Franklin pushed to have the book published between paper covers. He had to threaten Knopf with refusing to update the text for the next edition before the company acceded to his demand, but once he had won this battle, the book's sales expanded dramatically as it was able to capitalize on the ferment of civil rights and Black Power activism. The "insatiable demand for the book," Franklin reflected in the mid-1980s, came about because "students wanted courses in Black history at the secondary and collegiate levels. Civil Rights workers were introducing such courses as part of their own preparation for the struggle.... Negro history was in the air."[62] Developments in the publishing industry thus overlapped with the ferment provided by the Black freedom struggle and helped transform the fortunes of *From Slavery to Freedom*.

For example, even before it appeared in paperback, the book made several appearances in the curricula of the "Freedom Schools" that were established during Freedom Summer, the multi-pronged effort launched by the Student

Nonviolent Coordinating Committee (SNCC) and other civil rights groups in 1964 to register African American voters in the South. Coordinated by radical scholar-activists Staughton Lynd, Howard Zinn, Margaret Burnham, and Robert Zangrando, the history curriculum for the Freedom School in Jackson, Mississippi, aimed "to explore the history of the Negro on the American scene in the hope of developing in the students an added appreciation of the strengths and weaknesses of American patterns of race relations," and listed Franklin's book as a key text for both teachers and students to consult.[63] A "Guide to Negro History" prepared by Lynd also suggested using the Amistad slave revolt as key moment in African American history, and set a chapter in *From Slavery to Freedom* on the history of the slave trade to illustrate "the economic basis of slavery, as well as the various nations involved in the trade."[64] Part of the radical generation whose politics were forged via participation in the civil rights movement and the New Left, these historians demonstrated their intellectual debts to Franklin's work, at the same time as they highlighted the political utility of his most famous book. This version of "popularity," rooted in the political uses that the book was put to by activist readers, was radically different from those that transformed Hofstadter and Boorstin into household names.

From Slavery to Freedom remained enduringly popular in the years that followed. For example, numerous scholars have attested to its influence on their intellectual and political development. Describing the book as "an instrument of liberation," the historian Debra Ham has recalled the profound impact it had on her when she encountered it as a radical student at Howard University in the late 1960s: "That book reached into my past . . . made me heir to the riches of Mansa Musa, and taught me that Sojourner Truth was not just the name of a dorm."[65] African American studies professor Lillian Williams has reflected on the significance of the book during her days as an undergraduate at the University of Buffalo: "Militant students . . . walked around campus with *From Slavery to Freedom* under their arms in case they needed a quick reference in an impromptu debate over the nature of 'the black struggle.'" The book consequently provided "a historical explanation for the collective demands for social change and social justice" on campuses during the 1970s.[66] Historian Robin Kelley has recollected that when he pledged his Black fraternity, Alpha Phi Alpha, in 1981, he "proudly" included Franklin's name alongside Paul Robeson and Du Bois in a list of "big brothers" he was expected to recite loudly "under the duress of hazing." Kelley also noted that *From Slavery to Freedom* remained vital to the Black history courses he taught in his early career: "cloaked in the protective armor of judicious prose was a surprisingly radical interpretation of American history."[67] These testimonies demonstrate not only the longevity of the book's influence and the significance of its utility as a class text, but also its ideological malleability in the hands of an enthusiastic reader.

These encounters with Franklin's book took place during a period in which cultural nationalist approaches to Black intellectual and political life held considerable sway on college campuses. From the mid-1960s, the Black Arts Movement, led by intellectuals and artists such as Amiri Baraka and Larry Neal, theorized cultural nationalism as a vital corollary to Black Power politics. They called for artistic and cultural output that would cater directly to Black Americans and their demands for self-determination and nationhood.[68] In this understanding, the quality of an intellectual or artist's work would be judged by their ability to create a political vision that was of practical use to the Black community.[69] As well as conceptualizing the radical political implications of poetry, theater, and music, cultural nationalism also encompassed the world of scholarship, with the establishment of organizations such as the Institute of the Black World (IBW) in Atlanta, Georgia, in 1968 to institutionalize the interdisciplinary study of African American history in order to further the goals of radical political change.[70]

Alongside these developments, Black student numbers on college campuses across the United States underwent significant expansion. Student strikes and other forms of activism allowed campus radicals affiliated with the Black Power movement to successfully advocate for the establishment of African American studies programs, amounting to a "Black revolution on campus." As soon as the field was instituted, it immediately became a site of intellectual and political struggle, with arguments about disciplinary makeup, program content, and the nature of African American cultural identity rising to the fore.[71]

This was a struggle in which *From Slavery to Freedom* played a critical role as the most widely read and well-respected survey of African American history available for college-level courses. This influence is demonstrated in part by the expanded presence of the book on university campuses. In the period immediately after it was first published in 1947, the number of course adoptions at universities and high schools remained relatively low, at a total of thirty-one institutions, with the vast majority (twenty-four) of these being historically Black colleges and universities (HBCUs) in the South. However, by the late 1970s, the situation had changed dramatically, with a total of 351 universities, community colleges, and high schools having adopted the book for teaching purposes, representing a wide range of institutional types and a nationwide geographical distribution.[72]

Readers' encounters with *From Slavery to Freedom* as part of educational efforts in African American studies further demonstrate its significance within the contexts provided by the parallel emergence of Black cultural nationalism and African American studies. In March 1961, for example, Franklin received correspondence from as far afield as Nigeria, from where a schoolteacher wrote to praise the "great literary achievement" the book represented. The correspondent, Edward Ejon Onwuzike, described his first encounter with the book in a public library: "I . . . leapt to my feet several times when I saw the names of the immortals of the Negro Race within it," before attesting to Franklin's status as a "great son of Africa."[73] Closer to home and more than a decade later, in 1974 a student enrolled in her first Afro-American studies course at the University of Maryland wrote to Franklin to tell him that "a thorough reading, evaluation and study of . . . *From Slavery to Freedom*" had been vital to her learning: "Although I am a mere undergraduate student I am sure your book is a genius credit to this new and important area of study. . . . I have found it most helpful in understanding Black History and the African culture."[74] These testimonies highlight how readers of *From Slavery to Freedom* viewed the book through the prism of cultural nationalism: this was not simply American history, but history that connected people of color as part of a diasporic community.

Another example of this phenomenon is provided by the newsletter of the John Marshall Metro High School in Chicago from 1983, which announced the establishment of a "John Hope Franklin Afro-American History Club." The newsletter provided a synopsis of *From Slavery to Freedom*, which emphasized the book's arguments about the African origins of Black culture, before featuring a timeline of African American history from the seventeenth century to the 1980s. Two contributions sat alongside these pieces, the first of which was penned by George Crockett, a history teacher at the school, who argued that "history is KNOWLEDGE, IDENTITY, and POWER," and emphasized that an understanding of the past "is a matter of life and death to the oppressed, who cannot find themselves or free themselves without first finding and freeing their history."[75] This archetypal argument in favor of a cultural nationalist approach to Black history was published by a high school that also actively embraced the legacy of a liberal and integrationist scholar such as Franklin. His place in an educational initiative infused with the rhetoric of Black Power and cultural nationalism therefore highlights not only the deep roots of the African American studies movement in secondary as well as higher education, but also the way his ideas were compatible with a radical approach to Black history.

These various entanglements between Franklin's book and the activism of the post-1960s period complicate one of the key narratives in postwar Black intellectual life: that of generational conflict. The central story in post-1945 Black historiography revolves around the encounter that took place between

Franklin's generation, who were born in the first two decades of the twentieth century and came of age during the Great Depression, and those born in the 1930s and 1940s, whose politics were forged during the Black freedom struggle. After World War II, Black scholars like Franklin, Charles Wesley, and Benjamin Quarles, as well as a host of white historians who took Black history as their subject matter, were centrally interested locating the history of African Americans within the broader narrative of national history.[76] This involved emphasizing the theme of deep-seated oppression both during and after slavery and, as noted above, promoting a sense of responsibility and guilt in the minds of white readers.[77] This integrationist approach was subsequently challenged by the younger generation, who, influenced by the radical politics of Black Power, rejected integration and saw historical research as a tool of cultural nationalism.[78] Indeed, this was a view made popular by journalist Lerone Bennett Jr. as he used widely read articles in *Ebony* magazine to mobilize Black history in the service of revolutionary change.[79]

For radicalized young scholars, the moderate, integrationist "Negro history" needed to be replaced with a radical, separatist "Black history" more attuned to the times, and Franklin was very often a target as they sought to define their new approach. In an influential collection of essays published in 1970, Vincent Harding, head of the IBW and a key proponent of radical Black history, suggested that the younger generation saw themselves "as part of a new people, the formerly colonized, the wretched of the earth." They rejected the faith in "the basic goodness and greatness of American society" espoused by Franklin and his contemporaries.[80] For Harding, a generational reckoning with *From Slavery to Freedom* was vital. He wrote:

> In the text of the work one constantly feels that Franklin knows far more than he says about the ways in which the story of black people might need to rip apart the white fabric of American history. Indeed, he often comes to the brink of such total revaluation and then draws back. . . . The final impact, though, is still one of optimism about the movement of blacks into the mainstream of America, carrying with them certain gifts, but bearing no essential threat to the status quo.[81]

The radical intellectual Harold Cruse was less caustic about the political implications of Franklin's work in an unpublished essay written in 1979, but nonetheless critiqued the historian's approach for not being "provocative" or "original" enough to "defend his immense reputation against the searching criticism of those among us who yearn for . . . seminal ideas."[82] For proponents of radical Black history, Franklin's position of respectability in the historical profession was not one to be emulated.

The rift between Franklin and scholars such as Harding and Cruse no doubt existed, and not only in the minds of his radical opponents. As early as 1968, Franklin sought to justify the publication of a paperback edition of *From Slavery to Freedom* to his publisher by arguing that

> many advocates of "black history" are seeking a work that is more polemical than my own. At a time when courses in Negro history are multiplying daily, and when the demand for cheap books is increasing, someone is going to come forward with a cheap polemical book that will put us out of business.[83]

In making this point, Franklin highlighted his desire to protect his book's status as *the* African American history textbook. However, the reference to "cheap, polemical" approaches that might come to supersede his own serves as a reminder that he remained firmly wedded to his integrationist approach to history, was largely opposed to the multidisciplinary project offered by Black studies, and, at the same time, was skeptical of Black cultural nationalism.

This latter point is illustrated by his involvement in the Haverford Discussions in 1969. Convened by the sociologists Kenneth Clark and Mamie Clark at Haverford College, the discussions involved a range of high-profile integrationist African American intellectuals, including Ralph Ellison, St. Clair Drake, and J. Saunders Redding. Disagreements emerged among the group during their conversations, but all rejected the label of "conservative" that they believed had been imposed on them by intellectual proponents of Black Power. "We do not subscribe to a kind of separatist ideology that seeks an endowment of special racial talents," Franklin argued with characteristic directness, before going on, "I think it is very important as intellectuals and as academics that what we have to say, we say to the whole world, and not to this little Jim Crow bunch of Negro kids."[84]

While much of the success of *From Slavery to Freedom* derived from the reputation it developed among activist audiences involved in the civil rights and Black Power movements, Franklin was not uncritical of the most outspoken proponents of radical Black history and African American studies. Indeed, in making the case that his historical writing was not aimed simply at a "little Jim Crow bunch of Negro kids," his disappointments with Black cultural nationalism in 1969 echoed his critique of white racial liberalism in 1948. Both intellectual currents had contributed to his success and influence, but he remained firm in charting a middle course between them, producing popular historical writing that was attuned to the needs of Black activist audiences, but not craven in its attempts to win their sympathies. At a watershed moment in Black intellectual history, then, it is striking how successful he was in achieving this goal, and that the stock of *From Slavery to Freedom*, a book that stood as the distillation of continuity with a previous age, continued to rise.

If Franklin's work played an important role in shaping the emerging fields of Black history and African American studies during the 1960s and 1970s, those fields in turn shaped his approach as he revised the book over the course of six decades, and especially in the 1980s and 1990s. In undertaking this task, he was influenced by debates and developments that he synthesized for his readers, who, as the decades passed, became more firmly rooted in college classrooms.[85] The preface to the seventh edition, published in 1994 and co-authored with Alfred A. Moss, summarized this process:

> We have made every effort to keep abreast of the wide-ranging and significant scholarship in the field. It has affected our thinking, our approach, even our perspective. At times, its effect is quite obvious in the correction of statements of "facts" in earlier editions and in new interpretations gained from new re-search. Most often its effect is in the way it informs our view of the problem with which we deal and the sense of security it provides in helping us sort out the complexities and meanings of those problems. These effects are at times so subtle as not to be discernible, but this does not diminish their importance.[86]

As a part of this process, various elements of the book changed in ways that were significant not only for their scholarly value, but also for their engage-ment with the racial politics of post-1960s America.

The evolution of Black history and African American studies impacted the substance of the book significantly, especially its treatment of the Afri-can roots of Black history in America. The first three editions of *From Slav-ery to Freedom*—published in 1947, 1956, and 1967, respectively—contained an opening chapter entitled "A Cradle of Civilization," which showed no change between the three editions. In it, Franklin argued that the essential starting points for African American history were the ancient civilizations of Egypt and Ethiopia. Egyptian civilization, he argued, had developed not only because of the influence of "Mediterranean" people, but also due to the "constant infiltration of Negroid peoples from the south," the influence of whom should not be "regarded lightly in any final evaluation of the sources of culture and civilization in ancient Egypt." After 741 BC, Ethiopians came to dominate Egyptian social and political life and, because of the persistent presence of Black people for hundreds of years before this date, "felt them-selves part of a civilization whose custodians they now were." This narrative led Franklin to argue that Egyptian and Ethiopian culture moved westward across the continent and fundamentally shaped the identities of those Africans who were transported to the Americas between the sixteenth and nineteenth centuries as enslaved people.[87] These assumptions, which were widely held among other prominent Black historians at midcentury, placed Franklin as part of a tradition of "messianic assimilationism" in African American popular history, which used the perceived "greatness" of Black contributions to ancient civilizations to argue for integration.[88]

However, as radical approaches to Black history developed, this form of popular Afrocentrism became outdated. For example, in 1971 the radical sociologist Orlando Patterson criticized Franklin for his "contributionist" perspective on Black history, which aimed simply to demonstrate the achievements and inherent civilization of African Americans. He singled out *From Slavery to Freedom* in order to criticize the opening chapters of the book and their attempts to "establish continuities between black American and North African civilizations," by disregarding facts and exaggerating the influence of Egyptian and Ethiopian indigenous cultures on those communities who were brought to North America in enslavement. "It is to whites that these historically-conscious blacks seek to measure up," Patterson argued, grouping Franklin with Woodson, Wesley, and Bontemps as the equivalent of subaltern "colonial administrators" justifying their privileged position within a system that was nonetheless oppressing them.[89]

Patterson's critique highlighted not only his alignment with the radical Black historians who rejected Franklin's integrationist politics, but also how outdated the text of *From Slavery to Freedom* had become. Three years later, when the fourth edition was published in 1974, Franklin removed the chapter on ancient Egypt and Ethiopia. Instead, the book opened with material that had appeared in the first three editions under the heading "Early Negro States of Africa," now retitled "Land of Their Fathers." The chapter itself started with a newly composed paragraph, which, while not directly alerting the reader to the change, placed the book's discussion of African history against the backdrop of the recent process of decolonization. It was now "commonplace for Negro Americans to speak and write sensitively" about West Africa, Franklin argued, before suggesting that the emergence of "modern independent states" such as Ghana, Mali, Chad, Niger, and Nigeria "evoked a deep sense of identification" because they were "the land of the fathers of the New World slaves, as indeed, they were the land of the fathers of their twentieth-century descendants."[90] In making this case, Franklin continued to highlight what he saw as the deep roots of African Americans in Africa, but shifted the geographical origins of his story westward. As such, *From Slavery to Freedom* retained the diasporic approach to African American history that Franklin had identified as a central historiographical concern in 1947, even as it lost its references to Egypt and Ethiopia.

Another way in which the book responded to historiographical developments was in its coverage of Black music and culture. Discussion of these topics was relatively limited in the 1947 edition of the book. Early in the text, Franklin weighed in on a debate that raged between midcentury social scientists about the extent to which African Americans were influenced by their African cultural ancestry. He summarized the views of scholars such as Robert Park and E. Franklin Frazier, who "failed to see anything in Negro life today which can be traced to the African background," and, conversely, the scholarship of Carter Woodson and Melville Herskovits, "who insist that African cultural heritage can still be seen in many aspects of American life today." Seeking a characteristic middle ground between these positions, Franklin argued that some customs and traditions had remained, and that these surviving "Africanisms" existed primarily because of "the refusal of the dominant group in America to extend, without reservations, their own culture to the Negroes whom they brought over."[91] This argument demonstrated Franklin's ability to synthesize a large and complex body of sociological and anthropological research, but also chimed with his integrationist political views: as the book's original subtitle *A History of American Negroes* suggested, African Americans were essentially Black people who happened to find themselves in the United States with an as-yet-unfulfilled desire to participate fully and equally in the mainstream of national life.

Nonetheless, it was clear that Franklin, like most American historians, was not as confident discussing culture as he was political and social developments. For example, there were only two very brief references to Black music in the first edition of *From Slavery to Freedom* before the chapter on "A Harlem Renaissance," which then only briefly discussed singers such as Paul Robeson as examples of the "New Negro" sensibility, before dismissing jazz and swing in a short paragraph that made it clear that they should not be considered "serious" forms of music.[92] In subsequent editions, Franklin's treatment of the Harlem Renaissance expanded.[93] As the so-called "flowering" of Black culture in New York City in the 1920s and 1930s became a legitimate object of study for historians, Franklin was able to build on this new knowledge to improve his coverage of the arts.

However, it was Franklin's collaboration with Alfred A. Moss and the revisions they made during the 1980s that made the most significant difference to the book's treatment of popular music. Moss was hired as a coauthor in 1985 not only to lighten the load of the near-constant process of revision, but also because the older historian wanted to work with someone who "would be honest and forthright in stating his agreements and disagreements."[94] The educational publisher McGraw-Hill had bought the rights to publish *From Slavery to Freedom* as a textbook, and as its editors planned new editions, they commissioned reader reports from a range of Black history and African American studies educators. As a part of this process, Franklin and Moss started to receive critical reports from scholars suggesting that they needed to integrate the findings of cultural historians who studied Black music. One anonymous reviewer was surprised to have read "a book in black history that has five references to Benjamin Franklin but none to Aretha" and went on to argue that *From Slavery to Freedom* needed to pay more attention to "the enormous impact Afro-Americans have had on the culture of Euro-Americans, particularly in the area of popular culture."[95] The historian of slavery Leon Litwack offered a similar critique, suggesting that the book needed to "explore in larger and more imaginative ways Black expression, that is, how the great mass of Black Americans were forced to articulate their disillusionment, alienation, and frustration."[96] These reviews led Franklin and Moss's editor at McGraw-Hill to suggest that a widespread expansion of the book's coverage of "black popular culture, black religion, the blues and black pop music" was required.[97]

The subsequent sixth edition of *From Slavery to Freedom*, published in 1986, duly addressed these concerns. The number of index entries for "music" increased dramatically from five to twenty-one, with Franklin and Moss adding, among other topics, serious discussion of African American spirituals and their place within the culture of slavery.[98] However, most affected by these changes was the treatment of jazz music, with the authors expanding coverage of early musicians such as Jelly Roll Morton and Louis Armstrong, before recognizing the achievements of later instrumentalists such as Charlie Parker, Thelonious Monk, Miles Davis, and John Coltrane as "innovative developers of the jazz idiom," and praising Wynton Marsalis as the most up-to-date example of "the versatility and musical sensitivity of black artists."[99] Gone was Franklin's initial reluctance to describe jazz as a "serious" form of American music: it was now a central component in twentieth-century African American cultural identity.

Franklin claimed credit for writing about Morton and Armstrong based on his own experience as a "former jazz trumpeter."[100] But it is clear that Moss's brief, from McGraw-Hill as much as from Franklin himself, was to help his senior coauthor modernize the text with this type of reference, which reflected not only a desire for the book to be "up-to-date," but also an effort to chime in with the latest developments in African American cultural history, which had shifted toward a position that took musical output seriously as source material.[101] The seventh edition, published in 1994, extended this treatment further by paying serious attention to rap music, acknowledging the controversy over its legitimacy as a cultural form before describing it as "an unmistakable reflection" of Black urban life in the 1980s and 1990s.[102] These developments represented *From Slavery to Freedom*'s evolution into a textbook that represented the interests and passions of modern students at the same time as it synthesized recent developments in African American studies.

Franklin and Moss were also forced to respond to criticism of the book's use of racial terminology, especially the presence of "Negro" in its title. When *From Slavery to Freedom* was first published, its initial subtitle of *A History of American Negroes* was entirely appropriate. For African American intellectuals at midcentury, the capitalized term "Negro" was a hard-won advance on the previous designation of "colored," and its advocates hoped that it would define Black Americans as a specific racial grouping with concrete aspirations for equal treatment under the law. When Franklin first used the term, then, it was commonly understood as a politicized assertion of racial pride.[103] As the Black freedom struggle developed, however, younger activists and intellectuals shifted their preferences to the term "Black." The new designation stood in turn as a radical alternative to "Negro," which SNCC leader and Black Power activist Stokely Carmichael argued had been co-opted and redefined by liberal integrationists.[104] Nuancing this perspective through examination of the centuries-long "names controversy" among descendants of enslaved people, the radical Black historian Sterling Stuckey nonetheless argued that the history of the term "Negro" meant that it was inextricably linked with the experience of slavery in a way that designations such as "Black" and "Afro-American" were not.[105] In the ten years separating Carmichael's and Stuckey's arguments, it had become clear that Franklin's preferred term was viewed by most African Americans as outdated.

Throughout this period, Franklin started to integrate the term "Black" as a descriptor in the body of *From Slavery to Freedom* but did not change the book's subtitle in order to replace the term "Negro." Unlike the historian Rayford Logan, who was eighteen years his senior and rejected the use of "Black" absolutely, Franklin was clearly more flexible in the face of changing terminology.[106] Nonetheless, as those who knew him have attested, the continued use of "Negro" was a "matter of principle," and he often became angry when the topic was raised.[107] Franklin remained fundamentally uncertain about the cultural nationalism that provided the foundation for the Black history and African American studies movements, even after they had catapulted *From Slavery to Freedom* to prominence.[108]

Nonetheless, during the 1980s and 1990s, the tide turned. A report commissioned by McGraw-Hill in 1985 questioned the legitimacy of the term

"Negro" in the book's early chapters, suggesting that students had regularly "voiced consternation" at the use of a term that tended to "obfuscate the picture" when discussing the African past.[109] By 1991, however, the critiques were broader, with another report giving an overview of shifting nomenclature before suggesting that "the name be changed on the front of the book to read 'From Slavery to Freedom: A History of Black Americans' or 'A History of Afro-Americans.'"[110] This type of approach was expressed more forcefully the same year, in a letter from an instructor at a California community college:

> I have taught Black History over 17 years, and I have used your text book, *From Slavery to Freedom.* . . . Your book has been revised several times and the word "Negro" is still used. It is better to use Black, African American, or Afro-American instead of Negro. If this is not done, I can *no longer use your book* as the text of my class in years to come. Students find the term repulsive. Enclosed, please find a list of signatures of students who find the term disgusting. Please contact the author about the *change* that is *needed.*[111]

Franklin and Moss subsequently took more conscious steps to engage with the problem. At an editorial meeting, they agreed that they would continue to approach the issue of terminology on a "case by case basis" in the main text, and that they would not "eliminate the term 'Negro,' but . . . reduce the frequency of its use."[112] They also decided to change the subtitle of the seventh edition of the book, published in 1994, to *A History of African Americans.* Explaining this in the preface, Franklin and Moss suggested:

> While African American is increasing in current usage, there is no reason to believe that this is a final designation; for the political and cultural winds that produced it continue to blow, perhaps sweeping before them earlier designations and bringing forth in some later time a designation as yet unknown. . . . In recognizing the changes that have come in recent years, we must take care not to impose recent designations on persons of an earlier period.[113]

In making this point, the authors recognized the controversy involved in continuing to use the term "Negro," but at the same time emphasized the fundamental contingencies of racial terminology.

At least part of the responsibility for this important change must lie with Moss. Born in 1943 and a former graduate student of Franklin's at the University of Chicago, he was part of the generation that experienced the emergence of Black Power and cultural nationalism firsthand. He was therefore able to act as a mediator between Franklin and his radical critics. Furthermore, Franklin's resistance to change was born less of his being wedded to "Negro" than of his resistance to the use of "Black," which, to many African Americans of his and earlier generations, had been a derogatory term. Once

"African American" had arrived as a plausible middle ground between the two, change was more palatable to him. This explanation is backed up by the fact that Franklin had subtly changed the book's subtitle from *A History of American Negroes* to *A History of Negro Americans* for the third edition in 1967, a shift that reflected the author's changing understanding of African Americans' legal and political status after the passage of the Civil Rights and Voting Rights Acts of 1964 and 1965, as well as a shifting emphasis away from biological and toward socially constructed definitions of race in American intellectual life.[114]

It is also important to recognize that Franklin maintained a career-long conviction that African American history did not make sense unless rooted in an understanding of the African past. This was not only a scholarly but also an emotional conviction. For example, in his autobiography Franklin described how his first visit to Nigeria filled him with a "fraternal feeling" and a realization that he had "adopted Africa as my true motherland."[115] As Stuckey observed in 1977, the use of terms such as "Afro-American" and "African American" often allowed "people of African ancestry in the Americas" to feel a connection to the "land, history, and culture of their forebears, while recognizing their presence as an unassimilated people in America."[116] The abiding nature of Franklin's liberal Afrocentrism should therefore not be underestimated as another factor that shaped his decision to embrace "African American" in *From Slavery to Freedom*'s subtitle after years of resistance to adopting the designation "Black."

Overall, the substantive historiographical changes made to the text, along with the alterations of its subtitle, show how the development of Black history and African American studies impacted Franklin's relationship to his readers. By 1994 these fields were more dynamic and diverse than they had been when he first published *From Slavery to Freedom*. They were also now dominated by scholars whose approaches were informed by the politics of cultural nationalism. Rather than doing battle with young radicals as he had done in the 1960s and 1970s, Franklin was forced to recognize that the book's continuing status as the most widely read popular history of Black Americans depended not only on his authority and status as an individual historian, but also on its ability to adapt to new historiographical and political climates, and to attract new readers among activist audiences who were now most likely to be college students in African American studies programs. Ultimately, millions of Black readers had read *From Slavery to Freedom* and developed a close personal connection to its content. This was exactly what Franklin had hoped for upon publication of the first edition in 1947. However, it would have been hard for him to imagine the way the book's fortunes were transformed by the interventions of its activist readers as they reinvented its intellectual and political significance throughout the postwar period.

Franklin died two years before the ninth edition of *From Slavery to Freedom* was published in 2011. He had taken a back seat in the latest revisions process, allowing his new coauthor, the Harvard historian Evelyn Brooks Higginbotham, to take the text in new directions. There was a somber tone to the volume's foreword, which was written by the literary critic Henry Louis Gates Jr. Gates summarized *From Slavery to Freedom*'s importance when he wrote that "every scholar of my generation studied Franklin's book in a survey course in African American history; in this sense, we are all his godchildren."[117] Gates's metaphor drew attention to the vast influence of Franklin's popular history, which had sold more than three million copies since its first publication in 1947; had been translated into Chinese, French, German, Japanese, and Portuguese; and consequently remained a staple of university classrooms around the world.

From Slavery to Freedom came to develop this influence because its interpretation of African American history initially captured the mood of midcentury racial liberalism, before expanding its credibility as this liberal perspective fractured during the 1960s and 1970s in response to both the successes and failures of the Black freedom struggle. Subsequently, as radical approaches to Black history and African American studies were institutionalized during the 1980s and 1990s, Franklin was successful in adapting the book to new historiographical and political realities. This was a fundamentally different type of popular history to that written and published by Richard Hofstadter and Daniel Boorstin, to the extent that it appealed directly to a public conceptualized not as "general" readers, comfortable in their relationship to the liberal consensus, but to "activist" readers who were eager to use the insights derived from the history they consumed to imagine a more equal society. These were readers who were much more likely to challenge the perspectives offered by the authors who wrote for them. Indeed, Franklin was forced to grapple with a range of criticisms motivated not only by scholarly disagreements, but also by fundamental disputes over questions of racial politics. In this sense, then, Gates's idea of Franklin as the "godparent" of popular understandings of African American history is not as apt as it first seems. Many of his readers did not view him as an altogether benevolent force in their intellectual upbringing. Instead, they grappled with, revised, and sometimes rejected his ideas, using them to clarify their fundamental understandings of racial identity and political activism.

In navigating the controversy of the book's reception by these activist readers, Franklin was not alone among postwar historians. If all popular historical writing was inherently political, the writing embodied in *From Slavery to Freedom* was politicized in a very different way to that of Hofstadter and Boorstin. Instead of existing firmly within the framework of the postwar liberal consensus, Franklin's ideas actively challenged its assumptions about the significance of race and racism in American history. His personality, prose style, and the way Knopf framed his place in the literary marketplace all mitigated against controversy. Nonetheless, he found himself caught up in it, and the book's popularity was increased by the tumult of the Black freedom struggle. Another writer who found his work catapulted into the spotlight by the upheavals of the 1960s and 1970s was Howard Zinn. But in his case, causing controversy was the very meaning of the historian's craft. A natural radical, he wrote a very different type of popular history for activist audiences.

4

Howard Zinn: Popular History as Controversy

In April 1987, the conservative economist and public intellectual Thomas Sowell wrote a widely syndicated newspaper column about the problem of bias in American higher education. Imagining a situation in which like-minded Americans were seeking college places for their children, he asked, "Since nothing serious is being done about the continuing degeneration of education into propaganda, what can students and their parents do?" The answer was to engage in "comparison shopping," by probing chosen universities to discover how deep the influence of left-wing faculty members ran. One measure of this influence was whether Howard Zinn's *A People's History of the United States* (1980) was a visible presence on campus. "If you go to a college bookstore during your visit and find this textbook," Sowell suggested, "that tells you all you need to know." He went on to argue that the presence of scholars like Zinn on university curricula "can make the difference between getting a good education . . . and wasting a lot of time and money on something shallow and dishonest." In this argument, the reception of Zinn's book was a key measure of the extent to which the humanities and social sciences had been corrupted by the forces of the Left. For Sowell, *A People's History* was biased, anti-American, and contained arguments that "would embarrass *Pravda*."[1] It was, ultimately, an example of popular history gone spectacularly wrong.

However, for many other Americans, Zinn's book was a revelatory piece of historical writing. It provided them with their first opportunity to read history from "the bottom up" and to see, as the historian framed it in the book's opening chapter,

the story of the discovery of America from the viewpoint of the Arawaks, of the Constitution from the standpoint of the slaves, of Andrew Jackson as seen by the Cherokees, of the Civil War as seen by the New York Irish, of the Mexican war as seen by the deserting soldiers of Scott's army, of the rise of industrialism as seen by the young women in the Lowell textile mills, of the Spanish-American war as seen by the Cubans, the conquest of the Philippines as seen by black soldiers on Luzon, the Gilded Age as seen by Southern farmers, the First World War as seen by socialists, the Second World War as seen by pacifists, the New Deal as seen by blacks in Harlem, the postwar American empire as seen by peons in Latin America.[2]

This was a highly politicized history, one that questioned established scholarly conventions of objectivity. It found an enormous readership, attracting fans with experience of activism during the 1960s and 1970s. But more than anyone else, the book captured the attention of that generation's children and grandchildren, who interpreted it as an antidote to the insipid history presented in their high school classrooms.

Published by Harper & Row, A People's History has sold more than two million copies and been translated into numerous foreign languages. It therefore stands as another example of the enduring popularity of historical writing aimed at activist audiences during the second half of the twentieth century. However, as Sowell's 1987 excoriation highlights, Zinn attracted a more partisan response from his readers than Hofstadter, Boorstin, or Franklin. How could a 600-page textbook synthesis of left-wing historical writing cause such consternation on the right (as well as in certain sections of the historical profession), while generating such devotion on the left? Part of the answer to this question lies in a matter of timing: Zinn's book emerged amid the "culture wars" of the 1980s and 1990s, a moment in which conservative advocates of "normative America" pushed back against the liberal and radical agendas forged by activists and intellectuals during the 1960s.[3] In part, these were debates about national history, and whether the purpose of learning about that history was to make students more patriotic about, or more critical of, their nation's past.[4]

Clearly, Zinn's vociferous interpretation of American history made a high-profile intervention in this debate. But close examination of A People's History and its place within the larger story of postwar popular historical writing highlights some more specific and complex explanations for its enduring popularity and controversy. The book generated such heated response because of Zinn's composite generational position between the Old and New Lefts, his ability to generate excitement among young readers, the way the book framed American history through the lens of an idiosyncratic popular radicalism, and, finally, the way its afterlives were shaped not only by a series of political controversies, but also by the resonance of Zinn's version of American history for producers of movies and television. The book was a product of the culture wars, then, but also of changing understandings of what popular historical writing could achieve as it engaged and politicized activist audiences whose understandings of US history had been shaped by post-1960s politics, education, and popular culture.

Richard Hofstadter, Daniel Boorstin, and John Hope Franklin all came of age as proponents of the radical and reformist politics of the 1930s and 1940s, only to find themselves in confrontation with the young activists of the 1960s and 1970s. In a range of ways both intellectual and political, Howard Zinn's historical sensibility was also shaped by his interstitial position between the Old and the New Lefts. But in contrast to his peers, Zinn maintained his radical credentials after World War II and became a high-profile spokesperson for the New Left. The generational liminality that ensued shaped all his writing, not least *A People's History*.[5] While the book is often thought of as a distillation of the "New Left" historiography that emerged from the activist movements of the 1960s, its author's biography highlights a much longer intellectual and political gestation.

Zinn was born in 1922 to a working-class family living in the slums of Brooklyn, New York. At the age of seventeen, he left school and took up employment in the nearby Navy Yard, where he developed a sense of "the dignity of being a workingman." At the same time, he encountered radical political ideas for the first time, both at work, where he participated in trade union organization, and in his free time on Bushwick Avenue, where he became fascinated by the "young Communists" who "talked politics into the night with anyone who was interested." He participated in protests and developed a radicalized understanding of politics that disabused him of the liberal notion that American democracy could be "self-correcting." Instead, he came to believe that "something fundamental" was wrong with a society in which the problems of poverty and racism were embedded in the experience of everyday life. While there is little evidence that Zinn was a member of the CPUSA, he was certainly a fellow traveler and unashamedly described the late 1930s and early 1940s as his "communist years."[6]

Like Hofstadter, this was also the period in which he developed a belief in the power of literature to shape political ideas. While working at the Navy Yard, Zinn participated in a reading group that met weekly to discuss political texts such as *The Communist Manifesto* (1848), but also fiction, including novels by Jack London, Upton Sinclair, John Steinbeck, and Richard Wright. These writers all dramatized his sense that "race and class oppression were

intertwined" in American society.[7] But the writer who had the most significant impact on Zinn was Charles Dickens:

> He aroused in me tumultuous emotions. First, an anger at arbitrary power
> puffed up with wealth and kept in place by law. But most of all, a profound
> compassion for the poor. . . . Dickens is sometimes criticized by literary snobs
> for sentimentality, melodrama, partisanship, exaggeration. But surely the state
> of the world makes fictional exaggeration unnecessary and partisanship vital.[8]

Zinn's political and literary sensibilities were thus shaped by his Depression-
era reading. Drawn to a range of nineteenth- and twentieth-century literature
featuring elements of social realism, these fueled his awareness of political
injustice. They also developed his understanding of emotion and partisanship as literary devices, features that would find their way into all of Zinn's
future writing. In arriving at these conclusions, he was a very young member
of the "cultural front" that emerged out of immigrant and African American
working-class neighborhoods in the 1930s and 1940s. This was a culture that
was centrally concerned with the overlapping politics of communism, anti-
racism, and anti-fascism, and committed to the idea that literary and intellectual culture should be shaped by these explicitly political ideas.[9]

As was so often the case for radicals of his generation, World War II
marked a significant turning point for Zinn. Though appalled by the Nazi-
Soviet Pact (1939), it was the experience of serving in the US Air Force that
most impacted his understanding of politics. Zinn joined the war effort out
of a sense of political duty, deciding that military service represented "a noble
crusade against racial superiority, militarism, fanatic nationalism, and ex-
pansionism." Indeed, in their enthusiastic anti-fascism, Zinn and his wife,
Roslyn, came to the agreement that, in the aftermath of D-Day and with the
end of the war approaching, he should trade places with other bombardiers
scheduled to go overseas before him, so as not to miss out on the opportunity
to fight against Nazi Germany.[10] In this sense, the politics of the war appeared
as a continuation of the politics of the Depression: an opportunity to practi-
cally commit to a radical fight against inequality, both at home and abroad.

However, as Zinn witnessed the complicity of the air force in catastrophic
human destruction, he quickly came to view this enthusiasm as naive. He was
personally involved in the April 1945 bombing of Royan, France, and returned
horrified at the effect of an experimental weapon he had been ordered to drop
on the city: napalm. Then, only months later, he learned of the destructive scale
of the nuclear weapons used against Japan at Hiroshima and Nagasaki. These
acts of violence were watershed moments for Zinn and started the process by

which he revised his view that the fight against fascism could be participated in with "absolute morality." Instead, he decided that "the atmosphere of war brutalizes everyone involved," and turned toward the anti-militarist mindset that would prove so significant during the Vietnam era.[11]

The experience of war also forced Zinn to rethink his ideas about communism. While serving in Europe, he became fascinated by the arguments of Arthur Koestler, especially his book *The Yogi and the Commissar* (1945). What attracted Zinn to Koestler was the way that the Hungarian writer arrived at a nuanced anti-communist standpoint, in which he was able to criticize the totalitarian Soviet ideology of the "Commissar," without slipping toward the relativizing position of the "Yogi," who could only view social inequality through a lens of "passive submission."[12] Koestler's book shook Zinn's political ideas forever and led, several years later, to a sympathetic reading of *The God That Failed* (1950), a set of essays edited by the British member of Parliament Richard Crossman that drew together anti-communist writers from Europe and the United States.[13] The book contained a range of political insights, including Koestler's own denunciation of Soviet backsliding toward the Nazi-Soviet Pact, after which he found himself able to voice wholehearted opposition to the USSR, and "no longer cared whether Hitler's allies called me a counter-revolutionary."[14] These were the foundations of Zinn's anti-Soviet mindset: not what Crossman called the "facile anti-communism of expediency," which sought to oppose all radical politics in the name of the Cold War, but an anti-communism rooted in continued commitment to the Left.[15]

Again, though, the lessons Zinn drew from this chapter in his life were also intellectual and literary. He was already aware of Richard Wright (via his 1940 novel *Native Son*) when he read the African American writer's contribution to *The God That Failed*. Wright's essay detailed his experience as a CPUSA member, describing his dismay at party comrades who viewed him with curiosity and exoticism, given what they saw as his peculiar status as a Black "intellectual." This experience of being treated as a "fantastic element" by both Black and white party members led Wright away from the party.[16] Nonetheless, he remained committed to documenting the struggles of working-class African Americans. In seeking to make the Black experience "more intelligible," Wright suggested that he would

> hurl words into this darkness and wait for an echo; and if an echo sounded, no matter how faintly, I would send other words to tell, to march, to fight, to create a sense of the hunger for life that gnaws in us all, to keep alive in our hearts a sense of the inexpressibly human.[17]

Wright's lyrical argument that the documentation of everyday life could service a political project that was radical at the same time as it was anti-Soviet
appealed to Zinn, and years later he referred to it directly in a chapter on
African American protest in *A People's History*.[18] Disillusioned with the Soviet Union but still believing in socialism, he felt that the analytical key to
understanding the world remained the entangled relationship between class,
race, and militarism.[19]

Informed by these values, Zinn made the decision to enroll at New York
University at the age of twenty-five, supported by the GI Bill. He completed
his undergraduate degree in 1951, before moving to Columbia University to
undertake doctoral study in history, which he completed in 1958. Coming to
academia from a working-class background, later in life than was traditional
and after military service, Zinn had a pressing sense of the political motivations behind his research. Furthermore, as he completed his dissertation,
he was influenced by the Columbia historian Richard Hofstadter. Given the
relatively recent publication of *The American Political Tradition* (1947), it is
hardly surprising that Zinn was inspired by the book's embrace of a popular
yet critical writing style. Indeed, Hofstadter's interpretation of the common
capitalist vision held by all American politicians, no matter their party affiliation, would significantly influence the arguments Zinn developed twenty
years later in *A People's History*.

However, a much more significant development in these years was Zinn's
appointment in 1956, two years before the completion of his PhD, as professor and chair of the History Department at Spelman College, a Black women's
university in Atlanta, Georgia. In moving south, Zinn and his family relocated
to the heart of American white supremacy, but also to one of the geographical
foci of a range of long-term political movements seeking to "defy Dixie" via
radical challenges to the racial and economic status quo.[20] Zinn's intertwined
preoccupations at Spelman were the teaching of US and world history, along
with the mentoring of students involved in civil rights activism. His diaries
from the time contain numerous insights into the day-to-day activities by
which this process developed. For example, Zinn regularly taught the history
of late nineteenth- and early twentieth-century America, ensuring that the
subject matter would speak to the contemporary struggles of his students. In
early 1963, he taught the 1886 Haymarket Affair, in which protesting workers
clashed with Chicago police, resulting in at least eleven deaths and numerous
injuries. This class, Zinn noted, was an opportunity to engage his students
in discussion of the "invisibility" of the poor in American history and the
way that working-class agency was forged in conflict with the state.[21] Then, a
week later, he discussed the Progressive Era with another group of students

and again found an opportunity to outline activism's ability to shape political outcomes, as well as the contemporary resonances of this historical process:

> In U.S. history class, discussed Progressive movement reforms, making point that TR [Theodore Roosevelt], Taft, Wilson were *reacting* to pressures of Populist heritage, IWW, Socialists, strikes, muckrakers, etc., but that they get credit, as Hartsfield does, in history books, though Hartsfield reacted to Negro upsurge.[22]

Zinn was developing the themes in political history he had been taught at Columbia by Hofstadter and others, molding them to suit his own political belief in the importance of working-class agency.

But the reference to former Atlanta mayor William B. Hartsfield—who had won reelection in 1957 by resisting the politics of his arch-segregationist opponent, Lester Maddox, and who popularized the notion that Atlanta was the only southern city in which citizens were "too busy to hate"—highlighted how Zinn tried to make the history he taught relevant to his students and their interest in the racial politics of the South.[23] The development of these ideas about class, race, and the power of protest to shape political outcomes provided the first clear articulation of the "bottom-up" perspective Zinn would pursue in *A People's History*.[24]

Zinn's teaching and mentorship was clearly registered by his students. He taught the activist Marian Wright Edelman when she was an undergraduate at Spelman in the late 1950s, encouraging her and other students to "think outside the box." At this time, Zinn was manifestly committed to "live what he taught in history class" by challenging racial segregation in Atlanta, especially when he took his students to sit in the white section of the public gallery at the Georgia State Legislature. This example, Edelman has suggested, taught her "to examine and apply the lessons of history in the context of daily political, social, and moral challenges like racial discrimination and income inequality."[25] Another notable alumna of Spelman was the poet and novelist Alice Walker, who enrolled in 1961 and quickly forged a close relationship with Zinn. In a 1996 poem entitled "My Teacher," Walker highlighted the significance of Zinn's decision to support his students in rising up "against the local bosses, the killers of dreams, the reactionary cowards." She continued, "My teacher has heard the cry of the hungry, of the cold, of the imprisoned, and the humiliated. He has listened to the sobbing loneliness of the youngest soldier. My teacher has opened his arms to all."[26] As they reflected on their time at Spelman, these former students viewed Zinn as an exemplar of politically engaged pedagogy.

This perspective was not always welcomed by the university's administration, and in 1963 Zinn was fired by Spelman president Albert E. Manley, a decision that shocked both the historian and his students, and led them to believe that his contract was terminated because of his visible involvement in antiracist activism.[27] Writing about the event in 1994, with three decades of hindsight, Zinn was able to claim "a certain sympathy" for Manley, given the historian's unpopularity among the university's board of trustees. But more important than these professional concerns, he claimed, was the fact that he was "moved by the students," whose courage in speaking out in opposition to his firing filled him with awe.[28] This deeply held commitment to shaping the minds and futures of young adults, even at the expense of job security and advancement, were developed via Zinn's engagement with the peculiarities of the Spelman campus. While it came to an abrupt and unhappy end, his time in Atlanta allowed him to hone the approach to popular history that would later appear in *A People's History*.

The early 1960s also marked the beginnings of Zinn's engagement with the New Left, as he participated in the activities of the Student Nonviolent Coordinating Committee (SNCC), first in Atlanta and then, in 1964, as part of the Mississippi Summer Project. The Summer Project was an attempt to meld activism with cultural work, and its leaders embraced the power of history education to shape the political consciousness of African American communities.[29] Along with his friend and fellow historian Staughton Lynd, Zinn helped frame the history curriculum for the project and, in doing so, emphasized the utility of the Black past. It was in this moment that they demonstrated the value of Franklin's *From Slavery to Freedom* for activist audiences by setting it as key reading for participants in the project. But they also had their own intellectual agenda. In particular, the pair chose to highlight how the long history of African American protest was "inherently American." This enabled them to "justify and elaborate" the activism of Black Mississippians in the present.[30] While they developed this "usable past" in the aid of a radically new form of grassroots youth activism, it also had clear connections to the ideas that Zinn had developed since his youthful engagement with the Old Left in Depression-era Brooklyn.

After his firing from Spelman and involvement with SNCC, Zinn moved in the fall of 1964 to a new position in the Department of Political Science at Boston University, where he would remain until the end of his career. Unsurprisingly, his New Left political connections drew him into the fold of Boston's activist scene, especially via friendships with prominent critics of the war in Vietnam, such as the linguist and political commentator Noam Chomsky, the historian Marilyn Young, and, several years later, the former RAND employee-turned-whistleblower Daniel Ellsberg. Zinn emerged as a key figure in the local anti-war movement, speaking regularly at protests and

teach-ins, as well as traveling across the country to testify at the trials of protesters arrested for their participation in anti-war activism. In this activity,
Zinn clearly sought to exemplify the demand made of intellectuals by Chomsky in his widely referenced 1967 essay "The Responsibility of Intellectuals":
to "speak the truth and to expose lies" and thus resist the government's attempt to lead the United States "towards a 'final solution' in Vietnam, and in
the many Vietnams that inevitably lie ahead."[31]

Zinn distilled a considerable amount of his thinking during this period
into *Disobedience and Democracy*, a short pamphlet published in 1968. Returning to his long-held belief in the insufficiency of the ballot box as a tool
to "rectify injustice," he argued that it was precisely because of liberalism's
weakness that "the citizen in a democracy needs the weapon of civil disobedience." In Zinn's view, it was vital to remember that the individual and the state
were separate in their interests, with the state seeking "power, influence, and
wealth" as "ends in themselves," while the individual sought "health, peace,
creative activity, and love."[32] Ultimately, he felt that the overarching message
of the anti-war movement, as well as the broader culture of New Left politics
that it represented, should be that

> most people in the world are hungry, have no decent place to sleep, no doctor
> when they are sick; and some are fleeing from attacking airplanes. Somehow,
> we must transcend our own tight, air-conditioned chambers and begin to feel
> their plight, their needs. It may become evident that, despite our wealth, we
> can have no real peace until they do. We might then join them in battering at
> the complacency of those who guard a false "order," with that healthy commo-
> tion that has always attended the growth of injustice.[33]

Once again, Zinn advanced the idea that the interests of the Left would be
best served through a process of knowing and understanding those marginalized by the system, both at home and abroad. This was a vision not only of
political action, but also of historical writing as disobedience, and one that he
would pursue in *A People's History*.

Zinn's intellectual and political identities thus straddled the Old and New
Lefts. Explaining and resisting the overlapping phenomena of class, race, and
militarist oppressions were his overriding concerns as he wrote *A People's
History*, and these ideas developed not only as a response to the politics of the
civil rights and anti-war movements in the 1960s, but also as part of a much
longer intellectual formation that intersected Depression-era considerations
of poverty, racism, and communism with wartime reflections on anti-fascism
and militarism. *A People's History* was thus a synthesis of several generations
of left-wing attempts to describe and analyze American history and politics.

That it was so popular with young readers is testament to the long-standing appeal of these ideas, as well as to Zinn's particular ability to communicate them across another generational divide.

During his time in the South, Zinn decided that his professional standing could be "useful" to the civil rights movement if he devoted himself to writing projects that would blend "scholarship and activism."[34] This led him to sign with the Sterling Lord literary agency in New York, who supported him through the publication by Alfred A. Knopf of his second book, *The Southern Mystique* (1964). At a similar time, Zinn also began to publish essays in national political magazines such as *The Nation*, reporting on his experiences at Spelman and with SNCC.[35] He was beginning to project his voice beyond the academy in a serious and sustained way.

It was at this moment, and once again in collaboration with Sterling Lord and Knopf, that Zinn began to discuss the prospect of writing a book entitled "A Hidden History of the United States."[36] The work he pitched to his editor, Angus Cameron, was thematic rather than chronological, but it nonetheless bore similarities to the book that would become *A People's History*. Writing in 1961, Zinn told Cameron that the book would be synthetic, to the extent that he would not be "unearthing new data but selecting from available historical materials just those things that can be focused on present problems."[37] This was Zinn's version of a "usable past," and it fused ideas drawn from his long-standing radical sensibilities with those he was developing via participation in the New Left. He would highlight the entanglement between class and race in American history, presenting "the Negro as our last hope, from whose shoulders . . . the nation might be able to understand its backwardness not only in racial exclusiveness but in other forms." From this, he would build an argument, influenced by French existentialism, for the development in the United States of "the unpossessed man," who "does not allow himself to be captured by capitalism or socialism, by any organization or ideology, who even in the heat of the most fervent actions for social change always retains an inviolable part of himself which is critical and free."[38] This book proposal was fundamentally different in structure to *A People's History*, but its existence as a concept, and Zinn's attempt to foreground the contemporary political contributions that it would make, highlight his long-standing desire to write an overarching, synthetic national history linking past and present.

Another important theme in Zinn's early discussions of the project was the question of readership. The historian told Cameron that he wanted to provide bibliographical essays for each chapter, so that he could "put all the professional name-dropping and name-calling in a separate place so that the general reader needn't be bothered by . . . such insiders' talk."[39] In contrast, Cameron was keen for Zinn to emphasize, rather than downplay, the historiographical interventions the author had in mind, suggesting that the book's originality would be accentuated through the absorption of bibliographical comment into individual chapters.[40] This was a version of the midcentury publishers' refrain that, to be most marketable, popular historical writing should be both well written and intellectually serious. But what is more interesting about Cameron's observations is the way he conceptualized the readership for such history:

> It's always good to bear in mind that when you talk about writing for a "general public" you're writing for a very, very small percentage of it, a percentage which is perfectly capable of absorbing the arguments which you make to your peers.[41]

Cameron's observations show that his understanding of the readership for popular history mapped neatly onto those of Richard Hofstadter and Daniel Boorstin: there were both intellectual and commercial reasons for defining the intended reader narrowly, as well educated, intelligent, and fully embedded in the middlebrow liberal consensus. Zinn's response to these suggestions has not survived, but by the mid-1970s his relationship with Knopf had terminated.[42] Instead, as he reported to Cameron in a 1976 letter, he had reached an agreement with Harper & Row to publish a manuscript entitled *A People's History of the United States*, which would be "one-volume, easy to read, radical in viewpoint."[43]

Zinn's reference to the book being "easy to read" indicates a clear departure from the vision of popular history for "general" readers articulated by Cameron a decade earlier. In making this departure, the historian went in search of a different type of audience than that targeted by Hofstadter and Boorstin, one that was made up of younger readers who were restless with the middlebrow staples upheld by publishers such as Knopf and wanted to see their activist visions of the world represented in the history they read. This understanding was fundamental to the relationship Zinn developed with staff at Harper. The historian was first approached by the company's Junior Books Division in 1975 to publish an updated version of his book *Vietnam: The Logic of Withdrawal* (1967) aimed at young readers. The editor who initially engaged Zinn, Elaine Edelman, suggested that the material on America's most recent war circulating in high school textbooks was simply not accurate, and that this highlighted the emergence of a "post-Vietnam generation . . . that's turning away from the consciousness of the 1960s." In response, she told Zinn that it was "up to people like you to turn your understanding and talents to these kids—kids three and four years away from voting for the next President."[44]

It was out of these conversations that Zinn's relationship with Harper's Trade Division ultimately developed, along with his understanding of what it meant for popular writing to be "easy to read." When the manuscript of *A People's History* first arrived at the publisher, it was sent not only to readers willing to comment on its applicability for trade audiences, but also to high school teachers, who reported on its utility for classroom adoption. For example, in 1979 Cynthia Merman, Zinn's new editor, provided him with a list of revisions, before suggesting, "For high school students, you occasionally assume more historical knowledge than readers have."[45] Another reviewer for the press approached this topic with more positivity, suggesting that the book would appeal in a range of educational settings:

> Zinn's book . . . has a better chance than any of the competition I have seen, if properly marketed, of making history real and alive, especially to introductory students. . . . Harper & Row has an excellent opportunity to do some social good at the same time as it advances its own interests.[46]

For the publisher and its reviewers, then, the popular readership for Zinn's ideas was very different from that imagined by Knopf. This was decidedly *not* an attempt to engage historiographical complexity and court a middlebrow "general" readership. Instead, Merman and others at Harper understood that marketability and access to readers would come from framing the book as an all-new approach to US history, representing the values of 1960s activism, and rendering them accessible to school-age readers as well as adults.

In one sense, this was a set of stylistic decisions based around Zinn's talents as a writer: Harper viewed him as *the* person to communicate a radical version of national history to young Americans. But it was also a commercial decision taken by staff at the company who were determined to find a niche for the book in the youth market. Both judgments tapped into a generational sensibility embraced by those involved in the radical politics of the 1960s that emphasized the political radicalism of the young. Though linked to the greatly expanded number of Americans who came of age during the decade as part of the baby boom, this was not simply a demographic phenomenon. Instead, the decade's "youth frame" was one that told a larger story about the movements of the 1960s, emphasizing youth as a political identity, and underscoring "youthfulness" as a political choice as well as a by-product of being young.[47] These were values that the staff at Harper embraced when they courted Zinn, and the historian's own attitude about the political power of youth was evident in his commitment to politicized pedagogy, as well as his advocacy on behalf of student freedom, a continuing characteristic of his career at Boston University, where he regularly came into conflict with the administration of President John Silber.[48]

The book also arrived at an auspicious moment in the history of school textbooks. After the scholarly and political upheavals of the 1960s, authors of history texts lost faith in traditional narratives, which highlighted the singularity of the American people and way of life over multiple centuries. However, many publishers were cautious about the commercial implications of folding narratives of racism, sexism, and conquest into their texts. They were worried that doing so would alienate readers and close profitable markets, especially in southern states.[49] When *A People's History* was first published in 1980, then, the market was ripe for a book that confidently advanced a bottom-up perspective, especially if it was written by a historian with high-profile links to multiple 1960s movements. Author and publisher did not expect the book to instantly sell millions of copies by gaining access to highly profitable high school markets. Nonetheless, its publication demonstrates the afterlife of the "youth frame" as it was navigated by Zinn and his publishers in the post-1960s educational landscape, where the views of marginalized groups were not being effectively incorporated into the national narrative.

How did Zinn's readers respond to the book? The earliest reviewers positioned it in relation to school and university textbooks, arguing that it was distinguished by its radical perspective. Trailing *A People's History* in advance of its official publication date, for example, *Publishers Weekly* suggested that Zinn had interpreted American history as a "continuing class struggle" in order to "counter traditional history texts."[50] Similarly, Luther Spoehr in the *Saturday Review* described it as an "anti-textbook," while historian Bruce Kuklick, writing a critical review in *The Nation*, argued that Zinn had written "a radical textbook history . . . designed to give the left a usable past," and that the author hoped "to inculcate into students a certain view of America."[51] Other reviews chose to highlight the originality and clarity of Zinn's writing, which the reviewer for the *Grand Rapids Press* in Michigan described as "an antidote to the saccharine that clogs so many volumes of American history."[52] Similarly, the historian Eric Foner, writing for the *New York Times Book Review*, argued that "Zinn writes with an enthusiasm rarely encountered in the leaden prose of academic history."[53] In the twelve months after its publication, *A People's History* was widely reviewed, and, more importantly for staff at Harper & Row, it was regularly cited as an exciting crossover text that would appeal to both trade and educational markets.

In this context, it was the book's first chapter that garnered the most attention. Zinn opened his treatment of contact between European and Indigenous peoples in the Americas with a dramatic imagined narrative of the first encounter between Christopher Columbus and Arawak men and women, described as "naked, tawny, and full of wonder." From the outset, Zinn impressed upon his readers that this "beginning" was one rooted in "conquest, slavery, death." These were themes completely absent from "the history books given to children in the United States," in which such events were treated as a form of "heroic adventure," used to lull young readers into the "quiet acceptance of conquest and murder in the name of progress."[54] Going into more depth to elaborate the connections between economic and military conquest, he described the early colonization of Spanish America, Peru in particular, as driven by "the frenzy in the early capitalist states of Europe for gold, for slaves, for products of the soil," demands that were rooted in "that special powerful drive in civilizations based on property."[55] Again, it was not difficult to discern Zinn's overlapping emphasis on race, class, and conquest as key themes in American history.

This was not only an attempt to write from the romanticized perspective of the conquered, though. It was also an intervention in ongoing debates about Columbus, especially those centered on the national holiday held in his honor. Indeed, Zinn's coverage of these contemporary questions soon came to the attention of journalist Richard Cohen, who used the arguments in *A People's History* to rethink the Columbus Day holiday in 1982. On the front page of the *Washington Post*'s "Metro" section, Cohen praised Zinn's attempt to "turn over the rock of hero-worship and expose the gunk that lies underneath," before continuing:

> If Columbus is to be remembered, then it ought to be not only for accidentally discovering the New World, but also for enslaving and murdering the Arawak Indians he met there.... It is his time of year, and no newspaper column could possibly deprive him of his annual spotlight. But we would be better off as a nation if we extolled him for the good things he did, condemned him for the bad and learned, as he should have, from his mistakes. Happy Arawak Day.[56]

As well as publicizing Zinn's book, the article highlighted the contribution the historian made to a contentious national dialogue about the legitimacy of an annual holiday celebrating a historical figure viewed by some as the progenitor of violence and, in some cases, genocide.[57] To wish the readers of the *Washington Post* "happy Arawak Day" was to force them to at least consider adopting a radically alternative lens for viewing national history.

Indeed, over the coming decade, Zinn received numerous letters from readers engaging him on this topic. For example, one student who encountered *A People's History* as part of an advanced placement high school history class told Zinn that she had "always believed that Columbus was the hero who found America," but that since reading his chapter on the subject and having her view upturned, she had started to "gain interest in the subject of history which I used to dislike so much."[58] Another student, this time in a history class at the University of Massachusetts Boston, suggested that the chapter on Columbus was his "favorite" in the book, because he had grown up in the Caribbean and felt that Zinn's writing gave legitimacy to his outsider's sense that "Columbus was not a 'great man,'" before concluding, "Thanks for your honesty and having the courage to reveal the truth."[59]

Writing in 1992 to mark the quincentenary of contact, Zinn noted his surprise at the fact that he had received such a disproportionate amount of correspondence about the first chapter in a book that covered five hundred years of history. But as he made clear, this level of interest was rooted less in a fascination with Columbus then it was in a frustration with the empty "claims of pluralism and diversity in American culture."[60] In this argument, which Zinn continued two years later in his autobiography, the "problem" that his interpretation of contact created was not one of scholarly analysis. Instead, it grew out of his "entire approach to American history," which, for many readers, proved shocking and revelatory.[61]

As well as students, some of these readers were teachers, who found A People's History to be a provocative classroom tool. Writing in 1981, Roxanne Dunbar-Ortiz, a historian at California State University, Hayward, and an activist in the American Indian Movement, wrote to Zinn to tell him that she had used the book to "introduce radical ideas" to her students. Ultimately, she wanted to thank him for "this valuable contribution to our social revolution."[62] Zinn received further such letters, from, among others, an educator at a conservative college in Utah, who used the book to challenge his overwhelmingly Republican students, and the organizer of a series of "Summer Workshops on People's History" aimed at working-class residents of Lewisburg, Pennsylvania.[63]

Unsurprisingly, all this interest generated healthy year-on-year sales figures for the book. In 1992 Zinn was able to report that it had sold approximately 260,000 copies, with annual totals rising steadily from 16,000 in 1982 to 44,000 in 1991. He also reported an additional 30,000 sales of The Twentieth Century: A People's History, an abridgment of the original book first published in 1984.[64] This performance represented a success for both the author and his publisher. Harper & Row had recruited Zinn to write radical history for young readers, and he had delivered. The historian had signed up to write A People's History to produce a book that was "easy to read, radical in viewpoint," and a range of sympathetic responses from students and teachers demonstrated that he had done so.

This success was, in part, rooted in the talent exemplified by Zinn and the shrewdness of the editorial and marketing staff he worked with at Harper. But it also grew out of the contexts provided by the 1960s shift to a "youth frame" in radical politics, and the concurrent crisis in the history textbook market. These developments provided rich ground for Zinn to shift from the middle-brow conceptualization of popular history he encountered when working with Knopf, and toward an alternative vision, which, like that of John Hope Franklin, drew on an understanding of readers as members of a politicized community of activists. These readers did not always agree about the politics of radical historical writing, but they nonetheless saw significant value in the contribution made by *A People's History*.

Writing in 1981 for the liberal Catholic magazine *Commonweal*, historian David O'Brien found much to praise in *A People's History*. He described the book as "a fitting expression of its author: committed, angry, one-sided, polemical, and profoundly true."[65] Nonetheless, O'Brien's conclusion was critical. In his view, Zinn's work was as partial as the traditional textbook interpretations it sought to overturn:

> This is not the full story *of* the American people, and not a full story *for* the American people. It risks distorting both past and future. It results in alienation, or an existential gesture, rather than a serious democratic and socialist politics.[66]

Despite the book's popularity with non-academic readers, it provoked criticism from two overlapping constituencies represented by O'Brien: professional historians and advocates of left-wing politics. This criticism demonstrates not only the polarizing nature of Zinn's scholarship, but also the fundamental anxieties generated by its popularity, both of which were produced by the nature of the historian's engagement with the historiographical politics of the Old and New Lefts, as well as his idiosyncratic adoption of radicalism as an emotionally charged popular discourse.

As we have seen, Zinn made significant use of his former mentor Richard Hofstadter's critical framework for describing the consensus at work in American politics. Hofstadter was therefore one of Zinn's clearest influences as he wrote *A People's History*. However, based on in-text citations throughout the book, as well as references in its bibliography, Zinn owed an even greater historiographical and political debt to a group of historians who represented

a resolutely Old Left scholarly sensibility. In particular, the book's cumula-
tive references to historians Philip S. Foner (22) and Herbert Aptheker (13)
were equal to or greater than those to Hofstadter (13). Foner (b. 1910) and
Aptheker (b. 1915) were a little older than Zinn. However, both were shaped
by comparable political and intellectual biographies. The sons of European
immigrants to the United States and who trained as historians at Columbia
University while participating in radical politics, they publicly identified with
the CPUSA and remained members of the party for much of their lives. In
his ten-volume *History of the Labor Movement in the United States* (1947–94),
Foner approached American history with the goal of rescuing "from neglect
the great heroes and heroines" of America's working-class past, and, in doing
so, channeled the partisanship of his communist politics into an effort to "distinguish correct from incorrect policies, heroes from villains, and progressive
from regressive labor traditions."[67]

Aptheker, on the other hand, applied his comparable political commitment to another field: the history of slavery. The key insight of his pathbreaking *American Negro Slave Revolts* (1936) was that "revolts and rebellions"
against slavery were "only one manifestation of broad resistance" to the antebellum racial order among African Americans and that US history could not
be properly understood without reference to the Black struggle.[68] Like Foner,
Aptheker's research agenda was driven by political as well as scholarly commitment: he contributed to the culture of the CPUSA via his historical writing, by highlighting the radical progressive traditions in US history as a way
of providing the foundations for an American version of socialism.[69]

Zinn shared with historians such as Foner and Aptheker a vision of class
conflict, the heroism of protest, and the centrality of political struggle to the
development of American democracy. In clear and coherent ways, this model
of engaged historical scholarship, rooted in the desire to uncover the contributions made to political struggle by workers and African Americans, owed
much to conceptualizations of left-wing historical writing forged during the
1930s and 1940s. This was clear in a pivotal chapter of *A People's History*, which
covers the history of the Gilded Age and Progressive Era and was entitled "Rob-
ber Barons and Rebels." Woven into Zinn's narrative of post-Reconstruction
political and social life are several important observations that reflect an Old
Left understanding of history and politics. He wrote that the government of
the United States was "behaving almost exactly as Karl Marx described a capitalist state" to the extent that it maintained political order at the expense of
working-class rebellion, which meant that "whether Democrats or Republicans won, national policy would not change in any important way." This
thesis allowed Zinn to provide his readers with a series of other theoretical

pronouncements about the modern state. "Control in modern times requires more than force, more than law," he suggested. "It requires that a population dangerously concentrated in cities and factories, whose lives are filled with cause for rebellion, be taught that all is right as it is."[70] This led to the conclusion that the nation's education system was "developed as an aid to the industrial system," and that the teaching of history was "required . . . to foster patriotism," all of which was designed to stop individual Americans from "contemplating other possible ways of living."[71] Woven into celebratory accounts of the resistance mounted by Eugene Debs, Edward Bellamy, the Haymarket Martyrs, and Emma Goldman were a set of observations about the nature of the modern state that emphasized its ability to isolate pockets of resistance and maintain individual alienation via methods of cultural and social coercion as well as the rule of force and law.

The connection between these ideas and those of the Old Left is clear if *A People's History* is compared to socialist scholar Leo Huberman's *We, the People: The Drama of American History* (1932), a Depression-era work of popular history. The book, which included illustrations by the social realist painter Thomas Hart Benton, aimed to provide a "stirring account of the building of a nation through the efforts of men, women, and children of stout heart in the face of great odds." But as well as providing this working-class perspective on the past, it also interlaced Huberman's politicized understandings of capitalism into its narrative: it was "the saga of big business in America," and thus "a tale of the growing power of monopoly."[72] Viewed through this lens, his interpretation of the Gilded Age and Progressive Era bore striking similarity to that presented by Zinn almost a half century later. Huberman described the ruling ideology of the period as one in which "property was first, human life second," before extolling the heroism of working-class organizations, especially the Industrial Workers of the World (IWW), as the primary repositories of "class sentiment, as well as the means of cooperation and communication."[73] In spite of this positive view of radical politics, his overarching analysis struck a similar chord of pessimism to that of Zinn:

> The employing class saw in labor unions a challenge to its power. It was, accordingly, opposed to unions, and it used every means, fair or foul, to destroy them. Some of the most bitter struggles in American history—struggles in which thousands of dollars' worth of property was destroyed and scores of lives were lost—were the result, in the last analysis, of the refusal by the employers to recognize labor unions and bargain collectively with them.[74]

Like Zinn's popular history almost half a century later, this was a rendering of the national past in which the agency of "the people," workers in particular, was celebrated. But it was also one in which the power of capitalism to contain radical politics was, "in the last analysis," dominant.

Given the roots of Zinn's radicalism in the political and intellectual cultures of the 1930s and 1940s, this kinship is hardly surprising. His debts to historians such as Foner, Aptheker, and Huberman (the latter of whom Zinn did not cite in his book but could hardly have been unaware of) only make this point clearer.[75] In narrating American history in the way that he did, Zinn was thus replicating the strategies of left-wing authors and publishers of the Depression era, in particular the British Left Book Club, which, under the auspices of London-based publisher Victor Gollancz, had published titles such as socialist historian A. L. Morton's *A People's History of England* (1938). Although Zinn is often thought of as a popularizer of the historiography of the New Left, the politics of his work also shared deep-seated continuities with those of an older generation of American radicals.

This old-fashioned scholarly sensibility goes some way to explaining the criticism Zinn faced from liberal and left-wing historians who reviewed *A People's History*. Eric Foner's *New York Times* review, for example, took the book to task for its "strangely circumscribed" portrayal of "anonymous Americans." These people appeared only as "rebels or victims," Foner suggested, before arguing that "less dramatic but more typical lives" had been ignored.[76] Similarly, while he was supportive of the underlying impulse behind the idea of a "people's history," Michael Kammen sarcastically noted that Zinn mentioned Philip Foner more often than he did Thomas Jefferson. This resulted in a "simple-minded history . . . of Robin Hoods," that made no effort to delve into the complexities of working-class existence.[77] In making these points, Foner and Kammen echoed the proponents of the "new" social and labor histories of the 1970s and 1980s, which criticized Old Left scholars such as Foner and Aptheker for their simplistic portrayals of lives lived in romanticized struggle. Historians such as Herbert Gutman, David Montgomery, and David Brody all worked to highlight, in Brody's words, the "complexity and variety of working-class experience," thus emphasizing the patterns of everyday life as much as radical challenges to the status quo.[78] In this sense, Zinn's writing was decidedly *unrepresentative* of New Left social and labor history, and once again betrayed its debts to his intellectual and political formation in the 1930s and 1940s.

However, this is not to suggest that Zinn's interpretations went uninfluenced by the changes wrought on American historiography by the social movements of the 1960s and 1970s. Indeed, he cited work published by a wide range of historians associated with them: early Americanists such as Gary Nash, Staughton Lynd, and Jesse Lemisch; nineteenth-century historians such as Gutman, Eugene Genovese, and Nancy Cott; and scholars of the twentieth century such as Gabriel Kolko, Marilyn Young, and Gar Alperovitz. Zinn's intellectual debts to these scholars were multiple, and he littered his text with references to their work. In at least one instance, he even used such material without providing adequate citation.[79]

But Zinn's most important relationship to the New Left's historiography was as its first successful popularizer. Radical historians had wanted to make their new perspectives attractive to non-academic audiences as early as 1952, when Warren Susman worried that innovative left-wing approaches to the past would remain "isolated and unread" until their proponents understood that "it is the historian's obligation to improve his craft, to make meaning in his scholar's degree . . . to do what he can to aid man in passing from reality to even more meaningful reality."[80] This was a call for politically committed scholarship that disavowed Cold War ideology, but also for historical writing that aimed to engage readers beyond the academy. Indeed, a comparable theme emerged again in 1968, when New Left historian Barton Bernstein drew together a now-classic collection of "dissenting essays" in American history for Random House entitled *Towards a New Past*. In the book's introduction, he complained that most of this radical new scholarship had been "restricted to university monographs or tucked away in historical journals, usually beyond the public's reach."[81] While collections like *Towards a New Past* attempted to remedy this inaccessibility, it was not until the appearance of *A People's History* that the New Left historiography would find its popular voice.

The book's political valences and controversies are better understood when considered alongside Zinn's intellectual relationship with his Boston University colleague and fellow radical activist Frances Fox Piven. During the period that Zinn wrote *A People's History*, Piven was hard at work with coauthor and fellow sociologist Richard Cloward on *Poor People's Movements* (1977), a seminal study of radical activism from the 1930s through the 1970s as it emerged among radical trade unions, the civil rights movement, and the welfare rights movement. More academic than Zinn's popular history, the book was nonetheless published by Random House and released in a Vintage Books paperback edition in 1978. Its authors' key claim was that the development of long-term organizations to represent the interests of lower-class Americans would always result in disappointment and failure because, in short, "organizations endure . . . by abandoning their oppositional politics." By documenting this argument via a series of detailed case studies, Piven and Cloward reached the conclusion that the only way for coherent movements to emerge was for organizers to "proceed as if protest were possible," but at the same time understand that if it failed in a particular instance, this did not mean that radical political activism was not a valid way of doing politics.[82]

In 1978, after the publication of *Poor People's Movements* but while Zinn was still writing *A People's History*, the historian corresponded with Piven from a temporary teaching post in Paris. He relayed a conversation with mutual friend and radical historian Harvey Goldberg, also then in France, in which the two men had agreed that *Poor People's Movements* was important because it used "historical material to raise tactical and strategic questions for the movement—even if the answers are hard to get."[83] This approach clearly inspired Zinn as he wrote his book, a point that he made several years later when he reflected to Piven that they had both grappled with a comparable problem: "how plausibly to urge insurrection while we show how sophisticated is the set of controls in use." In the same letter, he went on to praise Piven and Cloward's analytical precision, before suggesting that his approach was "more emotional than analytical," in that it sought to "have a mix of history and hope (that is of control-history and revolt-history) in which the latter dominates, if not by hard count, by emotional effect."[84] While he channeled the scholarship of the New Left, then, he also embraced a passionate and engaged narrative style that necessarily avoided many of the complex questions raised by the new radical historiography. Very different in style to that of John Hope Franklin, this was Zinn's particular version of how to write popular history for "activist" audiences, one that signaled his debt to the literary influence of Charles Dickens as much as the professional influence of the New Left historians.

Indeed, it was precisely because of this avoidance of complexity that Zinn was subsequently criticized by a range of scholars who were otherwise sympathetic to his politics. In 2004, for example, historian Michael Kazin attacked Zinn from both a professional and a political perspective in an article in *Dissent*. Describing *A People's History* as "bad history, albeit gilded with virtuous intentions," Kazin criticized the book as a "Manichean fable." This was "history as cynicism," which did the thousands of students who engaged with it each year no good. But it was also a problematic vision of the nation's past for those who identified as radicals: it was "fatalistic" and could "only keep the left where it is: on the margins of American political life."[85] Coming at his critique from an educational perspective, Stanford historian Sam Wineburg furthered the condemnation of Zinn in 2018 by arguing that *A People's History* adopted a rhetorical strategy that relied on "the expected ignorance of the reader," and therefore used sources in misleading ways to substantiate arguments that were only partially true. This meant that the book simply replicated the mistakes of more traditional textbooks by relegating students to "roles as absorbers, not analysts, of information."[86]

These critiques marked another stage in the professional and political contestation of Zinn's work. The significance of *A People's History* and its im-

pact on young readers was never questioned, but from the moment of publication onward, the historian's peers regularly suggested that the popularity
of the book should be the cause of anxiety rather than celebration. In these
arguments, it represented an old-fashioned, romanticized view of radical
history and social change that did not map on to the approaches taken by
scholars at the cutting edge of labor and social history. Historians inclined
to take this view could not overlook the fact that Zinn was less interested in
these questions than he was in providing emotionally charged history that
would forge concrete links between the profession and popular audiences.
Ultimately, though, this was only one element of the controversy the book
would cause.

A significant contributing factor to the popularity of John Hope Franklin's
From Slavery to Freedom came in its "afterlife," as the book was revised by the
author and then adopted by students and activists across the United States. In
this process, its sales exploded, as new and diverse audiences found Franklin's
arguments directly relevant to their political and educational experiences. A
comparable phenomenon developed in the decades after the publication of *A
People's History*, whereby a series of controversies led to increased visibility
and augmented sales figures. Like Franklin, Zinn added chapters to extend
the book's chronological range via new editions in the 1990s and 2000s. However, the visibility of *A People's History* grew less because of these alterations
and more because, decades after its publication, it remained a potent symbol
of the educational and political battles being waged as part of the culture
wars. This meant that while the book reached a significantly expanded audience, its status as a signifier of polarized politics often caused its meanings to
be radically simplified.

A *People's History* garnered particularly disproportionate responses from
conservative critics. For example, in a review for the *American Scholar* printed
only months after the book's publication, Oscar Handlin described Zinn's
scholarship as having the "deranged quality" of a "fairy tale." He went on to
suggest that "the book pays only casual regard to factual accuracy" and described its method as "tearing evidence out of context and distorting it."[87] For
Zinn, this was a political rather than an intellectual attack. In a subsequent
issue of the journal, he replied to Handlin, arguing that as a "proponent of the
war in Vietnam and a supporter of Richard Nixon," it was no surprise that the
Harvard historian was critical of a radical work such as *A People's History*.[88]
In making this case, Zinn defended his book against attack. But by claiming
Handlin's views were based on his political beliefs rather than professional
judgment, he also went out of his way to court controversy.

Four years later, Zinn was targeted by the conservative organization Accuracy in Academia (AIA). A spin-off from the larger and more visible Accuracy in Media, AIA took a piece of right-wing common sense—that university campuses were safe havens for "tenured radicals" seeking to remake the minds of their students—and built an advocacy network around it. The group embedded conservative activists in college classrooms to draw attention to prominent radical professors in the hope of discrediting them. The goal was then to liaise with other right-wing campus groups such as College Republicans and Young Americans for Freedom to launch campaigns to return "truth and balance to the classroom."[89]

Given his national prominence as a spokesman for radical political causes, it is hardly surprising that Zinn quickly became an object of AIA's derision. In May 1985, his teaching style was publicly criticized, with a former student likening his classes to the "constant propaganda barrage" of a "police state."[90] As well as attacking Zinn's teaching, conservative campus activists took aim at what they saw as the pernicious influence of A People's History. At Virginia Tech, for example, the local branch of AIA argued that the book should be banned in the university's history classes. "Zinn's book . . . portrays American heroes as villains," their report argued, before criticizing the historian for interpreting the world "through Marxist eyes." After making this case, AIA suggested that students write to their college president to complain about the use of the book: its presence on reading lists meant that they were not presented with "the fundamental facts and interpretations of American history" as advertised by the course catalog.[91]

Zinn responded to these attacks in kind, by defending not only his individual reputation, but also the radicalism for which he was a national spokesman. For example, in a 1985 speech, he denounced AIA for wanting "obedience" and "subservience" from young people, before arguing against another shibboleth of conservative educational thought: the idea of educational neutrality. "We who teach have a responsibility," he suggested, before continuing:

> They talk about balance. The world is out of balance. The world is skewed and distorted in the direction of the people who have gone to war and wanted the new generations to go to war. And our problem is to restore that balance, and to teach about war.[92]

Then, in a 1986 interview with a Boston University campus newspaper, Zinn suggested that his conservative critics had "confused my criticism of government with being anti-American." He insisted that he was no such thing, and that A People's History was, in its own way, an expression of patriotic radicalism.[93]

In each of these instances, Zinn sought not only to defend his legitimacy as a professional academic, but also to extend the debate to encompass the politics of education, war, and national identity. Along with his conservative critics, the historian intervened in a series of "moral panics" over the well-being of young Americans that took place in the 1970s and 1980s.[94] Sometimes covering high-profile issues such as abuse, abduction, and gang violence, these panics just as often framed education as one of the key battle-fields of the culture wars, especially in response to a 1983 report released by the Reagan administration, which argued there had been "no measurable increase in student achievement despite sharp increases in school spending."[95] While right-wing critics used the opportunities provided by these panics to lambaste radical scholars such as Zinn for contributing to what Allan Bloom famously called "the closing of the American mind," the historian highlighted his ability to mold controversy into further opportunities to popularize his version of American history.[96] This was an opportunity for publicity, then, but one in which the significance of the arguments contained within *A People's History* were reduced to soundbites.

This relationship between the book's increased popularity and the simplification of its meaning was also evident in a range of references to it in popular culture during the 1990s and 2000s. The most high-profile of these came in the Oscar-nominated *Good Will Hunting* (dir. Gus Van Sant, 1997). The film was written by Matt Damon, who grew up in Boston as a neighbor and friend of the Zinn family, and tells the story of Will Hunting (Damon), a young working-class janitor at the Massachusetts Institute of Technology (MIT) whose mathematical gifts go unnoticed until he is discovered by Professor Gerald Lambeau (Stellan Skarsgård) and nurtured by therapist Dr. Sean Maguire (Robin Williams).[97] A key theme is the way Will's rough-edged intellect undermines traditional conceptions of credentialed knowledge, especially as it is represented by students and staff at Harvard and MIT. For example, in a scene set in a Harvard bar, Will demonstrates his knowledge of early American historiography by quoting historians such as Daniel Vickers, James Lemon, and Gordon Wood to put down an arrogant student who questions his intellectual faculties.[98] The scene culminates in Will's assertion that most Harvard graduates had spent "a hundred and fifty grand on a fuckin' education you could've got for a dollar fifty in late charges at the public library."

Will's historiographical literacy is demonstrated again shortly after this scene, when he encounters Maguire for their first therapy session. To demonstrate his intellectual superiority, Will paces around the therapist's office, assessing the contents of his bookshelves. Stopping to evaluate a book titled *The United States of America: A Complete History*, Will's eye is caught by a photograph of three military personnel posed in a jungle setting, a reference to Maguire's previous combat experience, presumably in Vietnam. In response to both the book and the photograph, Will says, "Jesus, if you want to read a real history book, read Howard Zinn's *A People's History of the United States*. That book will fuckin' knock you on your ass." The book thus serves as a marker of dissident knowledge for a young working-class autodidact—exactly the type of audience Zinn hoped to influence with his "easy to read" approach to radical popular history. The way Will presents his knowledge also establishes him as a participant in the "youth frame," to the extent that he, as a young man, is expressing the superiority of Zinn's history over the more conventional text on display in Maguire's office, but also because of the implicit reference to Vietnam: Will assumes that his therapist is a representative of the military-industrial complex that *A People's History* is so critical of. In this context, *A People's History* stood as a romanticized symbol of dissent, and, accordingly, the plug for the book provided by a young, handsome Matt Damon played a significant role in boosting its sales figures and Zinn's visibility as a public intellectual.[99]

Another fictional young reader of *A People's History* was Anthony Soprano Jr., the son of Tony Soprano, New Jersey Mafia boss and protagonist of the HBO drama series *The Sopranos* (1999–2007). The character's engagement with Zinn's book comes during a 2002 episode of the show's fourth season, entitled "Christopher," which centers on the importance to the Italian American community of the Columbus Day holiday. The baby-boomer generation represented by Tony, his wife, Carmela, and most of his Mafia associates are passionate advocates for the holiday, and for the glorified folk memory of Columbus as an Italian American hero. However, the seemingly self-evident facts of Columbus's contributions to US greatness are brought into question when a Native American protest takes place in Newark. The politics of cultural resentment and misunderstanding recur throughout the episode and build to a violent clash between a group of Soprano family Mafiosi and Native American protesters, who draw ire by lynching an effigy of Columbus near a statue commemorating the explorer.

It is in the aftermath of this fierce encounter that Anthony Jr. is shown reading a copy of *A People's History* while eating breakfast in the Soprano family kitchen. The character gives voice to Zinn's arguments by quoting from the opening-chapter discussion of Columbus, before the following exchange with his parents:

CARMELA: His history teacher, Mr. Cushman, is teaching your son that if Columbus was alive today, he'd go on trial for crimes against humanity like Milosevic in, you know, Europe.

TONY: Your teacher said that?

ANTHONY: It's not just my teacher, it's the truth. It's in my history book.

TONY: So, you finally read a book and it's bullshit. You have to walk in Columbus's shoes to see what he went through. People thought the world was flat, for crying out loud. Then he lands on an island with a bunch of naked savages on it. That took a lot of guts. You remember when we went to Florida, the heat, and those bugs?

ANTHONY: Like it took guts to murder people and put them in chains.

CARMELA: He was a victim of his time.

ANTHONY: Who cares? It's what he did.

TONY: He discovered America, is what he did. He was a brave Italian explorer. And in this house, Christopher Columbus is a hero. End of story.

Again, then, *A People's History* provides the centerpiece for an intergenerational debate about the politics of history and memory, this time between two parents and their child.

In one sense, Zinn's ideas as introduced by Anthony are another example of dissident knowledge channeled through the generational conflict created by the "youth frame." However, they also function to legitimate a particular vision of the culture wars. Tony stands between the emotionalized cultural identities of the Italian Americans and Native Americans represented in the episode and, in its closing scene, laments what he sees as the unnecessary and destructive appeal by both groups to protected minority status. For Tony, the debates about Columbus Day are simply one example among many of the overriding power of political correctness in American life. "Where the fuck is our self-esteem," he asks in a rhetorical flourish redolent of conservative culture warriors. As one symbol among many, Tony believes national confidence has ebbed away because of the cultural force of the ideas represented by *A People's History*.

The popular connections between Zinn's book and the theme of overbearing political correctness are made even clearer in "That '90s Show," a 2008 episode of the Fox animated sitcom *The Simpsons* (1989–present). Here, *A People's History* is explicitly presented as a cornerstone of liberal elitism in higher education. In recounting Marge Simpson's time as a college student during the 1990s, the episode shows the character reading *A People's History* because she is taking a class in US history with the louche Professor August, who enthralls her with his presentation of the nation's past. He tells the students to throw away their textbook understandings of the subject because "everything you have been taught about history is a lie," before narrating a version of the American Revolution that emphasizes the identities of the Founding Fathers as "white,

Protestant, property-owning males." Marge quickly becomes captivated by this version of American history and starts a romantic relationship with August. Homer's response to being dumped is to form a Nirvana-like grunge band called Sadgasm who write a hit song called "Politically Incorrect" and revel in their resistance to liberal norms. However, Marge's relationship with August is short-lived: her attraction to his radical ideas comes to an abrupt halt when he tells her that marriage, an institution she values, is akin to "slavery." The episode draws to a close with Marge telling Homer, "I got so caught up in the world of college that I forgot how important your love was."

In this context, A People's History stood as a key symbol of the "world of college," representative of a high-minded liberalism that looked down on working-class high school dropouts like Homer. Rather than serving as a source of dissident knowledge, then, Zinn's book was presented through a conservative framework as an appendage of liberal elitism. Furthermore, Homer's response to it—to publicly rail against the forces of political correctness—was framed as heroic and justified in the face of the bad behavior of a disreputable college professor. In using A People's History in this way, the episode intervened in culture wars–era debates about higher education, which represented college campuses as bastions of an "elitist class of intellectuals" who sought to police the discourse of young Americans, thus endangering freedom of speech in the name of political correctness.[100] When Marge Simpson read Howard Zinn, she was not undergoing intellectual enlightenment, but instead being drawn into the shady world of radicalism that would upset the stranglehold of normative ideas about history, politics, and education.

Popular cultural references like these significantly expanded the visibility of Zinn and his ideas. Consequently, the book's status as a popular history cannot be disentangled from this peculiar form of reception. As it circulated in popular culture, A People's History retained some of the radical implications noted by readers in the 1980s: Will Hunting claimed that it could "knock you on your ass," while Anthony Soprano Jr. was clearly convinced by its reinterpretation of Columbus. Nonetheless, the meanings of the book were unstable, and it was just as likely to come unmoored from its original intellectual contexts, thus morphing into a vague symbol of, on the one hand, intergenerational conflict between dissident youths and their conservative elders, or, on the other, of culture wars arguments about the legitimacy of higher education and the type of credentialed knowledge represented by a radical professor like Zinn.

When conservative critics lampooned Zinn's historical perspective, they only drew more attention to his most famous book. In turn, the historian was able use their criticisms to demonstrate the continued relevance of a radical, convention-defying approach to national history. Then, when the book found its way into the hands of fictional readers in film and on television, its intellectual significance became even more slippery. In some hands, it was a foundation stone of dissident knowledge for young Americans seeking to defy the system, and thus exactly what Zinn and his publishers at Harper & Row intended. In others, it was a symbol of the decline of educational standards, the closing of the American mind. Either way, it appeared as an iconic text in a decades-long debate between Right and Left, and thus as an archetypal popular history for a polarized America.

Howard Zinn died in 2010. In one sympathetic obituary, fellow radical historian Paul Buhle described *A People's History* as "a popularization" that was made "still more popular" by the spin-off texts Zinn's book had spawned: abridged versions, a young people's edition, a film adaptation, and a graphic novel.[101] But Buhle's point can be extended much further than this. As well as these official follow-ups, the book had given indirect rise to a huge range of other "People's Histories"—of the accordion, of computing, and of the world, to name only three examples—that extended its unofficial intellectual franchise.[102] Furthermore, the range of responses to *A People's History* in popular culture have provided it with unprecedented visibility. While Buhle suggested that Zinn remained "rather astonished" at this success until his death, it was no fluke. Zinn's liminality between the Old and New Lefts allowed him to communicate a radical version of American history that drew together these distinct generational perspectives. Furthermore, the relationship he developed with Harper & Row to write popular history for young activist audiences demonstrated his publisher's ability to capitalize on the emergence of new readerships for popular history.

Of course, the other key element in the book's popularity was its peculiar ability to court controversy. This was demonstrated again in 2013, when it was revealed that three years previously, then-governor of Indiana Mitch Daniels had launched an email diatribe against the historian in the days immediately after his death. "This terrible anti-American academic has finally passed away," Daniels wrote to a group of colleagues, before continuing:

> The obits and commentaries mentioned that his book *A People's History of the United States* is "the textbook of choice in high schools and colleges around the country." It is a truly execrable, anti-factual piece of disinformation that misstates American history on every page. Can someone assure me that it is not in use anywhere in Indiana? If it is, how do we get rid of it before any more young people are force-fed a totally false version of history?[103]

The publication of Daniels's emails sparked a controversy within the Indiana education system, between professional historians, and among conservative critics. While ninety academics at Purdue University (where Daniels was then president) signed a letter condemning what they saw as his attack on the "legitimacy of academic discourse," the American Historical Association announced that "attempts to single out particular texts for suppression from a school or university curriculum have no place in a democratic society."[104] A range of right-wing pundits took the other side of the argument and jumped to Daniels's defense. One perspective, from the editors of *National Review*, typified the conservative response by arguing that "American education is a sewer of left-wing ideology, and Zinn's work is an especially ripe excretion. . . . Governor Daniels's office was right to bring attention to it."[105]

The Indiana controversy raised a series of knotty questions about the role of teachers, politicians, and state-mandated textbooks in American history education. In doing so, it involved a large and diverse range of interest groups.[106] However, the majority of coverage interpreted it through a starkly dualistic lens: as the conservative *Weekly Standard*'s headline characterized it, this was the case of "Mitch vs. Zinn."[107] In miniature, the episode highlighted the ultimate significance of *A People's History*: its peculiar ability to intersect radical politics and American history, approaches to education and the culture wars, and the ways in which history could be popularized among young audiences seeking alternatives to the "mainstream." That the response to the book was so often simplistic and highly politicized was not inevitable, but it was shaped in fundamental ways by the polarization of American intellectual life in the age of the culture wars. Popularity was synonymous with controversy.

One topic on which Zinn did not court controversy was the history of women. *A People's History* hardly dealt with the topic until it was revised for later editions, and even when these changes had been made, it did not do justice to women's contributions to American history. This was hardly surprising. While Zinn was by no means opposed to feminism, it was hardly a central plank in his political identity. It would take the career-long efforts of another historian to properly popularize women's history and the feminist politics underpinning it: Gerda Lerner. In doing so, she highlighted the uniqueness of the challenges she had to overcome as a woman working against the grain not only of the historical profession, but also of the publishing industry.

Gerda Lerner: The Struggle for
a Popular Women's History

In May 2002 Gerda Lerner traveled from her home in Madison, Wisconsin, to New York City. Eighty-two years old and retired from professional academia for more than a decade, the pioneering women's historian made the journey to receive the Bruce Catton Prize for Lifetime Achievement in the Writing of History from the Society of American Historians (SAH). The award, named after the renowned journalist and chronicler of the Civil War, had only been awarded on nine previous occasions, and never to a woman.[1] Introducing Lerner to the audience, fellow historian Linda Kerber emphasized the contribution she had made as one of the first scholars to "demand respect" for the subject of women's history:

> Nowadays, when feminist historians write books that publishers are proud to produce in substantial print runs, and prize committees are delighted to honor, it is easy to forget that not very long ago, women were a topic, not a subject.[2]

For Kerber, Lerner's achievement was to have played a signal role in bringing women's history to mainstream attention, both as an institution-builder and as a tireless advocate for her field.

In her own remarks, Lerner chose to focus not on the content of her work, but on its form. After all, she was accepting a prize for lifetime achievement in "the writing of history" from an organization that was committed to promoting not only high-quality scholarship, but also graceful and entertaining prose. Lerner told the audience that "academic historians are generally not rewarded for taking time and effort to impart literary skills. . . . That is a pity. In the long run, it deprives us of wider audiences and diminishes the impact of history on society in general." However, she felt that popular history was not simply a literary enterprise, and that its impact should be measured in political as well as commercial terms. Lerner situated her work as part of a twentieth-century "renaissance for women and other groups who have been denied their history." This new approach to the past required "not only rigorous analytic thought, but the creativity of the writer, the empathetic humanism that will lead to the creation of a truly representative society."[3] As she gratefully accepted the largesse of the SAH, Lerner reminded her audience that the history she wrote, while graceful and evocative in style, was also born of struggle. In this, she shared a vision of popular history with John Hope Franklin and Howard Zinn, who worked with their publishers to address popular history to explicitly activist audiences.

By the end of her career, then, Gerda Lerner was the most visible academic proponent and popularizer of women's history in the United States. This popularity was particularly rooted in the success of *The Creation of Patriarchy* (1986) and *The Creation of Feminist Consciousness* (1993), a two-part history of women from ancient Mesopotamia to the contemporaneous United States. The first volume set out to prove that "patriarchy as a system is historical: it has a beginning in history. If that is so, it can be ended by historical process,"[4] before the second volume highlighted the manifold ways in which "women transformed the concepts and assumptions of male thought . . . so as to incorporate women's cultural knowledge and viewpoint."[5] These were interventions in the fields of women's history and intellectual history, but in writing them, Lerner also had political intentions. The books were published by Oxford University Press and have since circulated widely among non-academic readers, at least in part via the distribution networks provided by the post-1960s feminist bookstore movement. However, to highlight the success of the books is also to confront the struggle Lerner faced to break into the mainstream of American historical writing. Unlike Hofstadter, Boorstin, and Zinn, she did not have easy access to the attention of trade publishers, and, in comparison to Franklin, she had to work much harder to convince the publishing industry that her field—women's history rather than African American history—could generate a broad following among both academic and non-academic readers.

The story of Lerner's rise to prominence as a popular historian is, in part, the story of her peculiar biography, which traversed continents, political contexts, and literary milieus. It is also the story of her place within a generation of activists and historians who sought to bring women's history to mainstream attention, not only via research and writing, but also by institution building of the kind that gave rise to women's studies as a legitimate program of scholarship across the United States. Furthermore, it is the story of how second-wave feminisms gave rise to publishing and book-selling contexts in which it was possible to talk of a popular audience for women's history. Finally, it is the story of how this popular version of women's history confronted fundamental divisions within feminist thought about whether it was desirable, or even possible, to write a history of *all women* that could transcend racial, ethnic, and class differences. In working to legitimize women's history in the eyes of both the historical profession and the publishing industry, and then in promoting the findings of a generation of feminist scholarship via her own writing, Lerner demonstrated to the world that women's history could be rigorous, political, and readable in equal measure.

Gerda Hedwig Kronstein's early life, like those of many in interwar central Europe, was shaped by the twin experiences of fascism and displacement. Born in 1920 in Vienna, Austria, her father was a successful pharmacist and her mother an avant-garde artist. Her early childhood was "bounded by rooms, balconies and gardens, circumscribed by concepts of childrearing derived from German middle-class culture."[6] Within this context, and by the age of fourteen, Kronstein had experimented with both Judaism (the religion of her father) and Catholicism (the religion of her mother), only to conclude that she was a "political person" rather than a religious one.[7] This realization coincided with a shift in Austrian politics that would mark her life forever: the rise of militant nationalism that led in 1938 to the Anschluss between Austria and Nazi Germany. Participation with the anti-fascist resistance led to Kronstein's arrest and brief imprisonment, before she moved with her mother to France to escape further persecution. She then arranged safe passage to the United States via engagement to a family acquaintance named Bobby Jensen, who, in 1939 in New York City, became her first husband.

However, the couple were divorced in 1941, shortly before Lerner married again, to theater director and CPUSA member Carl Lerner. This new relationship, which lasted until Carl's death in 1973, would play a significant role in shaping her radical political sensibilities. Lerner had first been introduced to left-wing ideas at the age of eighteen when she attended a summer camp in the United Kingdom organized by the communist scientist J. B. S. Haldane, and from which she returned with "a new interest in Marxist thought."[8] Then, after moving to the United States, she was part of a community of anti-fascist German and Austrian émigrés. However, Lerner subsequently described her alienation from this group: while they railed against the American political and economic system, she had, instead, "fallen in love with the country."[9] This sense of belonging, combined as it was with her continued radicalism, was better suited to the Popular Front political culture she found herself interacting with as she met Carl's friends and acquaintances in the worlds of theater and, after their move to Hollywood in 1941, filmmaking.

In 1946, motivated by the desire to participate in struggles to unionize Southern California and to fight against racism, as well as by opposition to the emergence of the Cold War, Lerner joined the CPUSA. At this moment, the party was experiencing a range of postwar tumults, but the one that most significantly shaped Lerner's future direction was the so-called "woman question." In 1940, prominent party member Mary Inman had caused controversy by arguing that "the labor of housewives in the homes of productive workers . . . is an indispensable part of production," and that housewives had "helped create the wealth that is America today . . . [and] part of it belongs to them by right of toil."[10] For Inman's opponents in the CPUSA, the problem with her arguments was not the implication that good communists should be committed to women's liberation, but that they could be used to justify and perpetuate women's place in the separate sphere of domestic life. This line, combined with Inman's intransigent opposition to criticism, led to her expulsion from the party in 1942.[11] Nonetheless, she remained a significant figure in Southern California radical circles, and Lerner encountered her polemics with great enthusiasm, especially the argument that all women, regardless of employment status, were exploited workers who needed to be organized. As she later explained, Inman provided "a theoretical foundation for . . . organizing women as *women*."[12] By deviating from the party line in this way, Lerner demonstrated her independence of thought: what mattered more than ideological fidelity was her ability to put feminist principles into action.

Building on this commitment, Lerner played a central role in the establishment of the California branch of the Congress of American Women (CAW). The CAW was the official US affiliate of the Women's International Democratic Federation (WIDF), a communist-front organization spanning both sides of the Iron Curtain, which worked toward the goals of "anti-fascism, lasting peace, women's rights, and better conditions for children."[13] The two groups thus represented a politically charged form of women's internationalism.[14] This element of their mission appealed to Lerner's sense of postwar geographical and psychological displacement, and she threw herself into communicating with women across Cold War lines, traveling, for example, to Budapest in 1948 as a CAW delegate to the third WIDF World Congress.[15]

However, women's associations such as the CAW were also deeply rooted in the *national* identities of their members.[16] Indeed, it is in this sense that Lerner's involvement with the organization had the most impact on her future political and intellectual direction. The CAW was genuinely committed to antiracist politics and had more Black women members than any other comparable peace organization before it. This would motivate Lerner's own commitment to intersectional feminism.[17] Furthermore, CAW publications emphasized the organizational power of American women, with one slogan from the late 1940s positing that "Ten Women Anywhere Can Organize Anything."[18] This fierce sense of women's organizing potential, independent of male-dominated political structures, was a theme that would recur throughout Lerner's written work.

Finally, and perhaps most significantly, the CAW laced its campaigns for women's equality with historical rhetoric. One of the organization's publications from 1949 framed this issue concisely by arguing that "in the past the fight for women's rights was part of the fight against slavery and economic exploitation. Today it is part of the fight for peace and security everywhere."[19] CAW pamphlets were replete with references to notable female figures in American history such as Anne Hutchinson, Sojourner Truth, and Lucretia Mott. The organization also sought to draw attention to the absence of women's history from school and college curricula around the country. Lerner's approach to women's history was fundamentally shaped by this viewpoint. In 1949, for example, she organized a seminar on the subject for the Los Angeles chapter of the organization.[20] She subsequently argued that it was her time with the CAW that developed her "interest in the history of American women," as well as her "future career as a historian."[21]

The CAW was short-lived. It ceased activity in 1950, struggling under the weight of anti-communist repression after being cited as a subversive organization by the US Attorney General two years earlier.[22] Then, in 1956, Lerner was one of a wave of members who left the CPUSA in the aftermath of Nikita Khrushchev's "Secret Speech" acknowledging the true crimes of Stalinism.[23] This combination of repression and disillusion, along with the understandable fear that a publicized communist past might hamper her professional future, prevented Lerner from speaking or writing about her formation against the backdrop of the political culture of the CPUSA until 2003. Nonetheless, the early Cold War was a period of enormous intellectual and political development for her. Lerner's early commitment to communist politics provided a backdrop for her dedication in later life not only to the intellectual project of women's history, but also the political belief that the overlapping oppressions of gender, race, and class could not be treated separately, either by historians or activists.

Lerner's experiences during the late 1940s and early 1950s provided a literary as well as a political education. Her childhood reading in Austria focused on "social fiction" that gave her insight into the lives of the poor, such as Gerhardt Hauptmann's play *The Weavers* (1892) and Maxim Gorki's novel *Mother* (1906).[24] She also spent time reading "the sagas of Greeks and Romans, of heroic Vikings and knights and noble warriors," which provided the opportunity to identify with "adventurers and heroes," but, just as importantly, to recognize that she was never presented with "a female heroine."[25] When, at age fourteen, Lerner's parents purged their library of "red books" in response to the spread of anti-communist and anti-Semitic political violence in Vienna, Lerner remembered finding solace in the writings of Anatole France, Émile Zola, and Romain Rolland, which helped her to "hold up the standard of social justice" amid a climate of fear and repression.[26] This was an intensely literary childhood, in which the imaginative world of fiction was fused with a focused interest in questions of political inequality. Like both Richard Hofstadter and Howard Zinn, Lerner's deep connection with fiction would later come to influence her historical writing.

However, it was her arrival in the United States—and, in particular, the new intellectual vistas opened up by her engagement with the late Cold War cultural Left—that provided Lerner with her most significant grounding as a literary intellectual. Along with her second husband, she read aloud the poetry of Walt Whitman, Carl Sandburg, and Langston Hughes, in order to introduce her to "the true progressive America."[27] Then, with her friend Virginia Brodine, a journalist and fellow CAW member, she attended classes organized by the League of American Writers, a CPUSA affiliate committed to highlighting left-wing traditions in American writing and acting as a bridge between communist, progressive, and liberal approaches to culture.[28] There, Lerner studied alongside legendary novelist Theodore Dreiser, and discovered the fiction of Ernest Hemingway, John Dos Passos, and Richard Wright. It was in this moment that she "gave up German literary models" and started to make the transition toward an avowedly American literary identity.[29]

This shift in Lerner's cultural citizenship was motivated not only by her reading habits, but also her developing sense of self as an author. Starting in 1941, she published short stories in literary magazines, a process by which she would make "the momentous decision to change my accidental immigrant status into a conscious choice—I would become a writer in the English language."[30] In doing so, Lerner combined her residual understanding of the power of fiction to illuminate political processes and social inequalities, which she had developed as a child in Austria, with her emergent sense of the significance of American literature and history for understanding her new life and surroundings. Her discovery of an "American voice" was thus a central foundation for her literary and political identity: while she felt a sense of belonging as a cultural citizen of the United States, which was derived through the process of writing in English, she nonetheless retained a sense of "otherness," rooted in her experiences as a Jewish refugee.[31] Ultimately, these experiences were part of a "continuing effort to assimilate" that helped her forge a close identification with those on the margins of mainstream political and intellectual life in her new home.[32] This complex dynamic, combined with her political work with the CAW, led her toward the topic of women's history.

Nowhere is this better exemplified than in *Singing of Women* (1951), an off-Broadway musical written and produced by Lerner in collaboration with her friend and fellow radical Eve Merriam. While it was only performed over three nights and did not receive wide critical attention, the show signposted the budding preoccupation with women's history that would drive Lerner's future intellectual development. *Singing of Women* was a dramatization of women's participation in American history, built around a dialogue between a married couple. "I wonder about this battle of the sexes," sang Mary, the wife, in the musical's prologue, before suggesting, "Could it boil down to the old cash nexus?"[33] The plot was thus framed around what Lerner subsequently described as "the Marxist concept" of gender dynamics in capitalism, with Joe, Mary's husband, playing the role of a worker with a good union job who needed enlightenment on the "woman question."[34]

What followed was, in act 1, a series of short scenes dramatizing key chapters in American women's history, from "Colonial Dames" through "Suffrage," and then, in act 2, several longer scenes focusing on contemporary politics. One of the central themes of act 1 was the importance of dissenting women in US history, from Abigail Adams, via Lucretia Mott, to Mother Jones and Susan B. Anthony. Unsurprisingly, given their radical political credentials, Lerner and Merriam placed significant emphasis on women's organizing, with an anonymous "Working Woman" at the 1848 Seneca Falls Convention expressing the theme particularly clearly: "The only way to get anything in the world is to ask for it good and loud. . . . [W]omen are only going to get better laws if we take a hand in making them."[35] The lack of specific identity given to this and several other of the musical's characters highlighted Lerner and Merriam's emphasis not only on the struggle of notable historical women, but also the grassroots tradition of organizing in which their political experiences were rooted.

Another vitally important theme was the presence of Black political agency in *Singing of Women*'s narrative. Frederick Douglass was presented as a key figure at Seneca Falls, for example: his experience as an enslaved person was used to show how the suggestion that women "must go slow" to achieve reform was based on "fallacious thinking and bad advice."[36] This theme continued in a later scene, when Harriet Tubman argued for women's centrality in the abolitionist movement, and Sojourner Truth performed an extended solo based around her famous "Ain't I a Woman?" speech.[37] In this way, Lerner and Merriam firmly located *Singing of Women* in both an interracial organizing tradition and a radical feminist approach to the American past.

The play was covered by the *Daily Worker*, whose reviewer was cautiously positive about its attempt to "tackle and open up" the "tremendously important subject" of women's history. *Singing of Women* was, the newspaper argued, "another important event in this year's renaissance of progressive theater."[38] Such praise was unsurprising from an organ of the CPUSA, but it does highlight the way in which the musical's script was shaped by the values of the party and, just as significantly, by the CAW's internationalist feminism. Furthermore, the musical's content demonstrates that Lerner's commitment to using her creative writing to make American history accessible to a broad activist audience significantly predated her professional accreditation as a historian.

In 1955 Lerner followed *Singing of Women* with the publication of her first novel, *No Farewell*, a loosely autobiographical account of family life amid the political turmoil of interwar Vienna. However, she failed to interest the trade publishers she approached with the manuscript, and it was eventually acquired by Associated Authors, the short-lived "cooperative publishing house" she established in 1953 with the radical historian Henry Kraus.[39] The novel was not a success, and by the late 1950s, Lerner was experiencing a deep crisis in her identity as an author. Then, in December 1960, she read an article in the *Saturday Review* written by Lillian Smith. The novelist, also a proponent of peace activism, reflected on her identities as both a writer and a citizen:

> It is difficult to separate the novelist from the person or the person from the citizen as I think of my writing and that of others. We must do one thing as citizen, another as writer; but—and this is important—both kinds of activities are fused in the person. What we believe, what we are, has a profound effect upon the quality of our writing.[40]

This struck a chord with Lerner, who started a short but important correspondence with Smith. In her first letter, Lerner described the feelings of dehumanization and alienation she had experienced because of her novel's lack of success. In response, Smith encouraged her to find further avenues for her writing to "make something new out of what was hackneyed, trite and false . . . to show the invisible things."[41]

This encouragement prompted Lerner to rethink her approach to writing and marked an important transitional moment. During the 1940s, she had developed a political identity as a radical, a communist, and a feminist. Just as significantly, she had developed a literary identity that helped make sense of her contradictory relationship with American culture: she had overcome her status as an outsider (as a Jew, a foreigner, and a woman) by becoming a writer. Authorship thus drew her political and intellectual personas together and provided a sense of much-needed cultural citizenship. However, by the late 1950s, Lerner's confidence in this new identity was faltering, and Smith's prompt to continue writing to "show the invisible things" provoked her to reassess her interest in women's history. She decided to find a "new mode of writing" via the historical novel, which led her to enroll as a mature student at the New School for Social Research.[42] Fundamentally and irrevocably shaped by both her political and literary educations during the early Cold War, she started the process by which she would become a professional historian.

In the fall of 1958, Lerner began her studies at the New School. She expected that undergraduate coursework in US history would furnish her with the skills required to write a novel about nineteenth-century southern abolitionists Sarah and Angelina Grimké. However, she soon found that she had a talent for academic study. Graduating in 1963 at the age of forty-three, she entered the doctoral program in history at Columbia University. In an intellectual culture in which "women did not seem to exist," Lerner's interest in women's history made her a "target of ridicule."[43] Nonetheless, her confidence as a writer played in her favor, and Columbia offered an accelerated route to the PhD, which she achieved in 1966, writing a dissertation on the Grimké sisters that was supervised by Robert Cross and Eric McKitrick.

Immediately after World War II, women were outsiders in the humanities. This status was derived from the markedly gendered impact of the GI Bill, which, while it provided unprecedented access to higher education, did so almost exclusively for men. At the same time, a range of fields, including history, moved toward scientific methodological approaches that discriminated against women and in favor of men.[44] Nonetheless, during the 1970s and 1980s, Lerner, as part of a generation of pioneering women scholars, was able to buck these trends to become a leading exemplar of feminist approaches to humanistic knowledge. In this, she had much in common with John Hope Franklin: they both built on the work of their predecessors in the late nineteenth- and early twentieth-century historical enterprise, and thus demonstrated the legitimacy of non-traditional subfields by placing them on solid academic ground at the same time as articulating their significance to a broad readership.[45] In both cases, their position as outsiders drove a desire to professionalize and popularize their approaches to history, goals that neither historian saw as incompatible.

In Lerner's case, this objective was also motivated by her activist political commitments. She had joined the National Organization for Women (NOW) as a charter member at its founding in 1966, telling her friend Carl Degler that she had done so in the hope of "getting something going on 'the absence of women from textbooks in American history.'"[46] This effort served two purposes: not only would it deepen awareness of developments in academic history and their relevance to feminist activism, but it would also continue the historical work that Lerner had undertaken as a member of the CAW in the late 1940s. Nonetheless, her involvement with NOW did not last. The organization's leaders were not interested in her proposals about a women's history program, but, more importantly, its movement culture felt "very elitist" and she did not feel "at home" within its ranks.[47]

Instead, Lerner advocated a grassroots approach to feminism, with a greater degree of focus on the struggles of working-class women and women of color than that offered by NOW. Indeed, this was a vision that she channeled into her early writings on the politics of history. Before she had completed her graduate studies, for example, Lerner published in the *Journal of Negro History* on what she described as the Grimké sisters' "lifelong struggle against race prejudice" and the way it intertwined with their belief in women's equality.[48] The subject matter of this article revealed her early interest in the intersections of race and gender. But Lerner's choice of venue also highlighted her commitment to publishing in a journal that, even in the early 1960s, was not seen as "mainstream" by the white historical profession. Another early article, "The Lady and the Mill Girl" (1969), which has since become a classic of women's history, documented the class antagonisms that emerged in the Jacksonian era as the "image of 'the lady' was elevated to the accepted ideal of femininity toward which all women would strive," thus severing any potential for cross-class solidarity in the face of patriarchy.[49] Both of these articles were written in a firmly academic style, but they fused Lerner's scholarly and political interests: to be fully effective, they both implied, women's history needed to treat the themes of race and class with the utmost seriousness.

Most significantly, in 1971 Lerner wrote the first of several manifestos for women's history. "Women's Rights and American Feminism" was published in the *American Scholar* and explored the overlapping problems of "how women fit into human history, how one is to conceptualize their role, and how one is to evaluate their contributions." In doing so, she argued, historians should distinguish between a narrow focus on "legal rights" and a much broader commitment to a feminism that embraced "the emancipation of American women."[50] Both traditions were visible in American history, but the former had been prioritized at the expense of the latter by historians preoccupied with the emergence of the suffrage movement. Lerner, on the other hand, argued in favor of the more capacious approach to women's history, which would allow for attention to be paid to the experiences of working class and poor women, as well as the "double oppression" of Black women.[51] Ultimately, this was the only vision that could lead to, Lerner explained, the kind of change in role expectations and psychological orientation women's liberationists have been talking about. It does not mean only women's rights. It means the emancipation of both men and women from a sex-dominated archaic division of labor and from the values that sustain it.[52]

In making this argument, Lerner effectively synthesized the views of the emergent women's history movement, of which she was perhaps the most visible member in the English-speaking world. At least in part, she owed this visibility to the fact that she was two decades older than the other prominent historians who worked alongside her to develop women's history, such as Kathryn Kish Sklar (b. 1939), Linda Gordon (b. 1940), Linda Kerber (b. 1940), Alice Kessler-Harris (b. 1941) and Nancy Cott (b. 1945) in the United States, and the British historians Sheila Rowbotham (b. 1943) and Sally Alexander (b. 1943). The intellectual and organizational gravitas this extra age and experience offered Lerner was vital to her success and made her a key spokesperson for women's history. As Sklar remembered shortly after Lerner's death:

> Gerda brought distinctive cultural and political weapons to the fight that loomed ahead—a graceful German accent, matronly sexuality, and a deep personal knowledge of how to resist illegitimate authority. These were potent weapons; arguably more powerful than the tools we were sharpening in the New Left and our consciousness-raising groups because they were wielded by an age-peer of the men who dominated our craft.[53]

In playing this vitally important leadership role, Lerner more clearly resembled women's historians of her own generation, such as Dorothy Thompson (b. 1923) in Britain and Michelle Perrot (b. 1928) in France. Like Howard Zinn, they all found themselves in liminal generational positions, navigating their experiences of communism before and during World War II with the new intellectual and political contexts of the 1950s and 1960s.[54] This was a powerful position, and it provided their scholarship with maximum visibility.

The next step was to make women's history accessible to nonspecialist readers. Lerner's first opportunity to do this was provided by the textbook company Addison-Wesley, who approached her in 1967 to write a short introductory book on US women's history. She was attracted to the project because she wanted to "open up the subject of women to high school students . . . who need it badly," and in 1971 the book was published as *The Woman in American History*.[55] In it, Lerner surveyed the revolutionary, early national, and postbellum periods to emphasize the substantial contribution to the nation's development made by women. The framing logic for the book mapped onto her earlier arguments about the subject:

If history has heroes, it also has heroines. More significant than isolated individuals, however, are the forces exerted by groups of people having similar
concerns and needs. One such force, a significant and generally constructive
one, has been the force of women in American history.[56]

The book ended with a focus on the question of "child and maternal protective legislation," an area in which the United States compared poorly to "most
industrialized nations." The problem was particularly acute, Lerner argued,
because America's "abundant society" could "well afford" overarching reform
of the welfare system.[57] The book's politics thus fused Lerner's long-standing
interest in maternity and childcare, which she had developed while a member
of the CAW, with the more recent concern developed by the student New Left
with the cruel ironies of midcentury American abundance, and the emerging
second-wave feminist interest in welfare rights.[58] Even when pitched at high
school students, her vision of popular history was highly politicized.

However, few aspects of the Addison-Wesley project went smoothly, and
Lerner's rocky relationship with her publisher reveals much about her approach to writing for non-academic audiences. As she worked on the manuscript, for example, the historian regularly felt that she had to push back
against the misunderstandings of her editor, Robert Keller. She was perplexed
when he relayed the suggestion of a peer reviewer that, as well as presenting
the contributions to US history of a range of important women, the book
should also tell the story of "female villains." To this, Lerner replied that while
she was not "blind to their faults," women were not "in a position to start wars
or embezzle vast sums of money." Their opportunities for villainy were simply
not historically significant.[59]

On various occasions, she also felt the need to push back against her editor's view that the book was "a brief for women's rights" that might capitalize
on the contemporary interest in the topic raised by Betty Freidan's *The Feminist Mystique* (1963). This was emphatically not what she was attempting to
do. Women's rights were only "a minor part" of her story, the historian was at
pains to remind Keller, and modern questions of "self-fulfillment, feminine
mystique, and battles of the sexes" were topics for "sociologists and psycholo-
gists" rather than historians.[60] In her efforts to make her subject matter accessible and popular, Lerner demonstrated that she was not willing to pander to
contemporary political sentiment at the expense of quality scholarship.

The mismatch between the historian's vision for her book and that of
Addison-Wesley came into even sharper relief over the question of marketing
and sales. Before publication, Lerner identified a "growing interest in feminist
literature" in American higher education, arguing that "we should not jeopar-

dize this possible market by treating *The Woman in American History* like a high school textbook."[61] In making this case, Lerner identified the early development of the women's studies movement. Building on legal and political developments such as the 1972 passage of Title IX of the Education Amendments Act, which protected students and staff in educational programs from discrimination on the basis of sex, and the 1974 Women's Educational Equity Act, which provided funds for research and professional development to combat gender inequality, by 1980 there would be more than three hundred women's studies programs at universities across the United States.[62] In turn, during the 1970s and 1980s, these developments drove rapid student recruitment, as well as the hiring of numerous faculty.[63] Lerner was at the forefront of this movement, establishing an MA program in women's history at Sarah Lawrence College in 1972, and was hired in 1980 to direct the PhD program in women's history at the University of Wisconsin–Madison.[64] She was thus well positioned to see that there was the beginnings of a captive audience for her new book.

However, after publication, Lerner felt that Addison-Wesley had not capitalized on this new market. In 1972 she told a sales executive at the company that the book would have "considerable sales appeal if it is put in the 'Women's Liberation' section of bookstores."[65] Two years later, and citing interest in the book from representatives of both NOW and the Girl Scouts of America, she wrote to another employee that because the book was not being stocked in mainstream bookstores, "where it properly belongs," thousands of extra sales were being lost. "It is very frustrating," she continued, "to have written a book which fills a unique need, for which there seems to be a ready market, only to find the publisher unable or unwilling to do the proper marketing."[66] In response, Addison-Wesley told Lerner that the book "zeroes in perfectly on the markets for which it was written, i.e., college and school markets." Going further, they argued that it would be "disastrous" to "toss the book into the maw of the trade paperback stands, and especially the burgeoning section on 'Women,' where it might well be lost." Ultimately, their advice to Lerner was as follows:

> If you want to write a book specifically for the trade market, you should approach it anew, study the kinds of books that are selling there—it's a very faddish market, and more fragmented than it might seem—and write such a book.[67]

For Addison-Wesley, this was an important conversation about the business of selling books, a complex process that they felt Lerner did not fully understand.

But it was also a disagreement about the paperback: what it was and how it came to be consumed by readers. For a textbook publisher like Addison-Wesley, *The Woman in American History* was not technically a paperback, even if it appeared between paper covers. Rather, it was a textbook, and, if marketed correctly, could generate concentrated sales that capitalized on specific market segmentation. For an author like Lerner, on the other hand, the book's inexpensive format meant that it had the potential to function as a vector of politicized knowledge. In this view, which was in keeping with those of both Franklin and Zinn, success would not simply be measured in sales figures, but also by the type of reader to whom the book sold: history was only truly "popular" if it found its way into the hands of activists as well as students.

This mindset was what feminist novelist June Arnold referred to in 1976 when she argued that for an author to "reach women" with their work was not "a passive event," but an active process of mediating between writers and activist audiences.[68] This meant that significant attention needed to be paid to the way that women's writing was shaped by the publishers they chose to work with. Indeed, she represented a widespread view in the women's movement when she railed against mainstream publishers, which she described as "the hard-cover of corporate America":

> Madison Avenue publishers are . . . the intellectuals who put the finishing touches on patriarchal politics to make it sell. . . . They will publish some of us—the least threatening, the most saleable, the most easily controlled or a few who cannot be ignored—until they cease publishing us because to be a woman is no longer in style. For a feminist, they are truly the impermanent press.[69]

These ideas fed into a broader understanding among second-wave feminists that there was a distinction between "publishing feminism," a business activity engaged in by many US publishers, and "feminist publishing," a more systematic attempt to transform the production and dissemination of books, as well as their contents.[70] By the mid-1970s, it was clear that Lerner shared this feminist sense of ambivalence toward mainstream publishers. Before her first nonfiction book was published by trade press Houghton Mifflin, she had endured more than twenty rejections from similar publishers, a process that she found deeply dispiriting.[71] This, added to her experience with Addison-Wesley, meant that she was actively willing to explore alternative means of distributing her work.

It was against this backdrop that Lerner began to conceptualize the project that would spawn *The Creation of Patriarchy* and *The Creation of Feminist Consciousness*. In a 1975 essay in *Feminist Studies*, for example, she turned her back on the approach to women's history she had taken in her Addison-Wesley project. Lerner argued that a new feminist theory was required that would take account of the fact that "women's subjection to patriarchal institutions antedates all other oppression and has outlasted all economic and social changes recorded in history."[72] This would necessitate massive geographical and chronological expansion: research was required that went well beyond the boundaries of the United States and back in time as far as the ancient world. As she phrased the problem in a follow-up essay:

> The new history must be based on the understanding that women are half of mankind and have always been essential to the making of history. Only a history based firmly on this recognition and equally concerned with men and women and with the establishment and the passing of patriarchy can claim to be a truly universal history.[73]

This was a grand ambition, but one that Lerner was determined to pursue.

The first step was to propose to Oxford University Press (OUP) a project entitled "Women in History: An Attempt at a Theory."[74] A year and a half later, and after much discussion, OUP offered Lerner a contract for the project, along with a $25,000 advance.[75] In 1983 the press agreed that it would be split into two distinct volumes, to be published separately and consecutively.[76] The results were *The Creation of Patriarchy* in 1986 and *The Creation of Feminist Consciousness* in 1993, both of which were treated by the press as trade rather than academic titles. During the postwar period, OUP had developed a brand of trade publishing that sought to capitalize on its reputation for intellectual excellence. This most often involved the publication of out-of-copyright classic texts, illustrated histories, and the like. But it also meant handling books that capitalized on their authors' academic identities at the same time as they sought a mass audience. One example was the British evolutionary biologist Richard Dawkins's *The Selfish Gene* (1976), which was circulated to great acclaim and huge sales after its author opted to publish with OUP rather than a trade press because its imprint "would confer a stamp of respectability" on his theories.[77]

This crossover approach to the trade market was ultimately characterized by a higher level of risk than traditional academic publishing: larger discounts were offered to booksellers, advances were paid to authors, and OUP ran the risk of significant numbers of unsold books if sales did not match expectations.[78] Nonetheless, these were risks that, during the course of the 1980s, the New York office of OUP needed to take in order to reverse a decline in profitability. The bitter experience of economic "stagflation"—rising costs met by languishing overall wage levels—meant that the price of books could not keep pace with inflation, and by 1982 the press was struggling to survive on both sides of the Atlantic. In that year, the New York office appointed a new president, Edward Barry, who moved from the more profitable publisher Macmillan. In his first decade in charge, Barry oversaw a significant increase in sales and profitability, resting on the assumption that profits would not "come at the expense" of high-quality scholarship, but would instead be driven by it.[79] In a period of economic constraint, this approach to the business of publishing repurposed the rhetoric of the postwar boom in popular nonfiction at companies like Knopf and Random House, which, as we have seen, continually sought to balance the priorities of academic quality and profitability.

Lerner's involvement with OUP overlapped directly with this period of upheaval, and her books slotted very effectively into the new "Academic Humanities" list developed by the press to highlight major contributions to scholarship that would also be of interest to non-academic readers. *The Creation of Patriarchy* and *The Creation of Feminist Consciousness* were marketed aggressively, with the historian sitting for numerous magazine and radio interviews in the weeks and months after their respective publications. When publicizing the books, OUP emphasized Lerner's contributions to women's history, as well as the relatability of her life story. As one publicity document for *The Creation of Feminist Consciousness* put it:

> Twenty years ago, historians viewed "women's history" as a trivial inquiry, and many lay people had never heard the phrase. In 1993, thanks to Gerda Lerner and other pioneering historians, women's history is a rich and meaningful subject for many of us. This brilliant and determined woman, who opened up the field of women's history for a generation to come, never set out to become a historian, and came to the study of history late in life.[80]

While underscoring the quality of Lerner's scholarship, the claim that she had "never set out to become a historian" and had only done so "late in life" framed her work as approachable for readers from a range of backgrounds: the book was presented as anything but an intimidating academic text.

If the historian was marketed as an outsider to the world of the academy, this was also an identity that she was forced to embrace as she navigated the pitfalls of expanding the scope of her scholarship beyond her primary field of expertise. As Lerner had predicted in her 1975 *Feminist Studies* essay, both books required her to shift away from US history and toward world history, and to dramatically expand her chronological frame of reference. In doing so, she actively adopted the persona of a "generalist surveying the field from secondary literature," thus stirring up controversy among specialists.[81]

In this act of scholarly redefinition, she was ably supported by her editor at OUP, Sheldon Meyer, who had worked at the press since 1956. During this time, he had developed a formidable reputation as a proponent of crossover

American history titles that won numerous Pulitzer and Bancroft Prizes. As executive editor for trade books during the 1980s and 1990s, Meyer played a significant role in shaping the success of Edward Barry's new direction for OUP. During this period, and under Meyer's aegis, OUP become the "dominant house" in New York for American history, surpassing even the literary reputations of trade publishers like Harper & Row and Alfred A. Knopf.[82] As well as commissioning landmark books in US political history, African American history, and the history of popular culture, Meyer was also a proponent of women's history and eagerly worked with Lerner on the development of her books.

In doing so, he supported her through a range of challenging feedback from ancient historians, classicists, and Assyriologists. One example came in an exchange between Lerner and a scholar of ancient languages, who was asked by Meyer to review several chapters of *The Creation of Patriarchy*. In a report submitted in January 1985, the scholar suggested that it was impossible for anyone, "no matter how intelligent and well-intentioned," to develop the skills required to "read their way" into a field like Assyriology. He was also "grossly offended by the stridency" of Lerner's feminism, continuing, "The kind of hyperbole that was necessary fifteen years ago to shake us all up and recognize how women were indeed oppressed, is gratuitous and insulting in 1985."[83] In reply, Lerner suggested that she was "not attempting the work of an Assyriologist," but was rather providing a study of the "ways in which concepts of sex and appropriate gender roles became incorporated in the major thought systems of Western Civilization." She also defended her articulation of feminism as an attempt to "not to be preachy and to convert . . . but to fulfil the ground rule by which historians work to check their own bias." Overall, she remonstrated, "you and I obviously have profound differences . . . in our understanding of what feminism means."[84]

In this type of exchange, it was not only the academic legitimacy of Lerner's work that was at stake; it was also her feminist politics. She was an intellectual outsider to the fields in which she was intervening, but she was also treated as a political outsider whose activism had the potential to distort her scholarship, an experience that echoed Franklin's treatment by Knopf in the 1940s. Again, Meyer encouraged Lerner to embrace her radicalism rather than hedge against it. For example, in reviewing an early version of the manuscript, he told the historian to confidently assert that in the past "male dominance was assumed" but that now, in the present, feminist scholarship had decisively proved the case that this was a distortion that needed to be corrected. "It should be part of your hubris," Meyer argued, "to make the assumption that anyone who has not embraced this viewpoint is part of the past."[85] As a publishing professional who aimed to attract a wide readership for nonfiction books, he could clearly see the value in Lerner's outspokenly politicized version of history.

Meyer's encouragement of Lerner's feminism is also revealing because of what it highlights about the changing publishing philosophy at OUP during the post-1960s period. In 1966, for example, the editor had been one of the numerous New York publishing professionals who turned down the opportunity to publish Lerner's first academic book, arguing that the historian's "complete involvement with the cause of women's rights," while "one of her most engaging qualities," meant that her work was inappropriate for publication by OUP, whose remit only extended as far as "more straightforward historical studies" that lacked such explicit political content.[86] If this was the case in the mid-1960s, the company's approach had changed in the subsequent two decades: by 1985 Meyer was not only keen to capitalize on Lerner's feminism, but willing to give her the intellectual and political space to articulate her vision of a women's history liberated from the criticism of academic specialists. In doing so, he demonstrated that OUP was not only committed to publishing feminism, but also to its own version of feminist publishing, one that gave authors the independence to experiment with controversial ideas while also benefiting from the prestige offered by one of the world's leading university presses.

The Creation of Patriarchy and *The Creation of Feminist Consciousness* were the culmination of Lerner's attempts to popularize women's history, and to move it from the margins to the mainstream of American intellectual life. In pursuing this goal, she battled with her outsider status, both as a woman in the humanities, and as a feminist historian in the public sphere. She was given considerable support by OUP, and by Sheldon Meyer in particular, whom she recognized as "a great risk-taker" in supporting her so ardently.[87] It is hard not to read in this compliment a direct contrast with her experiences at Addison-Wesley, where she felt that not enough risks were taken to put *The Woman in American History* in front of politically sympathetic readers. But the business model of a press like OUP, especially after its internal restructuring in 1982, was markedly different from that of a textbook publisher. It emphasized risk taking, as well as the potential marketability of the broad-ranging, field-defining approach Lerner took with her two books. This mutually beneficial relationship, born of intellectual creativity and business acumen, provided her with the opportunity to amplify her ideas about women's history well beyond the academy.

"Women's history is indispensable and essential to the emancipation of women."[88] With this short sentence at the start of *The Creation of Patriarchy*, Lerner laid out one of the foundational arguments not only of that book, but of the two-volume project of which it was a part. At once conceptual and empirical, the observation gave root to her account of how geographically and chronologically vast surveys of patriarchy and feminist consciousness could contribute to American women's understanding of their place in history at the end of the twentieth century. This was the basis of Lerner's historical politics of feminism. In part, it grew out of her dialogue with Marxism during the 1940s and 1950s, as well as her early attempts to popularize women's history in the 1960s and 1970s. More fundamentally, though, Lerner's approach centered on her attempt to render women's history powerfully visible to readers influenced by the intellectual cultures of second-wave feminism.

The Creation of Patriarchy started by signposting some of Lerner's most significant political ideas. For example, she drew her readers' attention to the question of biology and its impact on women's historical subordination to convince them of the limitations of Freudianism. While Lerner conceded that some of Sigmund Freud's ideas had fed into breakthroughs in feminist theory, she also argued that his "dictum that for the female 'anatomy is destiny' . . . gave new life and strength to . . . male supremacist arguments," the popularization of which had become "the prescriptive text for educators, social workers, and the general audiences of the mass media."[89] In making this point, her arguments intersected with those of second-wave feminist Betty Friedan, whose book The Feminine Mystique dedicated a chapter to popular discussions of Freud and their diffusion in everyday life, ultimately concluding that his ideas had "sounded a single, overprotective, life-restricting, future-denying note for women."[90] This was a foundational argument for many second-wave feminists, and Friedan's ideas overlapped with those of the more radical Kate Millett, who, in 1970, went on to suggest that Freud was "beyond question the strongest individual counter-revolutionary force in the ideology of sexual politics."[91]

Lerner's disavowal of Freud therefore reflected the late twentieth-century process by which psychoanalysis fell out of fashion in the United States, after enjoying more than half a century of popularity among Americans seeking to understand their unconscious selves.[92] Not surprisingly, this theme touched a chord with the book's reviewers. For example, a publicity piece in the style section of the New York Times shortly after the publication of The Creation of Patriarchy quoted the historian as arguing that "what Freud should have said is that for women, anatomy was once destiny. But it no longer is, and it should not be in the future."[93] The declining reputation of psychoanalysis provided popular traction for Lerner's argument that women's history was not determined by biology and was thus worthy of detailed and sustained attention from non-academic readers.

In discussing the role of class in women's history, Lerner confronted another important school of thought among second-wave feminists: Marxism. In particular, she critiqued the theories of Friedrich Engels, whose book *The Origin of the Family, Private Property and the State* (1884) stood as a landmark in historical materialist ideas about gender. Engels had argued that the monogamous family emerged as a result of "the victory of private property over primitive, natural communal property." This was a historical lesson with a distinctly political meaning: "The emancipation of woman will only be possible when woman can take part in production on a large, social scale, and domestic work no longer claims anything but an insignificant amount of her time."[94] For Lerner, the problems with this theory were manifold. It could not be substantiated by empirical evidence. It directed too much attention to "a single event," the establishment of relations of private property. Furthermore, it led generations of Marxists into the political "dead end" of identifying "the relation of the sexes as a class antagonism," leading to "the insistence . . . that questions of sex relations must be subordinated to questions of class relations." Lerner's goal was thus to "correct the errors" of Engels and other Marxists.[95]

Several reviews of *The Creation of Patriarchy* latched on to this facet of her arguments. Assuming its readers would understand the reference without explanation, for example, the *Toronto Globe & Mail* suggested that Lerner's book proved that "Engels got the order wrong" in his discussion of the relationship between patriarchy and private property, while the New York–based radical newspaper *The Guardian* went as far as suggesting that the historian was "more plausible than Engels" when she argued that "male domination predates private property."[96] As well as highlighting the significance of her reformulation of Marxist ideas about the development of patriarchy, this reception highlighted Lerner's intervention in historical and political debates that resonated with audiences beyond the academy. In viewing the book as a sign that she was, once and for all, "finished with Marxism," the historian was in tune with popular reviewers, who, in the final years of the Cold War, lauded what they perceived as her efforts to prioritize history over ideology.[97]

If Freud and Engels were the thinkers Lerner chose to argue against, her intellectual lodestar when writing *The Creation of Patriarchy* and *The Creation of Feminist Consciousness* was the historian Mary Ritter Beard. The coauthor of several notable works of American history with her husband Charles A. Beard, Mary also published the pathbreaking book *Woman as Force in History* (1946). Writing in the immediate aftermath of World War II, she wanted to convince her readers that women have done far more than exist and bear and rear children. They have played a great role in directing human events as thought and action. Women have been a force in making all the history that has been made.[98]

To substantiate this argument, she called for historians to write the "long history" of women over multiple centuries by using "excavated artefacts of a preliterate age, in folklore, in myths, in religious literature, in printed and unprinted manuscripts."[99] It would have been hard to imagine an individual scholar undertaking this work in the 1940s. But by the 1980s, so much research had been undertaken in feminist history, classics, Assyriology, and other related disciplines that Lerner was able to imagine a synthesis that would speak to Beard's goals. Indeed, she framed *The Creation of Feminist Consciousness* as an attempt at what Beard had called "long history" more than four decades earlier.[100]

Again, this was not only an academic frame of reference, but also one that had popular crossover potential. In a 1981 interview with iconic second-wave feminist magazine *Ms.*, Lerner went as far as drawing Beard into comparison with the French feminist Simone de Beauvoir:

> *The Second Sex* provided an intellectual explanation for the status quo without really touching it. Mary Beard's insight absolutely challenges the status quo. The funny part is that Mary Beard seemed to be conservative and Beauvoir radical, but Beard is much more radical. Beauvoir's description of patriarchal society and women in it was a tremendous contribution, but not a prescription for understanding the reality of women's role in the past.[101]

Again, Lerner's arguments demonstrated her assumption that readers of *Ms.* would be familiar with both Beard and Beauvoir as intellectual reference points. Just as important, though, is the way that she indicated her debt to the former's approach to women's history, whose argument that feminism would benefit more from historical research than abstract theory was exactly the type of "radicalism" that Lerner was willing to embrace.

Another vital question was the role of religion in the development of patriarchy. In a chapter on "The Goddesses," for example, Lerner suggested that "no matter how degraded and commodified the reproductive and sexual power of women," their agency could not be "banished from thought and feeling" as long as female deities were believed to retain spiritual power.[102] It was the book of Genesis and its representation of a shift from "matrilocal and matrilineal to patrilocal and patrilineal family organization" that prompted a shift away from this religious culture, leading to the widespread notion that only men could speak to God and were thus the sole agents of human history.[103] Lerner was at pains to highlight that this was a contradictory process:

The development of monotheism in the Book of Genesis was an enormous advance for human beings in the direction of abstract thought and the definition of universally valid symbols. It is a tragic accident of history that this advance occurred in a social setting and under circumstances which strengthened and affirmed patriarchy. Thus, the very process of symbol-making occurred in a form which marginalized women. . . . Here is the historical moment of the death of the Mother-Goddess and her replacement by God-the-Father and the metaphorical Mother under patriarchy.[104]

In highlighting the "enormous advance" of monotheism, as well as its significant contribution to patriarchy, Lerner worked to avoid alienating readers with liberal religious affiliations. In doing so, she was at least partially successful. A reviewer for the Mormon magazine *Sunstone*, for example, praised the historian's arguments, making a particular point of highlighting how careful she was in weighing evidence.[105] Going further, William A. Johnson, writing in *Christian Century*, suggested that "*The Creation of Patriarchy* ought to be read by all Jews and Christians attempting to be more faithful to what they have already found in the biblical record—namely, the equality of all humans in the eyes of God."[106] On the copy of this review that survives in her personal papers, Lerner annotated the quotation with a large handwritten cross, suggesting that she disagreed with the reviewer's sentiment. This is not surprising, given that she was no defender of the feminist credentials of the Bible. However, the existence of the review, and others like it, demonstrated her success in channeling liberal religious readers toward her work.

After Lerner established her historical argument about the origins of patriarchy, she turned *The Creation of Feminist Consciousness* into an act of feminist recovery, showing how women "transformed the concepts and assumptions of male thought and subtly subverted it" to incorporate their own "cultural knowledge and viewpoints."[107] The book detailed attempts at what the historian called "feminist Bible criticism" by a range of women throughout the Christian epoch. It also documented multiple attempts by women to write their own history, many of which were lost to historical memory.[108] The key lesson of these and other examples was that "women, ignorant of their history, had to reinvent the wheel over and over again." The only solution to this problem was a complex one and resided in the overlapping opportunities provided to women by universal access to education, clearly defined ideas about women's history, and, most significantly, "a social movement of women."[109] Lerner argued that by 1993 this moment had arrived:

The millennia of women's pre-history are at an end. We stand at the beginning of a new epoch in the history of humankind's thought, as we recognize that sex is irrelevant to thought, that gender is a social construct, and that woman, like man, makes and defines history.[110]

This hopeful message was an important endpoint for Lerner's arguments, and, as a reviewer for a local newspaper in her hometown of Madison, Wisconsin, put it, "If the 1990s is to be the decade of the woman, Professor Lerner has written its credo."[111]

The positive reception for *The Creation of Feminist Consciousness* was also rooted in Lerner's abilities as a writer. One of the book's most important narrative strategies was to root its analysis in examples drawn from US history. In the introduction, Lerner compared the roles of gender and race in the nation's past. To do so, she briefly narrated the history of the early republic, centering on the Constitution's "unresolved contradiction over the slavery issue," which "set in motion the ideas and expectation that would fuel the struggle for the slaves' eventual emancipation and their admission to full citizenship." In contrast, she argued that "it was different for women," because the founding documents of American democracy "embodied the patriarchal assumption, shared by the entire society, that women were not members of the polity."[112] While the canvas of *The Creation of Feminist Consciousness* was vast—covering Western history from the Middle Ages to the late nineteenth century—Lerner was thus careful to situate its significance in terms her American readers could readily engage with.

This strategy continued throughout the book, which was structured around the stories of multiple women that the historian argued had played a role in the development of feminist consciousness. Among them were American figures such as Abigail Adams, Sojourner Truth, Sarah Grimké, and Elizabeth Cady Stanton, all of whom were framed as pioneers of egalitarian ideas. The success of this approach was registered in multiple reviews. For example, the *New York Times* put the book on a list of summer reading for 1993.[113] The *Milwaukee Journal Sentinel* told readers that its tone was "unapologetically informal," continuing, "Lerner cares about these women, and understands their struggle to be hard. As a result, the book is compelling."[114] Writing for the *Women's Review of Books*, Mary McLaughlin praised Lerner's presentation of "a greatly enlarged city of ladies," describing the book as "a synthesis that will encompass women along with men in a truly usable past."[115] In making these points, reviewers framed Lerner's work as popular feminist history at its most accessible.

These responses were endorsed by readers. One woman, who described herself as "lower middle class," told Lerner that her reading of *The Creation of Patriarchy* had provided the "courage" to interrogate patriarchy. Another described the experience of reading the book as one that provided new perspectives on the world: "You have allowed me to connect the past with my personal life. . . . This is a true gift, and I am deeply grateful."[116] Going into more detail, Gabriella Bueno, a fifty-seven-year old architect, told Lerner in 1992 that reading the book had provided her with considerable intellectual and emotional support while she made the decision to resign from a job at a large corporation:

> Reading *The Creation of Patriarchy* at such a time was deeply rewarding. I found a clear and organized context that confirmed my life experience, reconciling and grounding me in the reality we face as women. . . . Your book embodies a powerful force that realigns everything I ever learned and experienced into a sobering pattern, one that reflects the interaction of men and women through the ages.[117]

The Creation of Feminist Consciousness generated comparable feedback, with one reader writing from Japan in 1994 to tell Lerner that the book's explication of feminist thought "gives me the courage to press on in my own studies, knowing that other women have struggled to be more than auxiliary persons. The book gives me a sense of place in history and confirms some suspicions I've had about the special challenges facing female achievers."[118]

The many letters Lerner received from grateful readers thus highlight the powerful combination of intellectual and emotional responses generated by her work. They were responding as both *interpretive* readers, to the extent that they processed the rational arguments of the books and related them to concrete political situations, but also as *implicated* readers, who experienced the process of reading as a form of romance, in which they fell in love with the text and generated a series of deeply personal connections to it. In doing so, these readers highlighted the marked complexity of the audiences Lerner engaged, who could not be characterized in the terms so often used by postwar authors, publishers, and critics when they imagined a general readership as "well-educated, respectable, and (if only symbolically) male."[119] Instead, Lerner's readers were actively implicated in the politics of second-wave feminism, but in ways that were powerfully affective as well as purely rational.

The Creation of Patriarchy and *The Creation of Feminist Consciousness* also proved successful at communicating feminist ideas to readers in a range of institutional contexts. For example, in 1986 a coordinator of the Prison Research Education Action Project, funded by the New York State Council of Churches, wrote to Lerner to tell her how useful *The Creation of Patriarchy* had been in the development of a new course for incarcerated women on the prevention of sexual assault.[120] Writing from a very different context in 1994, a group of senior citizens describing themselves as the "Feminist Issue Group" at the Morningside Retirement and Health Center in New York City told the historian how instructive *The Creation of Feminist Consciousness* had been in their discussions of "the development of an alternate vision for a feminist future."[121] Lerner's popular feminist history thus generated not only moments of enlightenment for individual readers, but also concrete grounds for debate and discussion between collective audiences hoping to reframe their understanding of the past.

This was most evident in the way the book circulated within the feminist bookstore movement, which had emerged in the 1970s as a key vector for the ideas of second-wave feminism. With more than one hundred feminist bookstores doing business across the United States, the period between the late 1980s and the mid-1990s was the peak of the movement. As well as assembling a wide range of feminist books, businesses such as the Amazon Bookstore in Minneapolis, Pride and Prejudice in Chicago, ICI: A Woman's Place in Oakland, California, and New Words Bookstore in Cambridge, Massachusetts, brought into being multiple communities of feminist readers.[122] In the words of Mary Farmer, the proprietor of Lamma, a Washington, DC, feminist bookstore, "We're not just talking about bookstores . . . we're talking about physical spaces where women can escape from an increasingly hostile world."[123]

OUP actively promoted Lerner's books within this context, taking out numerous advertisements in *Feminist Bookstore News* (*FBN*), the movement's leading publication. In turn, the *FBN* encouraged booksellers to engage with university presses to increase the audience of books that had crossover potential. In one 1987 article promoting the practice of ordering books from academic publishers, for example, the publication highlighted the quality of OUP's trade list and drew specific attention to Lerner, whose books it suggested were excellent sellers.[124] A 1993 article went on to describe *The Creation of Feminist Consciousness* as "the lead title on the Spring lists" with the potential to follow in the footsteps of *The Creation of Patriarchy* as "one of the most important books in women's history and theory published in the last two decades and one of the all-time best-selling books in the area of women's studies."[125] With the emergence of the feminist bookstore movement, Lerner had found the enthusiastic activist readership she had longed for two decades earlier.

However, the response to Lerner's books was not universally positive. As she circulated draft chapters of the book, some friends and colleagues praised the geographical and chronological scope of her research, but also questioned whether it was possible for Lerner to write a history that held true for all women in all cultures. For example, after reading an early draft of

The Creation of Feminist Consciousness in 1991, the historian of Africa Steven Feierman questioned her claims to "historical universality" and suggested that her approach was unfortunate to the extent that it accepted "the master-narrative of western history . . . that western ideas are the central ideas with which all of humanity must in the end live."[126] Even earlier, a hostile reviewer had described *The Creation of Patriarchy* as "history in the grand mode now abandoned by many historians," that made no effort to question "the modes of thought that got rigidified with Enlightenment rationalism and the emergence of modern science."[127]

These critiques came about in a moment when the very language of feminism was fundamentally in question. The best register of the impact of these developments on women's history is Joan W. Scott's essay "Gender: A Useful Category of Historical Analysis" (1986). Published the same year as *The Creation of Patriarchy*, and now a major historiographical landmark, it argued that effective use of the concept of "gender" would move historians away from "scholarship focused too narrowly and separately on women" and, instead, highlight the "relational nature" of the links between both women's and men's historical agency.[128] In this sense, to be a historian of *gender* was to be something materially different from a historian of *women*. Another important feature of Scott's essay was its injunction that a new history of gender needed to be "redefined and restructured in conjunction with a vision of political and social equality that includes not only sex, but class and race."[129] On its face, this was a similar argument to those made by Lerner in the 1970s about the relationships between forms of inequality and oppression. However, in Scott's post-structuralist reading of the problem, there could be no hierarchy of historical causation: she rejected ideas that provided "a vision of the path along which history has moved dialectically."[130]

This was not the vision of causality pursued by Lerner, even as she was at pains to integrate observations about class and race into her analysis. Instead, she argued for the uniquely determinative aspects of gender in history. This was clearest in one of the most important chapters in *The Creation of Patriarchy*, which focused on the development of slavery. In moving beyond Engels and other Marxist theorists, Lerner suggested that "the oppression of women antedates slavery and makes it possible."[131] To substantiate this point, she cited examples drawn from scholarship on Babylonia, Mesopotamia, and other ancient societies to argue that "men learned the power of sexual control" by subordinating women and were thus able to develop "the symbolic language in which to express dominance and create a class of psychologically enslaved persons."[132] This meant that "distinctions of class and race, both first

manifested in the institutionalization of slavery," rested upon "the inextrica-
ble linkage of sexual dominance and economic exploitation manifested in the
patriarchal family and the archaic state."[133] In making this case, Lerner chose
to de-emphasize the economic and racial dimensions of slavery, ultimately
subsuming them under the logic of patriarchy. In pursuing her synthesis of
women's history, Lerner was therefore bucking the new epistemological trends
represented by Scott.

Lerner addressed the issue directly in the introduction to *The Creation of
Feminist Consciousness:*

> Today, when historians and literary scholars are very much aware of the dif-
> ferences within large groups, that is, factors of race, ethnicity, class, religion,
> any attempt at making generalizations is suspect and full of pitfalls. Still, in
> order to understand differences between men and women *as groups* such gen-
> eralizations need to be attempted. It is quite true that the group of women I
> am studying in this book is largely white, upper-class, wealthy, or economi-
> cally privileged, but that is precisely the problematic of women's intellectual
> history: for women, far longer than for men, education was a class privilege. I
> have, throughout, included whatever I could find of the lives and works of less
> privileged women, of middle and lower-class women, of women of oppressed
> groups, such as African Americans and Jews.[134]

This was a defensive stance, and the very fact that Lerner found herself in
such a position was itself ironic. As we have seen, she built her political and
scholarly reputation on the observation that the oppressions of gender, race,
and class were intertwined. Indeed, in 1977 she had gone as far as arguing that
Black and white women had not been able to escape "the confines and limitations of a society in which a person's status and power are defined not only by
sex, but—more importantly—by race."[135]

However, this did not stop audiences from within the feminist movement
from questioning Lerner's approach. During a book talk at Macalester College in Saint Paul, Minnesota, for example, the historian was interrogated
by audience members who wanted to know where the experiences of Native American, Asian, and LGBT women fit into her narrative, and a report
on the talk described the historian's response to these questions as a "frustrated" one.[136] This makes sense when we consider that as well as creating
newfound opportunities for book sales, the feminist bookstore movement
was also rooted in a transnational approach to feminism that revised conventional understandings of gender identity and their intersection with race and
class.[137] As the skeptical audience at Macalester highlighted, this framework

was not entirely compatible with that pursued in *The Creation of Patriarchy* and *The Creation of Feminist Consciousness*.

Lerner's frustrated response was surely born of the fact that it tapped into a vein of criticism she was already familiar with. Indeed, she had always been attuned to the idea that feminism was a heterogeneous political enterprise, and in this she was more closely aligned with Black and Chicana women's activists than with the majority of white campaigners.[138] However, as the viewpoint that women's experiences were multiple rather than singular gained increasing traction in American intellectual life, Lerner swam against the tide by searching for a frame of analysis that could transcend the differences of race, class, and ethnicity. In a sense, this was less a political than an epistemological disagreement: while Lerner had no interest in downplaying the significance of class and race, she felt that it was necessary to highlight gender as the determinative factor in the development of Western history. In doing so, she rejected Freudianism, entered into critical dialogue with Marxism, and embraced an approach to the past that was deeply indebted to the intellectual cultures of second-wave feminism. The success of the book with reviewers and readers suggested that this was an ideal formula for the communication of feminist ideas to a broad readership.

However, the questions that were asked by those more skeptical of her field of vision suggest that Lerner's effort to forge a popular women's history was not completely successful. While she had rejected any intellectual or political debt to Marxism many years before, she nonetheless retained its commitment to grand narratives of historical development. In an intellectual moment that privileged the relational nature of concepts such as gender, hers was a singular and hierarchical vision. Just like that provided by Franklin and Zinn, this was a form of historical interpretation written in a grand mode, and it was precisely the type of popular history that had proved so successful throughout the age of the paperback.

In a 2003 interview discussing her life and career, Lerner was asked about her attitudes toward contemporary women's studies in the United States. The historian outlined what she viewed as the success of attempts to "critique the patriarchal intellectual edifice" of modern society, which had resulted in a radical shift in "the structure of the university system that's been with us since the eleventh century."[139] As an effort at institution building and ideational change, she saw women's studies as an important and positive enterprise. However, she was less convinced about the discipline's capacity to communicate its findings beyond the university. In making this point, she singled out feminist literary theorist Judith Butler as a cautionary example:

Butler, to me, is just like the old monks arguing about how many angels fit on the head of a pin. If I can't, with two advanced degrees and seventy years of intellectual life . . . read a page and comprehend it, excuse me, there's something wrong with her, not with me. . . . I'm picking on her, but it doesn't matter—I mean, that's a dead end. I don't care what she says. If you cannot translate what you say into something that is translatable to the ordinary person then you . . . might as well be talking Latin or Aramaic, okay?[140]

In making this point, Lerner underscored the fundamental difference between her thinking and that of the new generation of post-structuralist feminists. But she also highlighted her career-long dedication to popularizing women's history. Starting with her writing soon after she had arrived in the United States as an exile from central Europe, continuing through her struggles write popular, engaging women's history after earning a PhD and entering professional academia, and culminating in her efforts to reach broad activist audiences with *The Creation of Patriarchy* and *The Creation of Feminist Consciousness*, this was a long-term feature of her intellectual and political mission.

In this effort, she capitalized on the contexts provided by early Cold War radicalism and second-wave feminisms. She also built vitally important relationships with staff at her publisher OUP. These relationships allowed her to intervene in, and capitalize on, the market for feminist writing that developed between the 1970s and the 1990s, propelled by, among other developments, the emergence of the feminist bookstore movement. In a variety of ways, then, Gerda Lerner's popular history was born of struggle: personal struggle to assimilate into American intellectual life as an outsider and a woman; intellectual struggle to prove the significance of women's history as an important subfield for both academic and non-academic readerships; and political struggle via direct contributions to second-wave feminist movements.

However, Lerner's characteristically forthright dismissal of Butler also highlighted some of the challenges she faced as a popular historian. In making her point, she chose to disparage one of the most preeminent spokespeople for the argument that overarching concepts such as patriarchy and feminism needed to be radically deconstructed: as Butler had famously argued in her landmark 1990 book *Gender Trouble*, "The feminist 'we' is always and only a phantasmatic construction."[141] Lerner was highly attuned to questions of racial and ethnic difference. But in her work as a popular historian, she chose not to foreground these ideas. In writing a two-volume account of the transnational development of patriarchy and feminism from the ancient to the modern worlds that was broad ranging and appealed to a wide audience, Lerner worked in a mold that feminist readers were, at the very moment of publication, coming to view as outdated. This was a significant paradox, and one brought about by her struggle to popularize women's history.

Another challenge was posed by the evolution of American publishing and book selling at the end of the twentieth century. By the early 2000s, the distribution networks for women's writing provided by the feminist bookstore movement had all but evaporated. The rise of chain stores such as Barnes & Noble and Borders began this process by pushing independent booksellers out of business, and it was subsequently compounded by the rise of internet book selling, which, in turn, placed major pressure on the chains.[142] Of course, this was not only a crisis for avowedly feminist writers, but for all of those who relied on America's network of trade publishers and independent booksellers to reach audiences.[143] Eventually, then, many of the opportunities provided by the paperback revolution and its attendant shifts in marketing and distribution began to disappear, or, at the very least, to change beyond recognition.

The contexts in which popular national history was written and published had therefore shifted fundamentally from those that shaped the genre's invention in the 1940s. The upheavals of the 1960s and 1970s had created opportunities for writers such as Franklin, Zinn, and Lerner to intervene in pressing conversations about social inequality. This led to a diversification of popular historical writing and its audiences, as well as a series of new visions of the national past. However, by the end of the century, the generation these historians represented was no longer in the driving seat when it came to determining the key ideas that would shape the attitudes of activist audiences. Franklin was forced to pass the baton of *From Slavery to Freedom* to younger collaborators. Zinn lost control of the meaning of *A People's History of the United States*, even as it proved enduringly successful. And, in the capstone volumes of her career, Lerner articulated a version of feminist politics that, though popular, no longer represented the academic cutting edge. Ultimately, these developments raised questions about whether or not the legacies of postwar popular history would extend into the twenty-first century.

CONCLUSION

The Legacies of Postwar Popular History

What's the matter with history? I set out to write this book as a way of grappling with my own version of Allan Nevins's 1939 question. I wanted to use my expertise as a historian of the United States to historicize a specific government imperative in the United Kingdom (from where I write), known as the Research Excellence Framework, or REF. This immensely costly and time-consuming bureaucratic process, which has been running in one form or another since 1986, apportions funds from central government to universities based on metrics relating to research quality.[1] One of these metrics, known as "impact," is centrally concerned with pushing academics to reframe their work for the non-academic world and recognizes activities like consultancy and public engagement, but not popular writing. In fact, and as I can attest from multiple conversations with my colleagues and peers, when viewed from the perspective of the REF, popular scholarship appears inherently suspicious. In parallel to these conversations, when I discussed my research with colleagues in the United States, they expressed similar anxieties, suggesting that hiring and tenure committees often dismissed the value of writing they deemed too popular. Troubled by these developments, I wanted to understand more about what I came to see as the problem of popularity in historical writing.

My interest in this problem was also driven by an intense "bookishness," the term employed by the scholar of contemporary literature Jessica Pressman to describe the phenomenon by which readers demonstrate their dedication to books in an increasingly digital (and digitized) world.[2] Even though historians are all, in one way or another, authors as well as researchers, it is my belief that we do not have a strong-enough narrative about the history of our profession's entanglement with the business of book publishing and the experience of reading. Put simply, I wanted to find out how and why historians' popular writing mattered in the past, as well what it could tell us about the historian's craft in the present. Knowing more about these important topics, I thought, would provide better explanations for the periodic crises that grip the discipline of history on both sides of the Atlantic. I did not expect my research to bring an end to the rich tradition of high-profile complaints about the profession's overspecialization. However, I did have the more modest goal of providing a framework through which professional historians could more completely grasp the manifold challenges they face, but also the opportunities available to them, as they navigate their identities as researchers and writers to engage audiences beyond the academy.

This, of course, led me to the historians and writers profiled in this book. As well as being of historical interest, I am convinced that their efforts to popularize scholarly approaches to the national past retain their relevance today. After World War II, popular history was continually invented and reinvented in the United States. The postwar period provided a range of political, social, cultural, and educational contexts that transformed the ability of historians to write popular history books and, just as important, to have those books reach everyday readers. The emergence of the paperback, the rapid expansion of American higher education, and the political upheavals that took place alongside them all made the genre of popular national history particularly resonant, and for multiple audiences.

As they popularized the past, the most successful postwar historians continually emphasized their identities as writers. This identification did not come at the expense of scholarly rigor and erudition, but it is important to recognize that literary style was just as important as these other markers of quality. More than most professional historians, Hofstadter, Boorstin, Franklin, Zinn, and Lerner thought carefully and creatively about the words they used, the stories they told, the readers they were targeting, and what their books meant in the world. They thus embraced the historian's craft as a literary and political one.

Postwar popular historical writing also grew out of the close relationships that developed between these authors and the publishing professionals who worked with them to collaboratively design, produce, market, and sell popular history. In other words, Hofstadter, Boorstin, Franklin, Zinn, and Lerner were not reliant solely on their individual talent as they developed identities as public intellectuals. Instead, they were deeply enmeshed in the business of books as it was transacted in the second half of the twentieth century. They did not always fully understand this process, which sometimes caused them to feel that they were succeeding despite, rather than because of, the contributions of their publishers. Nonetheless, they benefited tremendously from such relationships.

The five historians were also committed to the process of connecting history with the politics of the present. Their lives were deeply political, and this fact indelibly shaped the books they wrote. Consequently, they conceptualized good popular history not simply as entertaining or well researched, but also as politically relevant, perhaps even controversial. It was this type of commitment that led them to decisions about subject matter and storytelling that were framed to attract specific types of popular audiences, and here they had to make choices: Were they writing for "general" readers embedded in the mainstream politics of consensus, or for "activist" readers who wanted to challenge the status quo? These decisions flowed, often productively, from the historians' political commitments, and they developed an organic sense of who their readers would be that, in some cases, changed over time (this was particularly the case for Boorstin and Lerner, who wrote multivolume works, and Franklin, whose signal popular history was regularly revised and reissued). They also emerged from the relationships the historians developed with their readers, who consumed popular national history voraciously and were at once informed, entertained, and emotionally affected by new understandings of the American past they developed from it. While the division between general and activist readers that emerged in the second half of the twentieth century was not set in stone, and there was always some fluidity between them, these categories help us to remember that there was *never* a single "mass" public for historians to engage with. Instead, they created their own publics through a collaborative process that involved the input of publishers and readers as well as professional scholars.

Ultimately, then, these postwar historians were important because of the contributions they made to public knowledge about the past in books that sold hundreds of thousands—sometimes millions—of copies. These were major contributions to the American historical profession and deserve to be recognized as such. But they were also something more. They were efforts, undertaken in moments of uncertainty and upheaval, to demonstrate the social and political significance of both historical knowledge and erudite storytelling.

What of our own moment of uncertainty and upheaval? The approaches taken by Hofstadter, Boorstin, Franklin, Zinn, and Lerner cannot simply be replicated by historians working today. Each of them owed their success to a set of overlapping literary, political, and social contexts that were specific to the second half of the twentieth century. The paperback revolution, along with the dramatic impact it had on the historical profession, cannot be reproduced.

Nor can the waves of expansion in higher education that took place during the postwar period, and which, in turn, created expansive new audiences of educated readers who had faith in the expertise provided by the American university. Furthermore, the culture wars of the early twenty-first century provide a different type of politically engaged readership for popular history than the social upheavals of the postwar period. Nevertheless, popular historical writing of the kind they produced is still possible, and it still has much to teach us. It reminds us that the persistence of a healthy historical imagination can, and should, be rooted in popular writing about the past by professional historians of the type invented and reinvented throughout the second half of the twentieth century.

Today, college enrollments in history, and in the humanities more generally, are on the decline, and the historical profession faces a jobs crisis.[3] What is more, in an era racked by political polarization, new attempts to challenge popular narratives about the American past, such as "The 1619 Project" launched by journalist Nikole Hannah-Jones and published by the *New York Times*, have met with trenchant conservative opposition from activists, journalists, and politicians.[4] Unsurprisingly, then, multiple scholars have latched on to an explanation of these overlapping crises that shares similarities with those of their professional predecessors: the apparent lack of connection between the historical profession and the reading public.

As we have seen, one of the most high-profile critics is Jill Lepore. Writing in 2019, she argued that historians had recently shied away from the type of popular national history that had characterized the postwar period. "Meanwhile," she asked, "who was doing the work of providing a legible past and a plausible future—a nation—to the people who lived in the United States?" Her answer, shaped no doubt by the presence of such "historians" as Bill Bryson and Bill O'Reilly on the bestseller lists, was a caustic one: "Charlatans, stooges, and tyrants." In making this case, Lepore was publicizing her own recently published work of popular national history, *These Truths: A History of the United States* (2018). Her intention in writing the book, she explained, was to return to a particular type of story about the past that had been ceded to nonspecialists because professional historians were afraid of the politics of nationalism: "When scholars stop trying to write a common history for a people, nationalism doesn't die. Instead, it eats liberalism."[5]

These Truths represented what Lepore described as the "capstone" of a career spent "figuring out a different way for a historian to offer a contribution" via her work as a staff writer for the *New Yorker*, a role she undertook alongside her position as a professor at Harvard University. Like many of the scholars who popularized the past between the 1940s and the 1990s, she explicitly identified as a *writer* as well as a professional historian, telling an interviewer in 2018, "For me writing is a complete and total joy, and if I'm not writing I'm miserable."[6] Much like Richard Hofstadter's approach in *The American Political Tradition* seventy years earlier, Lepore's version of popular national history was richly literary, something she underscored in the introduction to *These Truths*:

> History isn't only a subject; it's also a method. My method is, generally, to let the dead speak for themselves. The work of the historian is not the work of the critic or the moralist; it is the work of the sleuth and the storyteller, the philosopher and the scientist, the keeper of tales, the sayer of sooth, the teller of truth.[7]

This sense of self-consciously literary storytelling, Lepore argued, was vital if a trade book by an academic historian was to capture the attention of a "general readership" and thus engage meaningfully in the public life of the nation.[8]

Lepore framed *These Truths* as an intervention in the political moment dominated by the specter of President Donald Trump. Like the books for general audiences written by Hofstadter and Boorstin in the postwar period, while this was an expressly political undertaking, it was one pitched at a broad audience of educated Americans, rather than a more specific audience of activists. The book's key themes were the upheavals caused by technological change, the shifting nature of "truth" and who defines it, the contingencies of constitutional government, and, finally, the historical agency of women in the development of American politics. In a moment when the president repeatedly used social media sites such as Twitter to rail against "fake news," reject the basic premises of American democracy, and malign a range of high-profile women, the contemporary relevance of Lepore's popular national history was clear.

Unsurprisingly, *These Truths* was also an anxious book. This disquiet was rooted in Lepore's sense that populist politicians like Trump were molding the nation's historical imagination far more successfully than professional historians:

> All over the world, populists seeking solace from a troubled present sought refuge in imagined histories. The fate of the nation-state itself appearing uncertain, nationalists, who had few proposals for the future, gained power by telling fables about the greatness of the past.[9]

Lepore's response was to promote a robust and resurgent liberalism. She rejected the popular history of radicals like Howard Zinn as a simplistic "Marxist reckoning with American atrocity," as well as that written by journalists such as David McCullough, who only focused their attention on "men and power."[10]

Instead, she sought a middle ground, framing *These Truths* with a closing epigraph by the theologian Reinhold Niebuhr, who was also influential on Boorstin's historical writing in the 1950s. In *The Irony of American History* (1952), Niebuhr had suggested that, given the context of the early Cold War, the failure of the American experiment would most likely result not because of "the ruthlessness of the foe" but because the nation was led by "eyes too blind to see all the hazards of the struggle," and that the blindness was caused "not by some accident of nature or history but by hatred and vainglory."[11] Lepore's history was intensely critical of the type of populist nationalism espoused by modern conservatives. However, like Niebuhr, she also placed significant blame for the state of American politics on liberals, arguing that they had "failed to plot a course" for the nation and had consequently "lost sight of the horizon and their grasp on any compass."[12] The answer to this paradox lay in a form of historical writing that grappled with complexity at the same time as it articulated a singular national vision of an inclusive politics for twenty-first-century America.

The *New York Times* praised Lepore's "elegant, readable, sobering" prose, while the *Washington Post*'s reviewer, historian H. W. Brands, described the book as "an honest reckoning with America's past."[13] However, the book was not uniformly well received, and several of Lepore's fellow scholars found her approach to popularization unsettling. One problem was what the Stanford historian Richard White described as the book's "New Yorkerization of American history," rooted in the fact that much of its content was recycled from Lepore's journalistic writing. Ultimately, he argued, while Lepore's penchant for unexpected anecdote made the individual parts of the book a delight to read, they did not cohere together into a satisfactory whole. Instead, the book focused too much attention on entertaining historical characters and not enough on the development of long-term historical forces that transcended individual Americans.[14] This interpretation of the book emphasized one of the perils of popularization: the difficulties of navigating the thorny distinction between the journalistic writing required for a literary magazine, and the synthetic approach required for a popular national history.

Another problem with the book was that the boundaries of Lepore's approach to racial and ethnic inclusivity were clearly marked. As several professional historians pointed out in reviews of *These Truths*, its grand synthesis failed to integrate the new histories of Indigenous and Latinx Americans that had expanded dramatically in the opening decades of the twenty-first century.[15] Furthermore, the book did not embrace the transnational turn in US historiography that told the story of the nation's past against the backdrop of its multifarious and long-standing imperial entanglements.[16] These were, in the eyes of Lepore's professional peers, some of the book's most significant shortcomings. They highlighted another peril of popularization: the difficulties faced by a single author attempting to synthesize a massive, diffuse field of knowledge into a single and representative national narrative.

Lepore's approach to writing popular history, along with her conceptualization of its audiences, therefore demonstrated remarkable similarity to the postwar ideas of Richard Hofstadter and Daniel Boorstin. Like many midcentury scholars with ambitions to be public intellectuals, they wrote for readers who, they hoped, had the requisite status and skills to grapple with the complexity of the histories they wrote. These were "general" readers, imagined as comfortably placed in the American mainstream, and who wanted to better understand, rather than fundamentally question, its public cultures, as well as to be entertained by the history they consumed.

A radical alternative to this vision has recently been elaborated by Ibram X. Kendi. "It is possible for a book . . . to be deeply scholarly, and at the same time fully accessible to individuals of all intellectual backgrounds," he claimed in 2018, writing alongside fellow historian Keisha Blain. "Knowledge seekers and producers cannot retire to their silos and expect their intellectual values or academic communities to survive," the pair continued. "Public scholarship is the lifeline. It can and will prevent the creation of a post-scholar America."[17] Appearing only two years after the publication of Kendi's best-selling book, *Stamped from the Beginning: The Definitive History of Racist Ideas in America* (2016), this was a clarion call for popular scholarship in the humanities and social sciences that bridged the gap between scholarly excellence and public engagement.

As Kendi explained in the book's prologue, it had been written in, and responded to, the specific political moment provided by "the televised and non-televised killings of unarmed human beings at the hands of law enforcement officials, and with the televised and non-televised life of the shooting star of #BlackLivesMatter during America's stormiest nights."[18] *Stamped from the Beginning* therefore addressed a similarly specific audience: those committed not simply to defining themselves as "non-racist," but to going one step further to articulate a politics of "antiracism." Indeed, Kendi emphasized the futility of writing a book that would appeal to *all* Americans:

> I know that readers truly committed to racial equality will join me on this journey of interrogating and shedding our racist ideas. But if there is anything

I've learned during my research, it is that the principal producers and defend-
ers of racist ideas will not join us. And no logic or fact or history book can
change them, because logic and facts and scholarship have little to do with
why they are expressing racist ideas in the first place. *Stamped from the Beginning* is about these close-minded, cunning, captivating producers of racist
ideas. But it is not for them.[19]

In the twenty-first century, as activist-historians once again reinvented the
nation's past to make it intelligible for those seeking to challenge the status
quo, Kendi repurposed the vision of popular history first articulated by historians such as Franklin, Zinn, and Lerner.

A key theme in *Stamped from the Beginning* was the dynamic between
segregationist, assimilationist, and antiracist ideas, narrated via the lives of
racial thinkers whose lifetimes spanned five hundred years: Cotton Mather,
Thomas Jefferson, William Lloyd Garrison, W. E. B. Du Bois, and Angela Davis. If the lives of Mather and Jefferson highlighted how racist ideas became
embedded in American life, those of Garrison and Du Bois showed how, even
in seeking to rid the nation of the scourge of racism, assimilationist thinking
could have racist implications because of its assumption of fundamental differences between Black and white Americans. Kendi argued that it was only
Davis who was fully able to embrace antiracist thinking, but that in doing so,
she became alienated from a society and political system in which racist ideas
continued to circulate in the mainstream even as it elected a Black president
in 2008.

Stamped from the Beginning therefore used its account of the American
past, which was explicitly pitched at audiences beyond the academy, to articulate an antiracist politics:

> An antiracist America can only be guaranteed if principled antiracists are in
> power, and then antiracist policies become the law of the land, and then anti-
> racist ideas become the common sense of the people, and then the anti-
> racist common sense of the people holds those antiracist leaders and policies
> accountable.[20]

In making this case, Kendi set himself apart from John Hope Franklin. He suggested that Franklin's *From Slavery to Freedom* was a "milestone that pushed
hard against the racist version of history" prominent in 1940s and 1950s
American schools and universities. Nonetheless, Kendi critiqued Franklin
for his "racist historical conception that slavery had induced Black inferiority." While this assertion "did at least counteract Jim Crow historians' claims
of enslavement as a civilizing force," Kendi argued, "both pictures were wrong
and racist—one started Black people in inferiority before slavery, and the

other ended Black people in inferiority after slavery."[21] This disagreement highlights important differences in historical interpretation, and, in articulating it, Kendi placed himself in a long tradition of Black historians who sought to differentiate their scholarship and politics from Franklin's.

Nonetheless, these differences should not blind us to the way in which the two historians worked in a similar mold of popular historical writing: one that openly addressed an audience of activist readers and that led them both to considerable success. Published when Kendi was only thirty-three years old, *Stamped from the Beginning* won the National Book Award for Nonfiction for 2016 and launched the historian into a prominent national position as a public intellectual whose subsequent writing on antiracism resulted in a spin-off children's book and a deal with Netflix to produce an animated series.[22] This success was built, at least in part, on the reception of the book's arguments in the mainstream media. In the *Washington Post*, for example, the paper's literary critic Carlos Lozada described it as "engrossing and relentless," before making the case that its "grim vision" of American history was one "consistent with an era when the prison warden has supplanted the slave master, and when Black Lives Matter is the latest incarnation of a civil rights movement that has no reason to stop moving."[23] Not only was the book well written, then, but it also made a bold and specific intervention in the political culture of social upheaval.

However, *Stamped from the Beginning* was not without its critics, and the controversy it has engendered has also contributed to Kendi's prominence. While his peers in the historical profession blended praise and criticism of his work in their reviews, he received sustained attacks from conservatives, especially those writing for the *National Review*.[24] The publication featured a range of articles and blog posts attacking Kendi, each of which poured scorn on what one called his "sophomoric and indefensible" approach to the history and politics of racial inequality.[25] For conservative writer Christopher Caldwell, for example, Kendi was a "terrible *simplificateur*" whose ideas represented the intellectual bankruptcy of the modern American Left.[26] In this way, Kendi's experience of the problems of popularization mirrored those of Howard Zinn in the 1980s and 1990s. As the outspoken author of a series of controversial works rooted in a powerful combination of activism and scholarship, his version of popular history as controversy became a lightning rod in the contemporary American culture wars.

In their own ways, then, Lepore and Kendi continued the debates about popular historical writing that were initiated in the 1940s, and which evolved throughout the following five decades. Their examples demonstrate that the question of how the historical profession can make high-quality scholarship accessible to the public retains vital importance. Like so many postwar scholars, publishing professionals, and readers, Lepore and Kendi shared a fundamental commitment to popular national history as a literary genre. However, the way they conceptualized who their readers were, and what they would expect from the books they read, differed markedly, and in politicized ways. Their divergent approaches to writing about the past therefore highlight another legacy of post-1945 popular historical writing: the striking differences between books written for what I have argued are the ideal types of "general" and "activist" readers.

Whatever the strengths of Lepore's account of US history in *These Truths*, and they are many, her public statements since its publication have highlighted that she is committed to the conception of a single, national readership that, as this book has shown, was radically revised in the second half of the twentieth century. As readers of mainstream nonfiction became more diverse and more influenced by their experiences in the multiple social upheavals of the period, it became apparent, to historians, publishers, and readers alike, that the goal of uniting a "general" audience around a single national narrative was impossible. In place of this idea emerged the belief that, even though they might sometimes intersect or overlap, the publics for popular history were varied and multiple.

This did not mean that the idea of a general readership had somehow fractured, to the detriment of the historical profession, the publishing industry, and the nation. Instead, it had broadened and diversified to encompass a range of different perspectives. And far from being a recent turn of events, this broadening and diversification had its long roots in the development of postwar popular history. Segmented by race, class, gender, and age, among other factors, the new readers of popular history were by no means the cause of history's crisis. This was clear from the successes of historians such as Franklin, Zinn, and Lerner in the period after 1945. It is also clear from the success of a historian such as Kendi today, whose work in *Stamped from the Beginning* so candidly rejects the premise that it might be a book for *all* Americans.

The experiences of these historians, and many others like them, highlight how futile it is to rebuke the historical profession for not crafting a singular national narrative that speaks to the experience of every American. No such narrative can, or indeed should, exist. What can still exist, however, is thought-provoking, entertaining, and critically engaged popular writing about the past. And it can be authored by professional historians.

Acknowledgments

I worked on this book while making the transition from early career to established academic life. In navigating the inevitable tensions between teaching, institutional citizenship, and research, I was incredibly fortunate. Not only did I benefit from stable, long-term employment at two institutions—Canterbury Christ Church University (2012–15) and University College London (2015–present)—but I was also granted a range of funds to support visits to archives and participation in conferences. This took the form of generous research support from my two home departments: the School of Humanities at CCCU and the Institute of the Americas at UCL. It was also provided by various external organizations: the Arts and Humanities Research Council, in the form of an International Placement Fellowship at the Kluge Center, Library of Congress; the British Academy, in the form of a Small Research Grant; the UK-US Fulbright Commission, in the form of an American Studies Scholarship; the University of Edinburgh, in the form of a postdoctoral fellowship at the Institute for Advanced Studies in the Humanities; and Duke University, in the form of a John Hope Franklin Center for African American History and Culture Travel Grant. The structural privilege granted to me by steady employment and plentiful research funding therefore made a huge difference to the completion of the book.

I also benefited from the mentorship provided by two remarkable and generous historians: Andrew Hartman and Jonathan Bell. Andrew's work in US intellectual history has long inspired me, and his generous feedback on the manuscript was invaluable. As a British person studying American history outside of the United States, it is easy to feel like one is on the outside of the profession, looking in. Andrew has always made me feel welcome: inviting me to contribute to conference panels, introducing me to colleagues, and supporting me in first pitching the book to the University of Chicago Press. There is no better example of a genuinely warm and approachable scholar. Likewise, Jonathan's contributions to my progress since we first met in Middelburg in 2012 have been manifold. The combination he exhibits of intellectual seriousness, collegiality, and empathy is all too rare in contemporary higher education. He has supported the completion of the book directly via illuminating feedback on draft articles and chapters, and indirectly by creating a supportive environment at the Institute of the Americas during his time as head of department. I am privileged to call him a colleague, mentor, and friend.

Others have read, reread, and critiqued the manuscript in draft form. I am particularly indebted to the brilliant Nick Grant for establishing an informal American studies reading group amid a pandemic, and to its energetic and insightful participants: Sarah Dunstan, Lydia Plath, John Munro, and Jenny Woodley. All of them have helped me improve my ideas about popular history and have inspired me with the example of their own remarkable scholarship. Tom Arnold-Forster was an enthusiastic interlocutor, and his critical readings of the chapters on Richard Hofstadter and Daniel Boorstin were vital. Mary Dudziak and Brooke Blower both provided feedback that pushed me to include Gerda Lerner as a subject of the book alongside four male historians. A range of others provided much-needed insight along the way: Gareth Davies, Paulo Drinot, Zalfa Feghali, Dan Geary, Gary Gerstle, Nadia Hilliard, Zoe Hyman, Richard King, Dan Matlin, Kevin Middlebrook, Maxine Molyneux, Katharina Rietzler, Kate Saunders-Hastings, Barbara Savage, Adam Smith, James West, and Stephen Whitfield. Mark Storey and Bevan Sewell kept me on the straight and narrow, at academic conferences and in general, while my fortnightly conversations with Sinéad Moynihan as part of our work for the *Journal of American Studies* transformed the way I think about writing and editing. I am deeply thankful to them all.

During the time I worked on the book, I was inspired by the dozens of students whose BA, MA, and PhD theses and dissertations I supervised. Several of the doctoral candidates I have had the pleasure of working with are talented historians whose research and argumentation shaped my thinking in a range of ways, and whose company in supervisions, at conferences, and in bars and restaurants in London and beyond lifted my spirits on numerous occasions: thanks to Elliot Askew, Tom Cryer, Lizzie Evens, Emily Hull, Will Ranger, and Chris Sarjeant. Of my current and former PhD students, though, Josh Hollands deserves special mention: now a colleague at UCL as well as a gifted scholar, his combination of sparkling intellect and dry wit make working alongside him a singular pleasure.

I am grateful to librarians and archivists at the following institutions, all of whom helped me navigate my research and gave permission to quote from materials in their collections: the Rare Book and Manuscript Library at Columbia University, the Manuscripts Division at the Library of Congress, the David M. Rubenstein Rare Book and Manuscript Library at Duke University, the Tamiment Library and Robert F. Wagner Labor Archives at New York University, the Arthur and Elizabeth Schlesinger Library on the History of Women in America at Harvard University, the Harry Ransom Center at the University of Texas at Austin, the Manuscripts and Archives Division at the New York Public Library, Special Collections at Smith College, the Robert S. Cox Special Collections and University Archives Research Center at the University of Massachusetts Amherst, and the Bancroft Library at the University of California, Berkeley. I also want to thank Sarah Hofstadter, David Boorstin, John Whittington Franklin, and Myla Zinn for permission to quote from their respective fathers' personal papers. I am grateful to the Reverend Professor Emeritus Alfred A. Moss Jr., PhD, Eric Foner, Roxanne Dunbar-Ortiz, Theodora Chocos Dimitrakopoulos, Jerrold Cooper, and Linda Kerber for kindly granting me permission to quote from letters and other documents they authored, and to the Society of American Historians for an excerpt from a speech by Eric Goldman. I also owe a debt to Zalfa Feghali, Joshua Albury Tait, and Joe Street, each of whom shared copies of documents that I cite in the book and deserve special thanks for their generosity.

The letters between John Hope Franklin and his editors at Alfred A. Knopf are courtesy of Penguin Random House, copyright © 2023 by Penguin Random House LLC; from Penguin Random House Corporate Correspondence by Penguin Random House LLC. Used by permission of Alfred A. Knopf, an imprint of the Knopf Doubleday Publishing Group, a division of Penguin Random House LLC. All rights reserved.

At the University of Chicago Press, my editor Tim Mennel generously supported me after we first discussed the book in Dallas in 2017. He helped me to see its potential, as well as to navigate the peer-review process, and gave me the extra push (or two) that I needed to get over the finish line. In their capacities at the press, Susannah Engstrom and Fabiola Enriquez Flores helped smooth the process of turning a manuscript into the book you see before you, Erin DeWitt did a remarkable job of copyediting it, and June Sawyers created an index with great skill and insight. My research assistants Tom Cryer and Will Ranger also provided invaluable support in securing permissions to cite from archival collections (and, in the process, corrected a range of errors in my endnotes!). I am also grateful to the three readers whose critical responses to the manuscript in both proposal and draft form combined

encouragement and generative criticism in a way that exemplified the ben-
efits of the peer-review system: thanks to Aaron Lecklider, Robert Townsend,
and Peter Mandler.

As someone fascinated by books and their biographies, it could hardly
escape my attention that the biography of *this* book maps almost directly onto
the period I have known Lydia Plath. As we navigated the challenges the last
decade threw at us, Lydia's passion for and deep engagement with the politics
of the past has kept me going. To say simply that she has read the manuscript,
or that she has been a source of intellectual inspiration—even though she has,
multiple times—would be to underplay the significance of the contribution
she has made, one that I cannot adequately put into words. All I can say is
thank you.

Archival Abbreviations

AAKR Alfred A. Knopf, Inc. Records, Harry Ransom Center, University of Texas at Austin.

AKP Alfred Kazin Papers, Henry W. and Albert A. Berg Collection of English and American Literature, The New York Public Library, New York City.

ASJP Arthur Schlesinger, Jr. Papers, Archives & Manuscripts, The New York Public Library, New York City.

BMCR Book-of-the-Month Club Records, Manuscript Division, Library of Congress, Washington, DC.

DBP Daniel J. Boorstin Papers, Manuscripts Division, Library of Congress, Washington, DC.

EGP Eric Frederick Goldman Papers, Manuscript Division, Library of Congress, Washington, DC.

FFPP Frances Fox Piven Papers, Sophia Smith Collection of Women's History, Smith College, Northampton, Massachusetts.

GLP Papers of Gerda Lerner, Schlesinger Library on the History of Women in America, Radcliffe Institute, Harvard University, Cambridge, Massachusetts.

HZP Howard Zinn Papers, Tamiment Library and Robert F. Wagner Labor Archive, New York University, New York City.

JHFP John Hope Franklin Papers, David M. Rubenstein Rare Book & Manuscript Library, Duke University, Durham, North Carolina.

KSP Kenneth M. Stampp Papers, Bancroft Library, University of California, Berkeley.

LTP Lionel Trilling Papers, Rare Book & Manuscript Library, Columbia University, New York City.

RHP Richard Hofstadter Papers, Rare Book & Manuscript Library, Columbia University, New York City.

RHR Random House Records, Rare Book & Manuscript Library, Columbia University, New York City.

WEBDBP W. E. B. Du Bois Papers, Robert S. Cox Special Collections and University Archives Research Center, University of Massachusetts Amherst Libraries.

Notes

Introduction

1. Allan Nevins, "What's the Matter with History?" *Saturday Review of Literature*, February 4, 1939, 4–5. For a fuller account of the context of Nevins's "crusade against pedantry," see Ian Tyrrell, *Historians in Public: The Practice of American History, 1890–1970* (Chicago: University of Chicago Press, 2005), 62–74.

2. Eric Foner, "Popularizing the Past," *New York Times*, April 27, 1980, 13.

3. Herbert Gutman, "Whatever Happened to History?" *The Nation*, November 21, 1981, 553.

4. Gutman, 554. These anxieties were also taken up in the more rarefied pages of the *Journal of American History* by Thomas Bender. Writing in 1986, he argued that "if narrative was once accepted as inherent in the historian's craft, we are now nervous about it." Striking a poststructuralist note, Bender reminded his peers that "our task is not to decide whether or not to narrate, but, rather, to conceive of a plot that is adequate to our proliferating knowledge about society." His answer to this crisis of narration was a new "national synthesis" that conceptualized the nation "in a new way, as the ever changing, always contingent outcome of a continuing contest among social groups and ideas for the power to define . . . the nation itself." See Thomas Bender, "Wholes and Parts: The Need for Narrative Synthesis in American History," *Journal of American History* 73, no. 1 (June 1986): 120–36.

5. Jill Lepore quoted in Evan Goldstein, "The Academy Is Largely Itself Responsible for Its Own Peril," *Chronicle of Higher Education*, November 13, 2018.

6. The term "marketplace of print" was first coined by Alexandra Halasz in her work on early modern England. See Alexandra Halasz, *The Marketplace of Print: Pamphlets and the Public Sphere in Early Modern England* (Cambridge: University of Cambridge Press, 1997). It has been productively developed for the postwar American context in Matthew S. Hedstrom, *The Rise of Liberal Religion: Book Culture and American Spirituality in the Twentieth Century* (New York: Oxford University Press, 2012).

7. Hofstadter, Franklin, and Lerner fit both categories. Zinn earned a PhD in history but was employed for most of his career in the Department of Political Science at Boston University. Boorstin earned a JSD in law but spent over two decades working in the University of Chicago's Department of History before moving into public administration.

8. For a discussion of the "citizen-historian" concept, see Mary P. Ryan, "Narratives of Democracy, or History without Subjects," *American Literary History* 8, no. 2 (Summer 1996): 312.

9. On antiquarianism and the reprinting of historical writing and other documents in the nineteenth century, see Lindsay DiCuirci, *Colonial Revivals: The Nineteenth-Century Lives of Early American Books* (Philadelphia: University of Pennsylvania Press, 2019). On the rise of impartiality as a key value for nineteenth-century historical writers, see Eileen Ka-May Cheng, *Nationalism and Impartiality in American Historical Writing, 1784–1860* (Athens: University of Georgia Press, 2008).

10. On the lack of clear borders between history and fiction in the early national period, see Philip Gould, *Covenant and Republic: Historical Romance and the Politics of Puritanism* (New York: Cambridge University Press, 1996). On the idea of "time and modern nationhood" in the nineteenth century, see Thomas M. Allen, *A Republic in Time: Temporality and Social Imagination in Nineteenth-Century America* (Chapel Hill: University of North Carolina Press, 2008).

11. Gregory M. Pfitzer, *Popular History and the Literary Marketplace, 1840–1920* (Amherst: University of Massachusetts Press, 2008).

12. On the professionalization of the historical discipline, the classic text is Peter Novick, *That Noble Dream: The "Objectivity Question" and the American Historical Profession* (New York: Cambridge University Press, 1998). An important work that updates and revises some of Novick's arguments is Robert B. Townsend, *History's Babel: Scholarship, Professionalization, and the Historical Enterprise in the United States, 1880–1940* (Chicago: University of Chicago Press, 2013).

13. On Adams, see Allan Nevins, *James Truslow Adams: Historian of the American Dream* (Urbana: University of Illinois Press, 1968). On DeVoto, see Louis P. Masur, "Bernard DeVoto and the Making of *The Year of Decision: 1846*," *Reviews in American History* 18, no. 3 (September 1980): 436–51. On Beard, see Clyde Barrow, *More than a Historian: The Political and Economic Thought of Charles A. Beard* (New York: Routledge, 2000); and David S. Brown, *Beyond the Frontier: The Midwestern Voice in American Historical Writing* (Chicago: University of Chicago Press, 2009). On Commager, see Neil Jumonville, *Henry Steele Commager: Midcentury Liberalism and the History of the Present* (Chapel Hill: University of North Carolina Press, 1999).

14. For details on the founding of the SAH, see Tyrrell, *Historians in Public*, 64–68. While this account is excellent, it also forms a brief part of a much wider-ranging book. The SAH thus awaits sustained scholarly attention, and there is voluminous material in the papers of many of the historians involved in its development to substantiate a book-length treatment of the organization's rich history.

15. On Woodson and Greene, see Pero Gaglo Dagbovie, *The Early Black History Movement, Carter G. Woodson, and Lorenzo Johnston Greene* (Champaign: University of Illinois Press, 2007). On Beard, Debo, and others, see Julie Des Jardins, *Women and the Historical Enterprise in America: Gender, Race, and the Politics of Memory, 1880–1945* (Chapel Hill: University of North Carolina Press, 2003).

16. Kenneth C. Davis, *Two-Bit Culture: The Paperbacking of America* (Boston: Houghton Mifflin, 1984), xii.

17. The classic work on the Book-of-the-Month Club is Janice Radway, *A Feeling for Books: The Book-of-the-Month Club, Literary Taste, and Middle-Class Desire* (Chapel Hill: University of North Carolina Press, 1997). On the History Book Club, see Erik Christiansen, *Channeling the Past: Politicizing History in Postwar America* (Madison: University of Wisconsin Press, 2013), 21–52.

18. Beth Luey, "Modernity and Print: The United States, 1890–1970," in *A Companion to the History of the Book*, ed. Simon Eliot and Jonathan Roes (Oxford: Wiley Blackwell, 2009), 376.

19. Joan Shelley Rubin, *The Making of Middlebrow Culture* (Chapel Hill: University of North Carolina Press, 1992).

20. Tim Lacy, *The Dream of a Democratic Culture: Mortimer J. Adler and the Great Books Idea* (New York: Palgrave Macmillan, 2013), 11–13.

21. Hedstrom, *The Rise of Liberal Religion*.

22. Henry R. Luce, "The American Century," *Life*, February 17, 1941, 61–65.

23. The classic account of the "cultural Cold War" is Frances Stonor Saunders, *Who Paid the Piper? The CIA and the Cultural Cold War* (London: Granta, 1999). See also Volker R. Berghahn, *America and the Intellectual Cold Wars in Europe: Shepard Stone between Philanthropy, Academy, and Diplomacy* (Princeton, NJ: Princeton University Press, 2001); Giles Scott-Smith, *The Politics of Apolitical Culture: The Congress for Cultural Freedom and the Political Economy of American Hegemony, 1945–1955* (London: Routledge, 2002); Greg Barnhisel, *Cold War Modernists: Art, Literature, and American Cultural Diplomacy* (New York: Columbia University Press, 2015); Patrick Iber, *Neither Peace nor Freedom: The Cultural Cold War in Latin America* (Cambridge, MA: Harvard University Press, 2015).

24. On the circulation of popular history in Cold War culture, see Tyrrell, *Historians in Public*; Carolyn Kitch, *Pages from the Past: History and Memory in American Magazines* (Chapel Hill: University of North Carolina Press, 2005); Christiansen, *Channeling the Past*; M. J. Rymsza-Pawlowska, *History Comes Alive: Public History and Popular Culture in the 1970s* (Chapel Hill: University of North Carolina Press, 2017).

25. See Suzanne Mettler, *From Soldiers to Citizens: The G.I. Bill and the Making of the Greatest Generation* (New York: Oxford University Press, 2005); and Daniel A. Clark, "'The Two Joes Meet. Joe College, Joe Veteran': The G.I. Bill, College Education, and Postwar American Culture," *History of Education Quarterly* 38, no. 2 (Summer 1998): 165–89.

26. On the post-1960s expansion and diversification of university campuses, see Martha Biondi, *The Black Revolution on Campus* (Berkeley: University of California Press, 2012); Ibram X. Kendi, *The Black Campus Movement: Black Students and the Racial Reconstitution of Higher Education, 1965–1972* (New York: Palgrave Macmillan, 2012); Stefan M. Bradley, *Upending the Ivory Tower: Civil Rights, Black Power, and the Ivy League* (New York: New York University Press, 2018); and Ellen Schrecker, *The Lost Promise: American Universities in the 1960s* (Chicago: Chicago University Press, 2021).

27. David Welky, *Everything Was Better in America: Print Culture in the Great Depression* (Champaign: University of Illinois Press, 2008), 149–59.

28. Lawrence W. Levine, "The Folklore of Industrial Society: Popular Culture and Its Audiences," *American Historical Review* 97, no. 5 (December 1992): 1369–99.

29. Paula Rabinowitz, *American Pulp: How Paperbacks Brought Modernism to Main Street* (Princeton, NJ: Princeton University Press, 2014); Peter Mandler, "Good Reading for the Million: The 'Paperback Revolution' and the Co-Production to Academic Knowledge in Mid-Twentieth-Century Britain and America," *Past & Present* 244, no. 1 (August 2019): 237.

30. "Symposium on the Writing of American History," Transcript of Society of American Historians Annual Meeting, May 10, 1967, 2, EGP, box 45, folder 4.

31. David Riesman, with Nathan Glazer and Raul Denney, *The Lonely Crowd* (New York: Doubleday, 1950). For an important account of the book as a version of popular sociology, see Daniel Geary, "Children of *The Lonely Crowd*: David Riesman, the Young Radicals, and the Splitting of Liberalism in the 1960s," *Modern Intellectual History* 10, no. 3 (November 2013): 603–33. On Trilling, see Thomas Bender, "Lionel Trilling and American Culture," *American Quarterly*

42, no. 2 (June 1990): 324–47. On Mead, see Peter Mandler, *Return from the Natives: How Margaret Mead Won the Second World War and Lost the Cold War* (New Haven, CT: Yale University Press, 2013). On Morgenthau, see Campbell Craig, *Glimmer of a New Leviathan: Total War in the Realism of Niebuhr, Morgenthau, and Waltz* (New York: Columbia University Press, 2003).

32. On Carson, see Priscilla Coit Murphy, *What a Book Can Do: The Publication and Reception of "Silent Spring"* (Amherst: University of Massachusetts Press, 2005). On Freidan, see Stephanie Coontz, *A Strange Stirring: "The Feminine Mystique" and American Women at the Dawn of the 1960s* (New York: Basic Books, 2011).

33. On the postwar rise of expertise and its dissemination, see Wilfred McClay, *The Masterless: Self and Society in Modern America* (Chapel Hill: University of North Carolina Press, 1994); Sarah E. Igo, *The Averaged American: Surveys, Citizens, and the Making of a Mass Public* (Cambridge, MA: Harvard University Press, 2007); Alan Petigny, *The Permissive Society: America, 1941–1965* (New York: Cambridge University Press, 2009); Aaron Lecklider, *Inventing the Egghead: The Battle over Brainpower in American Culture* (Philadelphia: University of Pennsylvania Press, 2013); Andrew Jewett, *Science, Democracy, and the American University: From the Civil War to the Cold War* (New York: Cambridge University Press, 2014); and Michael J. Brown, *Hope and Scorn: Eggheads, Experts, and Elites in American Politics* (Chicago: University of Chicago Press, 2020).

34. Robert Darnton has argued that there are three fundamental questions that animate book history: "How do books come into being? How do they reach readers? What do readers make of them?" To the extent that the archival record allows, this book attempts to pay roughly equal attention to each of them as it navigates the process by which popular history came into being, was mediated for readers, and helped those readers remake their understandings of the past. See Robert Darnton, "'What Is the History of Books?' Revisited," *Modern Intellectual History* 4, no. 3 (November 2007): 495.

35. In developing this line of argument, I am indebted to the work of several literary historians, who have recently played close attention to the role of editors in the production of postwar American literary fiction. See, for example, Evan Brier, *A Novel Marketplace: Mass Culture, the Book Trade, and Postwar American Fiction* (Philadelphia: University of Pennsylvania Press, 2009); Daniel Robert King, *Cormac McCarthy's Literary Evolution: Editors, Agents, and the Crafting of a Prolific American Author* (Knoxville: University of Tennessee Press, 2016); and Tim Groenland, *The Art of Editing: Raymond Carver and David Foster Wallace* (New York: Bloomsbury, 2019).

36. In making this point, I am drawing on the work of political theorist Corey Robin, especially "How Intellectuals Create a Public," *Chronicle of Higher Education*, January 29, 2016, B10. Robin's approach is based in significant part on the classic arguments of John Dewey in his book *The Public and Its Problems* (New York: Henry Holt, 1927).

37. Schlesinger served in John F. Kennedy's administration, Goldman in Lyndon B. Johnson's. On Schlesinger, see Richard Aldous, *Schlesinger: The Imperial Historian* (New York: W. W. Norton, 2017). No satisfactory account of Goldman's varied career yet exists; it is ripe for further study.

38. On Catton, see Robert Cook, "Bruce Catton, Middlebrow Culture, and the Liberal Search for Purpose in Cold War America," *Journal of American Studies* 47, no. 1 (February 2013): 109–26. On Tuchman, see William Palmer, *Engagement with the Past: The Lives and Works of the World War II Generation of Historians* (Lexington: University Press of Kentucky, 2001), 29–30, 278–81.

39. On Du Bois, see Claire Parfait, "Rewriting History: The Publication of W. E. B. Du Bois's *Black Reconstruction in America* (1935)," *Book History* 12 (2009): 266–94. On Bennett, see E. James

West, *"Ebony" Magazine and Lerone Bennett Jr.: Popular Black History in Postwar America* (Champaign: University of Illinois Press, 2020).

40. Daniel Rodgers, *Age of Fracture* (Cambridge, MA: Belknap Press, 2011), 5–6.

41. The classic account of the "liberal consensus" is Godfrey Hodgson, *America in Our Time* (New York: Doubleday, 1976). For a more recent set of essays interrogating the concept, see Robert Mason and Iwan Morgan, eds., *The Liberal Consensus Reconsidered: American Politics and Society in the Postwar Era* (Gainesville: University Press of Florida, 2017).

42. For examples of scholars who situate the "academic" and the "popular" at a remove from each other, see Pfitzer, *Popular History and the Literary Marketplace*, 1–17; and Jerome de Groot, "Empathy and Enfranchisement: Popular Histories," *Rethinking History* 10, no. 3 (2006): 391–413. This theme is also explored in the journalist and historian Nicholas Lemann's contribution to a 1995 roundtable: "History Solo: Non-Academic Historians," *American Historical Review* 100, no. 3 (June 1995): 788–98. Scholars working in the subdiscipline of public history have made some of the strongest arguments for blurring, if not completely rejecting, such distinctions. See, for example, Joan Hoff Wilson, "Is the Historical Profession an 'Endangered Species?'" *Public Historian* 2, no. 2 (Winter 1980): 4–21; Patricia Mooney-Melvin, "Professional Historians and 'Destiny's Gate,'" *Public Historian* 17, no. 3 (Summer 1995): 8–24; David Glassberg, "Public History and the Study of Memory," *Public Historian* 18, no. 2 (Spring 1996): 7–23; and Madge Dresser, "Politics, Populism, and Professionalism: Reflections on the Role of the Academic Historian in the Production of Public History," *Public Historian* 32, no. 3 (Summer 2010): 39–63.

Chapter One

1. Merle Curti to Richard Hofstadter, April 15, 1948, AAKR, box 30, folder 12.

2. Richard Hofstadter, *The American Political Tradition and the Men Who Made It* (New York: Alfred A. Knopf, 1948), xxxvi–xxxvii.

3. Alfred Kazin, *On Native Grounds: An Interpretation of Modern American Prose Literature* (New York: Harcourt & Brace, 1942), 364, 376, 419.

4. Richard Hofstadter to Alfred Kazin, November 1, 1942, AKP, folder 1.

5. Susan Stout Baker, *Radical Beginnings: Richard Hofstadter and the 1930s* (Westport, CT: Greenwood Press, 1985), xix.

6. Thomas Bender, *New York Intellect: A History of Intellectual Life in New York City, from 1750 to the Beginnings of Our Own Time* (Baltimore: Johns Hopkins University Press, 1987), 245–46.

7. Mark Greif, *The Age of the Crisis of Man: Thought and Fiction in America, 1933–1973* (Princeton, NJ: Princeton University Press, 2015), 3–7.

8. "Richard Hofstadter Project: Alfred Kazin," Columbia University Oral History Research Office, 1973, no. 1594, 4.

9. Richard Hofstadter to Harvey Swados, c. October 1939, cited in Baker, *Radical Beginnings*, 151.

10. "Richard Hofstadter Project: Elizabeth Earley," Columbia University Oral History Research Office, 1973, no. 1463, 6.

11. Richard Hofstadter to Kenneth Stampp, April 8, 1947, KSP, carton 1, folder 28.

12. Richard H. Pells, *The Liberal Mind in a Conservative Age: American Intellectuals in the 1940s and 1950s* (Middletown, CT: Wesleyan University Press, 1989), 54–58.

13. Jonathan Bell, *The Liberal State on Trial: The Cold War and American Politics in the Truman Years* (New York: Columbia University Press, 2004), xiii–xvi.

14. Thomas W. Devine, *Henry Wallace's 1948 Presidential Campaign and the Future of Postwar Liberalism* (Chapel Hill: University of North Carolina Press, 2013), x. On the Wallace campaign and its significance for postwar liberalism, see also Alonzo L. Hamby, *Beyond the New Deal: Harry S. Truman and American Liberalism* (New York: Columbia University Press, 1973); Allen Yarnell, *Democrats and Progressives: The 1948 Presidential Election as a Test of Postwar Liberalism* (Berkeley: University of California Press, 1974); Jennifer Delton, "Rethinking Post-World War II Anticommunism," *Journal of the Historical Society* 10, no. 1 (March 2010): 1–41; and Eric Arnesen, "Civil Rights and the Cold War at Home: Postwar Activism, Anticommunism, and the Decline of the Left," *American Communist History* 11, no. 1 (April 2012): 5–44.

15. "Richard Hofstadter Project: Arthur M. Schlesinger, Jr.," Columbia University Oral History Research Office, 1973, no. 914, n.p. The reliability of Schlesinger's certainty on this point is perhaps belied by the fact that he was, himself, an adamant opponent of Wallace. See Richard Aldous, *Schlesinger: The Imperial Historian* (New York: W. W. Norton, 2017), 114–19.

16. Richard Hofstadter to Kenneth Stampp, April 8, 1947, KSP, carton 1, folder 28.

17. Hofstadter, *The American Political Tradition*, xxv.

18. Eric Foner, *Who Owns History? Rethinking the Past in a Changing World* (New York: Hill & Wang, 2002), 32–33.

19. James Kloppenberg, "Pragmatism and the Practice of History: From Turner and Du Bois to Today," *Metaphilosophy* 35, nos. 1/2 (January 2004): 211.

20. Hofstadter, *The American Political Tradition*, xl.

21. Bender, *New York Intellect*, 255, 260.

22. Kazin, *On Native Grounds*, 448.

23. David Hawke, "Interview: Richard Hofstadter," *History* 3 (1960): 140.

24. Edmund Wilson, "Marxism at the End of the Thirties," in *To the Finland Station* (New York: New York Review Books, 2003), 491.

25. Hofstadter, *The American Political Tradition*, xxxvii.

26. Hofstadter, 87, 106.

27. Hofstadter, 113.

28. Hofstadter, 178, 180, 210.

29. Hofstadter, 113, 179.

30. Harold Strauss, "Report on Men and Ideas in American Politics," June 6, 1947, 2, AAKR, box 30, folder 12.

31. Richard Hofstadter, *The Progressive Historians: Turner, Beard, Parrington* (New York: Alfred A. Knopf, 1968), 466.

32. Stanley Pargellis, "The Lasting Literature and Public Taste," *Chicago Sun*, December 2, 1945, clipping in ASJP, box 527.

33. Arthur Schlesinger Jr. to Roger L. Scaife, December 15, 1940, ASJP, box 407, folder 6.

34. Richard Hofstadter, "Democracy in the Making," *New Republic*, October 22, 1945, 541.

35. Richard Hofstadter to Alfred Kazin, c. November 1945, AKP, folder 3.

36. Knopf Fellowship Advertisement, 1945, AAKR, box 564, folder 1.

37. "Report on Hofstadter Application for Knopf Fellowship," AAKR, box 1377, folder 6.

38. "Report on *Men and Ideas in American Politics*," June 6, 1947, AAKR, box 30, folder 12.

39. Harold Strauss to Richard Hofstadter, December 12, 1947, AAKR, box 30, folder 12.

40. Richard Hofstadter to Harold Strauss, December 1, 1947, AAKR, box 30, folder 12.

41. For Hofstadter's "afterthought" comment, see Hofstadter, *The American Political Tradition*, xxvii.

42. Richard Hofstadter to Kenneth Stampp, August 1947, KSP, carton 1, folder 28.

43. Harold Strauss to Richard Hofstadter, December 12, 1947, AAKR, box 30, folder 12.

44. "Draft Introduction," c. summer 1947, 11, RHP, box 3.

45. Hofstadter, *The American Political Tradition*, 127–28, 160–61, 169.

46. Hofstadter, 123.

47. Hofstadter, 173.

48. Richard Hofstadter to Alfred Kazin, c. 1950–53, AKP, folder 3.

49. Richard Hofstadter, "The Fitzgerald Revival," 1951, 2, RHP, box 22.

50. Lionel Trilling, *The Liberal Imagination* (New York: Viking Press, 1950), xxi.

51. Lionel Trilling to Pascal Covici, August 8, 1949, LTP, box 6, folder 2.

52. Thomas Bender, "Lionel Trilling and American Culture," *American Quarterly* 42, no. 2 (June 1990): 324.

53. Bender, 324–25.

54. Thomas C. Cochran to Richard Hofstadter, April 13, 1948, RHP, box 20.

55. Matthew Josephson to Richard Hofstadter, May 18, 1948, RHP, box 20.

56. Richard Hofstadter to Howard K. Beale, February 11, 1948, RHP, box 1.

57. "Report on Hofstadter Application for Knopf Fellowship," AAKR, box 1377, folder 6.

58. Roger Shugg to Harold Strauss, September 1, 1947, AAKR, box 960, folder 1.

59. Wendy L. Wall, "The 1930s Roots of the Postwar 'Consensus,'" in *The Liberal Consensus Reconsidered: American Politics and Society in the Postwar Era*, ed. Robert Mason and Iwan Morgan (Gainesville: University Press of Florida, 2017), 69.

60. Harold Strauss to Richard Hofstadter, December 12, 1947, AAKR, box 30, folder 12.

61. For the title suggestions, see Harold Strauss to Richard Hofstadter, December 23, 1947, AAKR, box 30, folder 12. For the response, see Richard Hofstadter to Harold Strauss, December 30, 1947, AAKR, box 30, folder 12.

62. "Outline Table of Contents for *Eminent Americans*," January 23, 1948, AAKR, box 30 folder 12.

63. Richard Hofstadter to Harold Strauss, March 25, 1948, AAKR, box 30, folder 12.

64. David S. Brown, *Richard Hofstadter: An Intellectual Biography* (Chicago: University of Chicago Press, 2006), 52.

65. Richard Hofstadter to Alfred A. Knopf, October 16, 1948, AAKR, box 30, folder 12.

66. Richard Hofstadter to Alfred A. Knopf, October 19, 1948, AAKR, box 30, folder 12.

67. William A. Koshland to Richard Hofstadter, May 18, 1949, AAKR, box 49, folder 9.

68. Erik Christiansen, *Channeling the Past: Politicizing History in Postwar America* (Madison: University of Wisconsin Press, 2013), 25.

69. Christiansen, 24.

70. Janice Radway, *A Feeling for Books: The Book-of-the-Month Club, Literary Taste, and Middle-Class Desire* (Chapel Hill: University of North Carolina Press, 1997), 10.

71. Jason Epstein, "Views on Publishing," *Publisher's Weekly*, December 16, 1974, cited in Kenneth C. Davis, *Two-Bit Culture: The Paperbacking of America* (Boston: Houghton Mifflin, 1984), 209–10.

72. Hans Schmoller, "The Paperback Revolution," in *Essays in the History of Publishing: In Celebration of the 250th Anniversary of the House of Longman, 1724–1974*, ed. Asa Briggs (London: Longman, 1974), 305.

73. "Eggheads: Cracking the Enigma," *Newsweek*, October 8, 1956, 57, cited in Aaron S. Leck-lider, "Inventing the Egghead: The Paradoxes of Brainpower in Cold War American Culture," *Journal of American Studies* 45, no. 2 (May 2011): 250.

74. Harry N. Scheiber, "A Keen Sense of History and the Need to Act: Reflections on Richard Hofstadter and *The American Political Tradition*," *Reviews in American History* 2, no. 3 (September 1974): 446.

75. Richard Hofstadter to Ashbel Green, October 20, 1969, AAKR, box 833, folder 8.

76. Ashbel Green to Beatrice Hofstadter, December 21, 1972, AAKR, box 833, folder 8.

77. Dwight Macdonald, "Masscult and Midcult," in *Against the American Grain* (New York: Da Capo, 1962), 18–19.

78. Macdonald, 74.

79. Gerald W. Johnson, "Some Tenants of the White House: Shrewd Appraisals of Our Presidents, and Aspirants to That Trying Office," *New York Times Book Review*, September 19, 1948, 1.

80. "Our Greatest Politicians," *Newark News*, September 14, 1948, clipping in RHP, box 20.

81. Earl L. Shoup, "Some Idols Are Upset in a Study of Political Ideas," *Cleveland News*, September 15, 1948, clipping in RHP, box 20; Review of *The American Political Tradition*, by Richard Hofstadter, *Los Angeles Examiner*, n.d., clipping in RHP, box 20.

82. Oscar Handlin, "America's Political Tradition," *Commentary*, July 13, 1949, 98.

83. Daniel Aaron, review of *The American Political Tradition and the Men Who Made It*, by Richard Hofstadter, *American Quarterly* 1, no. 1 (Spring 1949): 96.

84. Matthew Josephson to Richard Hofstadter, May 18, 1948, RHP, box 20.

85. Fred V. Cahill, "Twelve Americans," *Yale Review* 38, no. 3 (Spring 1949): 565.

86. Louis Filler, "Tenets of Scientific Skepticism," *Antioch Review* 9, no. 1 (Spring 1949): 90, 91.

87. Filler, 92.

88. John K. Hutchens, "Books and Things," *New York Herald Tribune*, September 16, 1948, clipping in AAKR, box 1377, folder 2.

89. Robert Friedman, "American Political Tradition: Essays on the Men Who Made It," *Daily Worker*, n.d., clipping in AAKR, box 1377, folder 2.

90. C. Vann Woodward, review of *The American Political Tradition and the Men Who Made It*, by Richard Hofstadter, *Mississippi Valley Historical Review* 35, no. 4 (March 1949): 681, 682.

91. Hofstadter, *The American Political Tradition*, 372–73, 407.

92. Hofstadter, 412.

93. Hofstadter, 426, 440.

94. Hofstadter, 456.

95. Perry Miller, "The New History," *The Nation*, October 16, 1949, 440.

96. Arthur Mann, review of *The American Political Tradition and the Men Who Made It*, by Richard Hofstadter, *William and Mary Quarterly* 6, no. 2 (April 1949): 302.

97. Lecklider, "Inventing the Egghead," 248–52.

98. Howard Zinn, *The Politics of History* (Urbana: University of Illinois Press, 1970), 16, 32.

99. Howard Zinn, *A People's History of the United States*, 1st ed. (New York: Harper & Row, 1980); on Lincoln, see 187–92; on Wilson, see 362.

100. Howard Zinn, *A People's History of the United States*, 2nd ed. (New York: Harper & Row, 1995), 563.

101. John Higham, "The Cult of the 'American Consensus': Homogenizing Our History," *Commentary*, February 1, 1959, 94.

102. John Higham, "Beyond Consensus: The Historian as Moral Critic," *American Historical Review* 67, no. 3 (April 1962): 613.

103. Norman Pollack, "Hofstadter on Populism: A Critique of 'The Age of Reform,'" *Journal of Southern History* 26, no. 4 (November 1960): 480.

104. Aileen S. Kraditor, "The Abolitionists Rehabilitated," *Studies on the Left* 5, no. 2 (Spring 1965): 101.

105. Barton J. Bernstein, introduction to *Towards a New Past: Dissenting Essays in American History* (New York: Vintage, 1968), viii.

106. The radical historian Jesse Lemisch excoriated Hofstadter as "a leader of the pro-administration forces" during the Columbia dispute in *On Active Service in War and Peace: Politics and Ideology in the American Historical Profession* (Toronto: New Hogtown Press, 1969), 103. For a more balanced account of Hofstadter's encounters with the New Left, especially the controversy surrounding his 1969 commencement address at Columbia, see Brown, *Richard Hofstadter*, 176–87. On the AHA controversy, see Rich Yeselson, "What the New Left History Gave Us," *Democracy* 35 (2015): 33–35.

107. Pollack, "Hofstadter on Populism," 481.

108. Kraditor, "The Abolitionists Rehabilitated," 106; Bernstein, introduction to *Towards a New Past*, ix.

109. For examples of this, see Arthur Schlesinger Jr., "Richard Hofstadter," in *Pastmasters: Some Essays on American Historians*, ed. Marcus Cunliffe and Robin D. Winks (Westport, CT: Greenwood Press, 1969); Daniel Walker Howe and Peter Elliott Finn, "Richard Hofstadter: The Ironies of an American Historian," *Pacific Historical Review* 43, no. 1 (February 1974): 1–23; Daniel Joseph Singal, "Beyond Consensus: Richard Hofstadter and American Historiography," *American Historical Review* 89, no. 4 (October 1984): 976–1004; Jack Pole, "Richard Hofstadter," in *Clio's Favorites: Leading Historians of the United States, 1945–2000*, ed. Robert Allen Rutland (Columbia: University of Missouri Press, 2000); and James Livingston, "On Richard Hofstadter and the Politics of 'Consensus History,'" *boundary 2* 34, no. 3 (2007): 33–46.

110. Hofstadter, *The Progressive Historians*, 451.

111. Richard Hofstadter, *America at 1750: A Social Portrait* (New York: Alfred A. Knopf, 1971). For the description of the project, see "Proposal for a Three-Volume History of American Political Culture from 1750 to the Recent Past," May 15, 1969, AAKR, box 833, folder 7. For details of Knopf's advance, see Ray Mayer to William A. Koshland, February 27, 1970, AAKR, box 833, folder 7.

112. Hofstadter, "Proposal for a Three-Volume History."

113. Alfred Kazin, "Richard Hofstadter, 1916–1970," *American Scholar* 40, no. 3 (Summer 1971): 399.

Chapter Two

1. Daniel J. Boorstin, "Varieties of Historical Experience: Paper to American Historical Association," December 29, 1960, 3, DBP, box 227, folder 4.

2. Boorstin, 9.

3. Richard Hofstadter, *The Progressive Historians: Turner, Beard, Parrington* (New York: Alfred A. Knopf, 1968), 457–58.

4. Richard Hofstadter to Jack Pole, April 4, 1968, RHP, uncatalogued correspondence, box 7.

5. Daniel J. Boorstin, *The Americans: The Colonial Experience* (New York: Random House, 1958), 314, 294.

6. Daniel J. Boorstin, *The Americans: The Democratic Experience* (New York: Random House, 1973), ix, 107.

7. Lizabeth Cohen, *A Consumers' Republic: The Politics of Mass Consumption in Postwar America* (New York: Vintage, 2003), 6.

8. This portrait is drawn from Boorstin's own autobiographical writing, limited as it is, in Daniel J. Boorstin, *Cleopatra's Nose: Essays on the Unexpected* (New York: Random House, 1994), 181–90, and from the biographical details supplied in William Palmer, *Engagement with the Past: The Lives and Works of the World War II Generation of Historians* (Lexington: University Press of Kentucky, 2001), 33.

9. Mary Anne Dolan, "Go-Getters Like Daniel Boorstin Often Run into Trouble," *Washington Star*, July 27, 1975, in *Nomination of Daniel J. Boorstin of the District of Columbia to Be Librarian of Congress* (Washington, DC: US Government Printing Office, 1975), 431.

10. Daniel Boorstin quoted in *Nomination of Daniel J. Boorstin*, 369.

11. See Harvey Klehr, "Jews and American Communism," in *Jews and Leftist Politics: Judaism, Israel, Anti-Semitism, and Gender*, ed. Jack Jacobs (New York: Cambridge University Press, 2017), 175.

12. "Daniel Boorstin: 26 February 1953," in *Thirty Years of Treason: Excerpts from Hearings before the House Committee on Un-American Activities, 1938–1968*, ed. Eric Bentley (New York: Thunder's Mouth Press, 2002), 605.

13. Daniel Boorstin, *The Genius of American Politics* (Chicago: University of Chicago Press, 1953), 6, 1.

14. Boorstin, 188.

15. Jennifer Delton, "Rethinking Post–World War II Anticommunism," *Journal of the Historical Society* 10, no. 1 (March 2010): 1–41.

16. Boorstin, *The Genius of American Politics*, 189.

17. Daniel Boorstin, "America and the Image of Europe," *Perspectives USA* 14 (1956): 19.

18. Reinhold Niebuhr, *The Irony of American History* (1952; repr., Chicago: University of Chicago Press, 2008), 133. For important accounts of these themes in Niebuhr's postwar thinking, see Andrew S. Finstuen, *Original Sin and Everyday Protestants: The Theology of Reinhold Niebuhr, Billy Graham, and Paul Tillich in an Age of Anxiety* (Chapel Hill: University of North Carolina Press, 2009), 97–122; and Raymond Haberski Jr., *God and War: American Civil Religion since 1945* (New Brunswick, NJ: Rutgers University Press, 2012), 18–44.

19. Boorstin, *The Genius of American Politics*, 189.

20. H. Reuben Neptune, "The Irony of Un-American Historiography: Daniel J. Boorstin and the Rediscovery of a U.S. Archive of Decolonization," *American Historical Review* 120, no. 3 (June 2015): 936.

21. Daniel J. Boorstin, *The Lost World of Thomas Jefferson* (New York: Henry Holt, 1948), ix.

22. Boorstin, 6.

23. Daniel J. Boorstin, "American Liberalism," *Commentary* 20, no. 1 (July 1955): 99, 100.

24. Boorstin, *The Americans: The Colonial Experience*, 1.

25. Boorstin, 150–51.

26. Laura Belmonte, *Selling the American Way: U.S. Propaganda and the Cold War* (Philadelphia: University of Pennsylvania Press, 2008), 95–115.

27. Daniel J. Boorstin, "Democracy and its Discontents: The U.S.A.," *Encounter* 3, no. 5 (July 1954): 21.

28. Emily Dorothea Hull, "Beyond the Cultural Cold War: *Encounter* and the Post-War Emergence of Anglo-American Conservatism," *Journal of Transatlantic Studies* 19 (2021): 115–37.

29. David Hollinger, *Science, Jews, and Secular Culture: Studies in Mid-Twentieth-Century American Intellectual History* (Princeton, NJ: Princeton University Press, 1996), 33.

30. Hollinger, 19–28.

31. K. Healan Gaston, *Imagining Judeo-Christian America: Religion, Secularism, and the Redefinition of Democracy* (Chicago: University of Chicago Press, 2019).

32. These quotations and biographical details are all contained in Daniel Boorstin to A. H. Rabinowitz, May 11, 1957, DBP, box 343, folder 10.

33. Daniel Boorstin, "The Moral Mission of the Intellectual Jew," unpublished essay, c. 1947, DBP, box 225, folder 5.

34. Daniel J. Boorstin, "A Dialogue of Two Histories," *Commentary* 8, no. 4 (October 1949): 316.

35. W. E. B. Du Bois, *The Souls of Black Folk* (1903; repr., Boston: Bedford Books, 1997), 38.

36. For an important account of the ethnic and racial dimensions of the Frank case, from which this interpretation of its significance for the politics of Jewish whiteness is drawn, see Jeffrey Melnick, *Black-Jewish Relations on Trial: Leo Frank and Jim Conley in the New South* (Jackson: University Press of Mississippi, 2000), 30–46.

37. Nancy MacLean, "The Leo Frank Case Reconsidered: Gender and Sexual Politics in the Making of Reactionary Populism," *Journal of American History* 78, no. 3 (December 1991): 917–48.

38. Boorstin, *Cleopatra's Nose*, 192.

39. Daniel J. Boorstin, preface to *American Judaism*, by Nathan Glazer (Chicago: University of Chicago Press, 1957), viii.

40. The role of Glazer in constructing the idea of "ethnic America" is explored in detail in Lila Corwin Berman, *Speaking of Jews: Rabbis, Intellectuals, and the Creation of an American Public Identity* (Berkeley: University of California Press, 2009), 94–117.

41. Boorstin, *The Genius of American Politics*, 136, 157.

42. This argument about the links between Boorstin's consensus ideas and his Jewish identity builds on similar points made by Michael Rogin and Andrew Heinze. See Michael Rogin, *Ronald Reagan, the Movie: And Other Episodes in Political Demonology* (Berkeley: University of California Press, 1988), 276–80; and Andrew R. Heinze, "'Farther Away from New York': Jews in the Humanities after World War II," in *The Jewish Role in American Life 5: An Annual Review*, ed. Bruce Zuckerman and Jeremy Schoenberg (West Lafayette, IN: Purdue University Press, 2007), 35–37.

43. For detailed discussions of these phenomena, see Rachel Kranson, *Ambivalent Embrace: Jewish Upward Mobility in Postwar America* (Chapel Hill: University of North Carolina Press, 2017); and Lila Corwin Berman, "American Jews and the Ambivalence of Middle-Classness," *American Jewish History* 93, no. 4 (December 2007): 409–34.

44. Daniel Boorstin to John Fischer, June 20, 1952, DBP, box 343, folder 10.

45. John Fischer to Daniel Boorstin, July 24, 1952, DBP, box 343, folder 10.

46. Daniel J. Boorstin, "A Historical Study of the Role of Ideas in American Culture: Proposal to the Relm Foundation," December 20, 1955, 3–4, 10, DBP, box 243, folder 10.

47. Jess Stein to Daniel Boorstin, March 26, 1954, DBP, box 244, folder 7; Daniel Boorstin to Jess Stein, October 16, 1954, DBP, box 244, folder 7.

48. Jess Stein to Daniel Boorstin, January 11, 1955, DBP, box 378, folder 10.

49. Keith Berwick, "Comments on Second Draft," c. 1955, DBP, box 247, folder 4.

50. Boorstin, *The Americans: The Colonial Experience*, 9.

51. Leon Wilson, report on Daniel J. Boorstin, *The Americans: The Colonial Experience*, c. 1958, BMCR, box 49; John T. Winterich, report on Daniel J. Boorstin, *The Americans: The Colonial Experience*, c. 1958, BMCR, box 49.

52. Winterich, report on Boorstin, *The Americans: The Colonial Experience.*

53. Boorstin, *The Americans: The Democratic Experience*, 186, 175.

54. Daniel J. Boorstin, *The Americans: The National Experience* (New York: Random House, 1965), 11.

55. Boorstin, *The Americans: The Democratic Experience*, 41.

56. Boorstin, *The Americans: The National Experience*, 143, 147.

57. Boorstin, *The Americans: The Democratic Experience*, 101.

58. Boorstin, 107.

59. Boorstin, 393, 399.

60. Betty Friedan, *The Feminine Mystique* (1963; repr., London: Penguin, 2010), 5–20.

61. Advertisement for *The Americans: The Colonial Experience*, c. 1958, DBP, box 246, folder 5.

62. Lee Wright to Daniel Boorstin, July 12, 1965, DBP, box 257, folder 15.

63. "*The Americans* by Daniel J. Boorstin," *History Book Club News*, c. 1973, DBP, box 242, folder 11.

64. "What Makes a Quality Paperback," advertisement, *New York Times Book Review*, December 7, 1975, BR102.

65. Edward L. Bernays to Daniel Boorstin, August 10, 1965, DBP, box 257, folder 13.

66. Cohen, *A Consumers' Republic*, 295.

67. "The West Began with Beef: The Americans Volume 3 Press Release for Texas Newspapers," c. 1973, RHR, box 1123.

68. "Product or Package, Which Do We Buy? The Americans Volume 3 Press Release for the Women's Press," c. 1973, RHR, box 1123.

69. Daniel Boorstin to Jess Stein, April 13, 1963, DBP, box 244, folder 7.

70. Daniel Boorstin to Jess Stein, c. June 1963, DBP, box 244, folder 7.

71. André Schiffrin, *The Business of Books: How International Conglomerates Took over Publishing and Changed the Way We Read* (New York: Verso, 2000), 7.

72. Boorstin, *The Americans: The National Experience*, 105, 107, 112.

73. "The American Experience: Sales Presentation," February 23, 1971, DBP, box 245, folder 1.

74. "Outline Letter to Actors," July 22, 1971, DBP, box 245, folder 1.

75. "Getting There First: Revised Outline," January 13, 1972, 7, 11, DBP, box 245, folder 7.

76. "Getting There First: Revised Outline," 15–16.

77. Nicolas Noxon to Daniel Boorstin, April 2, 1972, DBP, box 245, folder 7.

78. Daniel J. Boorstin, "Television: More than We Suspect, It Has Changed All of Us," *Life*, September 10, 1972, 39.

79. "Remarks by Daniel J. Boorstin on Receiving the Bancroft Award, Columbia University," April 22, 1959, 3, DBP, box 246, folder 6.

80. Lisa McGirr, *Suburban Warriors: The Origins of the New American Right* (Princeton, NJ: Princeton University Press, 2001); Matthew D. Lassiter, *The Silent Majority: Suburban Politics in the Sunbelt South* (Princeton, NJ: Princeton University Press, 2006). On the politics of Nixon's famous "silent majority" speech, see Scott Laderman, *The "Silent Majority" Speech: Richard Nixon, the Vietnam War, and the Origins of the New Right* (New York: Routledge, 2019).

81. George H. Nash, *The Conservative Intellectual Movement in America since 1945* (Wilmington, DE: ISI Books, 2008), xvi–xvii.

82. On Buckley's contributions to the conservative movement, see Linda Bridges and John R. Coyne Jr., *Strictly Right: William F. Buckley Jr. and the American Conservative Movement* (Hoboken, NJ: John Wiley & Sons, 2007); Alvin S. Felzenberg, *A Man and His Presidents: The Political Odyssey of William F. Buckley Jr.* (New Haven, CT: Yale University Press, 2017); and Julian Nemeth, "The Passion of William F. Buckley: Academic Freedom, Conspiratorial Conservatism, and the Rise of the Postwar Right," *Journal of American Studies* 54, no. 2 (May 2020): 323–50.

83. Corey Robin, *The Reactionary Mind: Conservatism from Edmund Burke to Sarah Palin* (New York: Oxford University Press, 2011), 18.

84. Nash, *The Conservative Intellectual Movement in America*, 222–23.

85. Rowland Berthoff, "The American Social Order: A Conservative Hypothesis," *American Historical Review* 65, no. 3 (April 1960): 496.

86. Rowland Berthoff, *An Unsettled People: Social Order and Disorder in American History* (New York: Little, Brown, 1971), ix.

87. Berthoff, xiv, 477.

88. Reba Soffer, *History, Historians, and Conservatism in Britain and America: From the Great War to Thatcher and Reagan* (Oxford: Oxford University Press, 2008), 270.

89. Frederick J. Dobney, "The 'Everywhere' American," *St. Louis Post Dispatch*, June 24, 1973, DBP, box 295, folder 5.

90. John P. Roche, "History with No Politics?" *Philadelphia Bulletin*, October 2, 1973, DBP, box 295, folder 5.

91. Sheldon Wolin, "From Jamestown to San Clemente," *New York Review of Books*, September 19, 1974, 2.

92. Wolin, 3.

93. Michael Zorn to Daniel Boorstin, August 7, 1975, DBP, box 242, folder 14.

94. Dwight D. Eisenhower to Daniel Boorstin, October 19, 1965, DBP, box 257, folder 13.

95. Elizabeth Bagwell to Daniel Boorstin, c. March 1974, DBP, box 273, folder 7.

96. Boorstin, *The Americans: The Colonial Experience*, 5, 19.

97. Boorstin, *The Americans: The National Experience*, 42.

98. On the attack mounted by postwar conservatives on Dewey in the field of education, see Andrew Hartman, *Education and the Cold War: The Battle for the American School* (New York: Palgrave Macmillan, 2008).

99. Boorstin, *The Americans: The Democratic Experience*, 496.

100. Boorstin, *The Genius of American Politics*, 2.

101. Drew Maciag, *Edmund Burke in America: The Contested Career of the Father of Modern Conservatism* (Ithaca, NY: Cornell University Press, 2013), 213.

102. For a pithy summary of this position, see Russell Kirk, *The American Cause* (1957; repr., Wilmington, DE: ISI Press, 2002), 2.

103. Russell Kirk quoted in Joshua Albury Tait, "Making Conservatism: Conservative Intellectuals and the American Political Tradition" (PhD diss., University of North Carolina at Chapel Hill, 2020), 73.

104. Russell Kirk, "A Revolution Not Made but Prevented," *Modern Age* 29 (1985): 299.

105. Kirk, 302–3.

106. Irving Kristol, "American Historians and the Democratic Idea," *American Scholar* 39, no. 1 (Winter 1969–70): 101.

107. Kristol, 103.

108. Kristol, 104.

109. Boorstin, *The Americans: The Democratic Experience*, 148.

110. Boorstin, 291, 302.

111. On the conservative backlash against affirmative action, see Terry H. Anderson, *The Pursuit of Fairness: A History of Affirmative Action* (New York: Oxford University Press, 2004), 161–216.

112. Marc Dollinger, *Black Power, Jewish Politics: Reinventing the Alliance in the 1960s* (Waltham, MA: Brandeis University Press, 2018).

113. For an important account of debates among and between conservatives and liberals about the New Left, see Daniel Geary, "Children of *The Lonely Crowd*: David Riesman, the Young Liberals, and the Splitting of Liberalism in the 1960s," *Modern Intellectual History* 10, no. 3 (November 2013): 603–33.

114. Daniel J. Boorstin, *The Decline of Radicalism: Reflections on America Today* (New York: Vintage, 1969), 121, 123.

115. Boorstin, *The Americans: The Democratic Experience*, 219.

116. Boorstin, 598.

117. For discussion of George Will's place in the conservative intellectual movement, see J. David Hoeveler Jr., *The Postmodernist Turn: American Thought and Culture in the 1970s* (New York: Rowman & Littlefield, 1996), 156–58.

118. George F. Will, "Suffocating in the Open Air, July 9, 1979," in *The Pursuit of Virtue and Other Tory Notions* (New York: Touchstone, 1982), 215.

119. George F. Will, "The Virtues of Boldness, July 23, 1979," in *The Pursuit of Virtue*, 24.

120. George F. Will, *Statecraft as Soulcraft: What Government Does* (New York: Touchstone, 1983), 97.

121. Will, 120.

122. Henry Kissinger quoted in Tait, "Making Conservatism," 341–45.

123. "Statement by Daniel J. Boorstin, American Historian, to the Republican Platform Committee at Miami Beach, Florida," August 16, 1972, 1, 4, DBP, box 43, folder 2.

124. "Statement by Daniel J. Boorstin," 6–7.

125. "Daniel Boorstin," *The Economist*, March 20, 2004, 14.

Chapter Three

1. Roi Ottley, *Black Odyssey: The Story of the Negro in America* (New York: Charles Scribner's and Sons, 1948), vii.

2. Hugh H. Smythe, untitled review of Roi Ottley, *Black Odyssey*, c. 1948, WEBDBP, box 239, folder 27, http://credo.library.umass.edu/view/full/mums312-b239-i027.

3. Smythe, untitled review of Ottley, *Black Odyssey*.

4. On the pre–World War II context at Knopf, including discussions of the publisher's engagement with the Harlem Renaissance, see Amy Root Clements, *The Art of Prestige: The Formative Years at Knopf, 1915–1929* (Amherst: University of Massachusetts Press, 2014).

5. John Hope Franklin, *From Slavery to Freedom: A History of American Negros*, 1st ed. (New York: Alfred A. Knopf, 1947), viii.

6. Kenneth W. Warren, *What Was African American Literature?* (Cambridge, MA: Harvard University Press, 2011), 9, 42.

7. Dorothy Ross, *The Origins of American Social Science* (New York: Cambridge University Press, 1990), 314.

8. Peter Novick, *That Noble Dream: The "Objectivity Question" and the American Historical Profession* (New York: Cambridge University Press, 1998), 88–90.

9. Arthur Schlesinger, *New Viewpoints in American History* (New York: Macmillan, 1922).

10. John Hope Franklin, *Mirror to America: The Autobiography of John Hope Franklin* (New York: Farrar, Straus and Giroux, 2005), 76–77.

11. Franklin, *From Slavery to Freedom*, 1st ed., 593–94.

12. William M. Brewer, review of *From Slavery to Freedom*, by John Hope Franklin, *William and Mary Quarterly* 5, no. 3 (July 1948): 441.

13. Franklin, *From Slavery to Freedom*, 1st ed., 592.

14. For discussions of these and other important topics in midcentury social scientific thinking on race, see Walter A. Jackson, *Gunnar Myrdal and America's Conscience: Social Engineering and Racial Liberalism, 1938–1987* (Chapel Hill: University of North Carolina Press, 1990); Daryl Michael Scott, *Contempt and Pity: Social Policy and the Image of the Damaged Black Psyche, 1880–1996* (Chapel Hill: University of North Carolina Press, 1997); Alice O'Connor, *Poverty Knowledge: Social Science, Social Policy, and the Poor in Twentieth-Century U.S. History* (Princeton, NJ: Princeton University Press, 2001); Jonathan Scott Holloway, *Confronting the Veil: Abram Harris Jr., E. Franklin Frazier, and Ralph Bunche, 1919–1941* (Chapel Hill: University of North Carolina Press, 2002); Jerry Gershenhorn, *Melville J. Herskovits and the Racial Politics of Knowledge* (Lincoln: University of Nebraska Press, 2004); Daniel Matlin, *On the Corner: African American Intellectuals and the Urban Crisis* (Cambridge, MA: Harvard University Press, 2013); Stephen J. Whitfield, "Out of Anarchism and into the Academy: The Many Lives of Frank Tannenbaum," *Journal for the Study of Radicalism* 7, no. 2 (2013): 93–123; and Daniel Geary, *Beyond Civil Rights: The Moynihan Report and Its Legacy* (Philadelphia: University of Pennsylvania Press, 2015).

15. John Hope Franklin, "On the Evolution of Scholarship in Afro-American History (1986)," in *Race and History: Selected Essays, 1938–1988* (Baton Rouge: Louisiana State University Press, 1989), 50.

16. Maghan Keita, *Race and the Writing of History* (New York: Oxford University Press, 2000), 50.

17. Franklin, "On the Evolution of Scholarship in Afro-American History," 51.

18. Carter G. Woodson, *The Negro in Our History* (Washington, DC: Associated Publishers, 1922), ix.

19. Franklin, *From Slavery to Freedom*, 1st ed., 591–92.

20. The key texts mentioned by Franklin were W. E. B. Du Bois, *The Suppression of the African Slave Trade to the United States* (New York: Longman's, Green and Co., 1896); C. L. R. James, *The Black Jacobins: Toussaint L'Ouverture and the San Domingo Revolution* (New York: Dial Press, 1938); and Eric Williams, *Slavery and Capitalism* (Chapel Hill: University of North Carolina Press, 1944). See Franklin, *From Slavery to Freedom*, 1st ed., 596–97.

21. Pero Gaglo Dagbovie, *The Early Black History Movement, Carter G. Woodson, and Lorenzo Johnston Greene* (Urbana: University of Illinois Press, 2007), 2. See also Stephen G. Hall, *A Faithful Account of the Race: African American Historical Writing in Nineteenth-Century America* (Chapel Hill: University of North Carolina Press, 2009).

22. Dagbovie, *The Early Black History Movement*, 50.

23. Nahum Daniel Brascher, "This Is Negro History Week. Read. Think!!!" *Chicago Defender*, February 14, 1942, 15.

24. "How Shall We Celebrate Negro History Week?" *Negro History Bulletin*, January 1, 1945, 90–91.

25. Lloyd L. Brown, "Trampling Out the Vintage," *New Masses*, February 11, 1947, 8.

26. Franklin, *From Slavery to Freedom*, 1st ed., 550.

27. John Hope Franklin, "The New Negro History," *Journal of Negro History* 42, no. 2 (April 1957): 89, 90.

28. Franklin, 96–97.

29. Roger W. Shugg to John Hope Franklin, February 6, 1946, JHFP, box W06, folder "FSF Correspondence 1943–1947."

30. Roger W. Shugg to John Hope Franklin, February 25, 1946, JHFP, box W06, folder "FSF Correspondence 1943–1947."

31. John Hope Franklin to Roger W. Shugg, May 4, 1946, JHFP, box W06, folder "FSF Correspondence 1943–1947."

32. John Hope Franklin to Roger W. Shugg, March 5, 1946, JHFP, box W06, folder "FSF Correspondence 1943–1947." In this way, his ideas about the global scope of the text chimed with other examples of transnational thinking in African American midcentury thought and culture. For more on this, see Robin D. G. Kelley, "'But a Local Phase of a World Problem': Black History's Global Vision, 1883–1950," *Journal of American History* 86, no. 3 (December 1999): 1045–77.

33. Roger W. Shugg to John Hope Franklin, May 31, 1946, JHFP, box W06, folder "FSF Correspondence 1943–1947."

34. R. W. Shugg memo, June 20, 1946, AAKR, box 3, folder 1.

35. Roger W. Shugg to John Hope Franklin, June 7, 1946, JHFP, box W06, folder "FSF Correspondence 1943–1947."

36. R. W. Shugg memo, June 20, 1946, AAKR, box 3, folder 1.

37. C. Vann Woodward to John Simon Guggenheim Memorial Foundation, November 1949, in *The Letters of C. Vann Woodward*, ed. Michael O'Brien (New Haven, CT: Yale University Press, 2013), 124.

38. Ben Keppel, *The Work of Democracy: Ralph Bunche, Kenneth B. Clark, Lorraine Hansberry, and the Cultural Politics of Race* (Cambridge, MA: Harvard University Press, 1995), 8.

39. Jay Garcia, *Psychology Comes to Harlem: Rethinking the Race Question in Twentieth-Century America* (Baltimore: Johns Hopkins University Press, 2012), 3–4.

40. Roger W. Shugg to John Hope Franklin, November 25, 1946, JHFP, box W06, folder "FSF Correspondence 1943–1947."

41. Madge E. Pickard to John Hope Franklin, June 11, 1947, JHFP, box W06, folder "FSF Correspondence 1943–1947."

42. "Toward Justice," *Atlanta Journal*, September 25, 1947, clipping in JHFP, box W05, folder "FSF Reviews 1947."

43. Edward B. Orr, "An Inside Story," *Christian Science Monitor*, September 22, 1947, clipping in JHFP, box W05, folder "FSF Reviews 1947."

44. Youra Qualls, "Record of the American Negro," *New York Herald Tribune*, December 14, 1947, clipping in JHFP, box W05, folder "FSF Reviews 1947."

45. Frank F. Bauer Jr., "Negro Saga Objectively Described," *Hartford Times*, September 27, 1947, clipping in JHFP, box W05, folder "FSF Reviews 1947."

46. Untitled review, *New Haven Register*, October 5, 1947, clipping in JHFP, box W05, folder "FSF Reviews 1947."

47. Alain Locke, "Moral Pivot," *Saturday Review of Literature*, November 8, 1947, 16.

48. Leah N. Gordon, *From Power to Prejudice: The Rise of Racial Individualism in Midcentury America* (Chicago: University of Chicago Press, 2015), 2.

49. James J. Marshall, untitled review, *Christian Register*, November 1947, 448.

50. Ernest Rice McKinney, "Negro Struggle in History," *New International*, February 1948, 63.

51. Eugene C. Holmes, untitled review, *Bookshopper*, February 1948, clipping in JHFP, box W06, folder "FSF Reviews 1948." For more detail on the store and its book club, see Robert Justin Goldstein, "Watching the Books: The Federal Government's Suppression of the Washington Cooperative Bookshop, 1939–1950," *American Communist History* 12, no. 3 (2013): 237–65.

52. Roi Ottley, "Genesis of the American Negro," *New York Times*, October 12, 1947.

53. John Hope Franklin to Roger Shugg, October 14, 1947, JHFP, box W06, folder "FSF Correspondence 1943–1947."

54. John Hope Franklin to Roger Shugg, August 7, 1946, JHFP, box W06, folder "FSF Correspondence 1943–1947."

55. John Hope Franklin to Roger Shugg, December 15, 1947, JHFP, box W06, folder "FSF Correspondence 1943–1947."

56. "Letter to College Presidents," February 18, 1949, JHFP, box W06, folder "FSF Correspondence 1943–1947."

57. "*From Slavery to Freedom* Publicity Sheet," February 1949, JHFP, box W06, folder "FSF Correspondence 1943–1947."

58. John Hope Franklin to Walter White, August 21, 1947, JHFP, box W06, folder "FSF Correspondence 1943–1947."

59. John Hope Franklin to Roger Shugg, September 9, 1947, JHFP, box W06, folder "FSF Correspondence 1943–1947."

60. For Franklin's account of his involvement with Marshall and the Legal Defense Fund, see Franklin, *Mirror to America*, 143, 156–59.

61. These figures are drawn from royalty statements in the Franklin Papers. See JHFP, box W21.

62. John Hope Franklin, "A Heady Experience: Writing *From Slavery to Freedom*," c. 1987, 5–6, JHFP, box W05, folder "FSF Biography of a Book."

63. Freedom Schools Curriculum, c. March 1964, Student Non-Violent Coordinating Committee Papers, microfilm, reel 67, file 337, 640, King Center for Nonviolent Social Change, Atlanta, Georgia.

64. Staughton Lynd, "Guide to Negro History, 1964," in *Freedom School Curriculum: Mississippi Freedom Summer, 1964*, ed. Kathy Emery, Sylvia Braselmann and Linda Gold, http://www.educationanddemocracy.org/FSCpdf/CurrTextOnlyAll.pdf.

65. Debra Newman Ham, "John Hope Franklin and the Year of Jubilee," *Journal of Negro History* 85, nos. 1–2 (Winter–Spring 2000): 13–14.

66. Lillian Serece Williams, "Participant-Observer of History: John Hope Franklin," *Journal of African American History* 94, no. 3 (Summer 2009): 372–73.

67. Robin D. G. Kelley, "A Historian in the World," *Journal of African American History* 94, no. 3 (Summer 2009): 362–63.

68. Larry Neal, "The Black Arts Movement," *Drama Review* 12, no. 4 (Summer 1968): 28.

69. James Edward Smethurst, *The Black Arts Movement: Literary Nationalism in the 1960s and 1970s* (Chapel Hill: University of North Carolina Press, 2005); Amy Abugo Ongiri, *Spectacular Blackness: The Cultural Politics of the Black Power Movement and the Search for a Black Aesthetic* (Charlottesville: University of Virginia Press, 2010).

70. Stephen Ward, "'Scholarship in the Context of Struggle': Activist Intellectuals, the Institute of the Black World (IBW), and the Contours of Black Power Radicalism," *Black Scholar* 31, nos. 3/4 (Fall/Winter 2001): 42–53.

71. Martha Biondi, *The Black Revolution on Campus* (Berkeley: University of California Press, 2012). See also Fabio Rojas, *From Black Power to Black Studies: How a Radical Social Movement Became an Academic Discipline* (Baltimore: Johns Hopkins University Press, 2007); and Noliwe M. Rooks, *White Money/Black Power: The Surprising History of African American Studies and the Crisis of Race in Higher Education* (Boston: Beacon Press, 2006).

72. This data is drawn from "Adoption List for From Slavery to Freedom, 19 October 1948" and "Adoption List for From Slavery to Freedom, October 1978 to September 1979," JHFP, box W05.

73. Edward Ejon Onwuzike to John Hope Franklin, March 21, 1961, JHFP, box W06, folder "FSF Correspondence 1961–1974."

74. Sharon Cole to John Hope Franklin, September 30, 1974, JHFP, box W06, folder "FSF Correspondence 1961–1974."

75. George Crockett, "A Historical Analysis," *John Marshall Metro High School Newsletter*, 6, February 1983, JHFP, box W06, folder "FSF Correspondence 1981–1985."

76. August Maier and Elliott Rudwick, *Black History and the Historical Profession, 1915–1980* (Urbana: University of Illinois Press, 1986), 119.

77. Novick, *That Noble Dream*, 480.

78. Novick, 476–77; Pero Gaglo Dagbovie, *African American History Reconsidered* (Urbana: University of Illinois Press, 2010), 34.

79. E. James West, "Lerone Bennett, Jr.: A Life in Popular Black History," *Black Scholar* 47, no. 4 (2017): 3–17.

80. Vincent Harding, "Beyond Chaos: Black History and the Search for the New Land," in *Amistad 1*, ed. John A. Williams and Charles F. Harris (New York: Vintage, 1970), 278, 279.

81. Harding, 274.

82. Harold Cruse, "The New Negro History of John Hope Franklin—Promise and Progress" (unpublished, c. 1979), in *The Essential Harold Cruse: A Reader*, ed. William Jelani Cobb (New York: St Martin's Griffin, 2002), 208.

83. John Hope Franklin to William A. Frohlich, May 27, 1968, JHFP, box WC25, folder "Alfred A. Knopf, Inc."

84. Transcript of "Friday Afternoon Discussion (30 May 1969)," in *The Haverford Discussions: A Black Integrationist Manifesto for Racial Justice*, ed. Michael Lackey (Charlotte: University of Virginia Press, 2013), 34.

85. It is difficult to establish exactly what percentage of the book's total sales went to college students, but it is likely to have been very high from the late 1970s onward. For example, between September 1978 and September 1979, a total of 16,097 copies were shipped to college bookstores, and in the twelve months ending in March 1980, Franklin received royalties on sales totaling 19,260 copies. This means that even allowing for a significant number of returns from college bookstores, at least 75 percent of total sales took place on campus.

86. John Hope Franklin and Alfred A. Moss, *From Slavery to Freedom: A History of African Americans*, 7th ed. (New York: McGraw-Hill, 1994), xx.

87. Franklin, *From Slavery to Freedom*, 1st ed., 4–10.

88. Wilson Jeremiah Moses, *Afrotopia: The Roots of African American Popular History* (New York: Cambridge University Press, 1998), 238. See also Jonathan Fenderson, "Evolving Conceptions of Pan-African Scholarship: W. E. B. Du Bois, Carter G. Woodson, and the 'Encyclopedia Africana,' 1909–1963," *Journal of African American History* 95, no. 1 (Winter 2010): 71–91.

89. Orlando Patterson, "Rethinking Black History," in *Harvard Educational Review* 41, no. 3 (August 1971): 305, 308.

90. John Hope Franklin, *From Slavery to Freedom: A History of Negro Americans*, 4th ed. (New York: Alfred A. Knopf, 1974), 39–41.

91. Franklin, *From Slavery to Freedom*, 1st ed., 39–41.

92. Franklin, 509.

93. Andrew M. Fearnley, "When the Harlem Renaissance Became Vogue: Periodization and the Organization of Postwar American Historiography," *Modern Intellectual History*, 11, no. 1 (April 2014): 72–74.

94. Alfred Moss, "Address on John Hope Franklin at 2002 OAH Meeting, 13 April 2002," JHFP, box C19, folder "Moss, Alfred."

95. "Report on John Hope Franklin's *From Slavery to Freedom*," c. 1985, JHFP, box W05, folder "FSF Critical Appraisals, 1980–85."

96. Leon Litwack, "An Assessment of John Hope Franklin, *From Slavery to Freedom*," c. 1985, JHFP, box W05, folder "FSF Critical Appraisals, 1980–85."

97. Christopher J. Rogers to John Hope Franklin, October 1, 1985, JHFP, box W06, folder "FSF Correspondence 1981–1985."

98. John Hope Franklin and Alfred A. Moss, *From Slavery to Freedom: A History of Negro Americans*, 6th ed. (New York: McGraw-Hill, 1986), 130.

99. On Morton, see Franklin and Moss, 334; on Armstrong, 369; on Parker et al., 430–31.

100. Franklin, "A Heady Experience," 9.

101. Two important examples of this vein of scholarship are Lawrence W. Levine, *Black Culture and Black Consciousness: Afro-American Folk Thought from Slavery to Freedom* (New York: Oxford University Press, 1977); and Sterling Stuckey, *Slave Culture: Nationalist Theory and the Foundations of Black America* (New York: Oxford University Press, 1987). These books are first cited by Franklin and Moss in the sixth and seventh editions, respectively.

102. Franklin and Moss, *From Slavery to Freedom*, 7th ed., 552.

103. For a useful discussion of shifting racial nomenclature in the twentieth-century United States, see Tom W. Smith, "Changing Racial Labels: From 'Colored' to 'Negro' to 'Black' to 'African American,'" *Public Opinion Quarterly* 56, no. 4 (Winter 1992): 496–514.

104. Stokely Carmichael and Charles V. Hamilton, *Black Power: The Politics of Liberation* (New York: Random House, 1967), 36.

105. Stuckey, *Slave Culture*, 217–84.

106. For a discussion of Logan's approach to the question, see Kenneth Robert Janken, *Rayford W. Logan and the Dilemma of the African-American Intellectual* (Amherst: University of Massachusetts Press, 1993), 3–4, 229–32.

107. Robert L. Harris Jr., "We Can Best Honor the Past . . . by Facing It Squarely, Honestly, and Above All Openly," *Journal of African American History* 94, no. 3 (Summer 2009): 391.

108. See Brian Purnell, "Interview with John Hope Franklin," *Journal of African American History* 94, no. 13 (Summer 2009), on Black history, 411; on African American studies, 416–17.

109. Donald Spivey, "Report on *From Slavery to Freedom*, 5th Edition," c. 1985, 3, JHFP, box W05, folder "FSF Critical Appraisals, 1980–85."

110. John L. Dabney, "Critical Review: *From Slavery to Freedom*," 1991, JHFP, box W02, folder "FSF 7th Edition Correspondence and Revisions Folder 1."

111. Jeanette Baidoo to Alfred A. Knopf, April 22, 1991, JHFP, box W02, folder "FSF 7th Edition Correspondence and Revisions Folder 1."

112. "John Hope Franklin and Alfred Moss confer about FSTF, 7th Edition (28–31 May 1992)," JHFP, box W02, folder "FSF 7th Edition Correspondence and Revisions Folder 1."

113. Franklin and Moss, *From Slavery to Freedom*, 7th ed., xix–xx.

114. For a broader discussion of this shift, see Richard H. King, *Race, Culture and the Intellectuals, 1940–1970* (Baltimore: Johns Hopkins University Press, 2004), 268. For a brief discussion of the change made to the subtitle of the third edition, see Harris, "We Can Best Honor the Past," 393–94.

115. Franklin, *Mirror to America*, 193.

116. Stuckey, *Slave Culture*, 273.

117. Henry Louis Gates Jr., foreword to *From Slavery to Freedom: A History of African Americans*, by John Hope Franklin and Evelyn Brooks Higginbotham, 9th ed. (New York: McGraw Hill, 2011), xv.

Chapter Four

1. Thomas Sowell, "Shining Light on Irresponsible Faculty Bias," *Indianapolis Star*, April 3, 1987, 32.

2. Howard Zinn, *A People's History of the United States*, 1st ed. (New York: Harper & Row, 1980), 10.

3. Andrew Hartman, *A War for the Soul of America: A History of the Culture Wars* (Chicago: University of Chicago Press, 2015), 5.

4. Hartman, 7.

5. I owe the idea of generational liminality, if not the precise term, to historian Ambre Ivol, who has perceptively deconstructed Howard Zinn's biography in order to "complexify our understanding" of the Old and New Lefts. See Ambre Ivol, "The U.S. Left in Generational Perspective: A Study of Howard Zinn's Trajectory," in *Agitation with a Smile: Howard Zinn's Legacies and the Future of Activism*, ed. Stephen Bird, Adam Silver, and Joshua C. Yesnowitz (Boulder, CO: Paradigm, 2013), 35–50. The porous intellectual and political boundaries between the two generational sensibilities is highlighted in Maurice Isserman, *If I Had a Hammer: The Death of the Old Left and the Birth of the New Left* (New York: Basic Books, 1987).

6. Howard Zinn, *You Can't Be Neutral on a Moving Train: A Personal History of Our Times* (Boston: Beacon Press, 2002), 177, 171, 173.

7. Zinn, 17.

8. Zinn, 169.

9. Michael Denning, *The Cultural Front: The Laboring of American Culture in the Twentieth Century* (London: Verso Books, 1997), xv. For a comparable analysis of the origins of the "intellectual people's front," see Judy Kutulas, *The Long War: The Intellectual People's Front and Anti-Stalinism, 1930–1940* (Durham, NC: Duke University Press, 1995), 2–4.

10. Zinn, *You Can't Be Neutral on a Moving Train*, 87–89.

11. Zinn, 98.

12. Arthur Koestler, *The Yogi and the Commissar and Other Essays* (London: Jonathan Cape, 1945), 12.

13. Zinn, *You Can't Be Neutral on a Moving Train*, 178.

14. Arthur Koestler in *The God That Failed*, ed. Richard Crossman (London: Hamilton, 1950), 74.

15. Richard Crossman in *The God That Failed*, ed. Crossman, 4.

16. Richard Wright in *The God That Failed*, ed. Crossman, 127.

17. Wright, 162.

18. Zinn, *A People's History*, 1st ed., 438.

19. Zinn, *You Can't Be Neutral on a Moving Train*, 178.

20. Glenda Gilmore, *Defying Dixie: The Radical Roots of Civil Rights, 1919–1950* (New York: Norton, 2009).

21. Howard Zinn, diary entry, January 3, 1963, in *Howard Zinn's Southern Diary: Sit-Ins, Civil Rights and Black Women's Student Activism*, ed. Robert Cohen (Athens: University of Georgia Press, 2018), 88–89.

22. Howard Zinn, diary entry, January 10, 1963, in *Howard Zinn's Southern Diary*, ed. Cohen, 95.

23. For discussions of late 1950s and early 1960s Atlanta racial politics, see Bradley R. Rice, "If Dixie Were Atlanta," in *Sunbelt Cities: Politics and Growth since World War II*, ed. Richard M. Bernard and Bradley R. Rice (Austin: University of Texas Press, 1983), 31–57; and Stephen Tuck, *Beyond Atlanta: The Struggle for Racial Equality in Georgia, 1940–1980* (Athens: University of Georgia Press, 2001), 96–98.

24. Robert Cohen, "Mentor to the Movement: Howard Zinn, SNCC, and the Spelman College Freedom Struggle," in *Howard Zinn's Southern Diary*, ed. Cohen, 18.

25. Marian Wright Edelman, *Lanterns: A Memoir of Mentors* (New York: Harper, 1999), 30–31.

26. Alice Walker, "My Teacher," in *The World Has Changed: Conversations with Alice Walker*, ed. Rudolph P. Byrd (New York: New Press, 2010), 146.

27. For detailed accounts of the firing, see Davis D. Joyce, *Howard Zinn: A Radical American Vision* (Amherst, MA: Prometheus Books, 2003), 71–73; Martin Duberman, *Howard Zinn: A Life on the Left* (New York: New Press, 2012), 77–93; and Cohen, "Mentor to the Movement," 42–49.

28. Zinn, *You Can't Be Neutral on a Moving Train*, 41.

29. Joe Street, *The Culture War in the Civil Rights Movement* (Gainesville: University Press of Florida, 2007), 81.

30. Street, 85–86.

31. Noam Chomsky, "The Responsibility of Intellectuals," *New York Review of Books*, February 23, 1967, https://www.nybooks.com/articles/1967/02/23/a-special-supplement-the-responsibility-of-intelle/.

32. Howard Zinn, *Disobedience and Democracy: Nine Fallacies on Law and Order* (New York: Random House, 1968), 68, 122.

33. Zinn, 123–24.

34. Howard Zinn, "The Making of a Public Intellectual," *Antipode* 40, no. 3 (2008): 489.

35. See, for example, Howard Zinn, "Finishing School for Pickets," *The Nation*, August 6, 1960, reprinted in Howard Zinn, *The Zinn Reader: Writings on Disobedience and Democracy* (New York: Seven Stories Press, 2009), 40–46.

36. This title is first mentioned in a letter from Knopf editor Angus Cameron to Zinn dated July 5, 1961, AAKR, box 338, folder 7.

37. Howard Zinn to Angus Cameron, October 5, 1961, AAKR, box 338, folder 7.

38. Howard Zinn to Angus Cameron, May 27, 1962, AAKR, box 429, folder 13. For more on Zinn's debt to existentialism and its relationship to his idiosyncratic interpretation of Marxism, see Nick Witham, "A People's History of Howard Zinn: Radical Popular History and Its Readers," in *Marxism and America: New Appraisals*, ed. Christopher Phelps and Robin Vandome (Manchester: University of Manchester Press, 2021), 195–216.

39. Howard Zinn to Angus Cameron, May 27, 1962, AAKR, box 429, folder 13.

40. Angus Cameron to Howard Zinn, August 22, 1962, AAKR, box 429, folder 13.

41. Angus Cameron to Howard Zinn, October 8, 1962, AAKR, box 429, folder 13.

42. Zinn biographer Martin Duberman suggests that the severing of this relationship was based on "disappointment" from Knopf and Sterling Lord at the sluggish sales of *The Southern Mystique*. See Duberman, *Howard Zinn*, 69.

43. Howard Zinn to Angus Cameron, July 30, 1976, AAKR, box 447, folder 3.

44. Elaine Edelman to Howard Zinn, May 22, 1975, HZP, box 5, folder 2.

45. Cynthia Merman to Howard Zinn, March 7, 1979, HZP, box 5, folder 4.

46. Robert C. Twombly, "Reader's Report on 'Struggle for Democracy: A People's History of the United States,'" March 10, 1979, HZP, box 10, folder 32.

47. Holly V. Scott, *Younger than That Now: The Politics of Age in the 1960s* (Amherst: University of Massachusetts Press, 2016), 2–3.

48. For detailed accounts of Zinn's numerous battles with Silber, see Joyce, *Howard Zinn*, 85–89; and Duberman, *Howard Zinn*, 217–23.

49. Joseph Moreau, *Schoolbook Nation: Conflicts over American History Textbook from the Civil War to the Present* (Ann Arbor: University of Michigan Press, 2003), 305–18.

50. Review of *A People's History of the United States*, by Howard Zinn, *Publisher's Weekly*, November 5, 1979, 63.

51. Luther Spoehr, review of *A People's History of the United States*, by Howard Zinn, *Saturday Review*, February 2, 1980, 37; Bruce Kuklick, "The People? Yes," *The Nation*, May 24, 1980, 635.

52. Herbert L. Carson, "People's History, or . . . Indictment?" *Grand Rapids Press*, February 17, 1980.

53. Eric Foner, "Majority Report," *New York Times Book Review*, March 2, 1980, 10.

54. Zinn, *A People's History*, 1st ed., 1, 7.

55. Zinn, 12, 16.

56. Richard Cohen, "Columbus," *Washington Post*, October 12, 1982.

57. For one radical exploration of these questions from the period, see Ward Churchill, "Deconstructing the Columbus Myth: Was the 'Great Discoverer' Italian or Spanish, Nazi or Jew?" *Social Forces* 19, no. 2 (Summer 1992): 39–55. For a historical account of debates about and protests against the holiday, see Sam Hitchmough, "'It's Not Your Country Anymore': Contested National Narratives and the Columbus Day Parade Protests in Denver," *European Journal of American Culture* 32, no. 3 (September 2013): 263–83.

58. Saki Uechi to Howard Zinn, February 1, 1998, HZP, box 8, folder 7.

59. Student response quoted in a letter by Teddy Chocos to Howard Zinn, April 15, 1999, HZP, box 8, folder 16.

60. Howard Zinn, "Columbus, the Indians, and Human Progress, 1492–1992," May 1992, HZP, box 12, folder 27.

61. Zinn, *You Can't Be Neutral on a Moving Train*, 2.

62. Roxanne Dunbar-Ortiz to Howard Zinn, December 9, 1981, HZP, box 5, folder 7.

63. M. J. Ogden to Howard Zinn, January 8, 2004, HZP, box 10, folder 31; Charles Sackey to Howard Zinn, June 30, 1982, HZP, box 5, folder 8.

64. Howard Zinn to Richard Balkin, March 10, 1992, HZP, box 11, folder 8.

65. David O'Brien, "Out of Anger, Out of Hope," *Commonweal*, January 16, 1981, 25.

66. O'Brien, 26.

67. Melvyn Dubofsky, "Give Us That Old Time Labor History: Philip S. Foner and the American Worker," *Labor History* 26, no. 1 (1985): 120. See also Sally M. Miller, "Philip Foner

and 'Integrating' Women into Labor History and African-American History," *Labor History* 33, no. 4 (1992): 456–69.

68. Guy Morrell, *"The Most Dangerous Communist in the United States": A Biography of Herbert Aptheker* (Amherst: University of Massachusetts Press, 2015), 44–46.

69. Guy Morrell, "Herbert Aptheker's Unity of Theory and Practice in the Communist Party USA: On the Last Night, and during the First Two Decades," *Science and Society* 70, no. 1 (January 2006): 111.

70. Zinn, *A People's History*, 1st ed., 258, 262.

71. Zinn, 263–64.

72. Leo Huberman, *We, the People: The Drama of America* (New York: Monthly Review Press, 1960), xi.

73. Huberman, 223–24.

74. Huberman, 234.

75. The connection between Zinn and Huberman is noted briefly but not elaborated on in Staughton Lynd, *Doing History from the Bottom Up: On E. P. Thompson, Howard Zinn, and Rebuilding the Labor Movement from Below* (Chicago: Haymarket Books, 2014), 29.

76. Foner, "Majority Report," 10.

77. Michael Kammen, "How the Other Half Lived," *Washington Post Book World*, March 23, 1980, 7.

78. As well as being the source for this quotation, Brody's article is also an excellent overview of the "new" labor history and is distinctive identity. See David Brody, "The Old Labor History and the New: In Search of an American Working Class," *Labor History* 20, no. 1 (1979): 111–26, quotation at 122.

79. The victim was historian of the American Revolution Edward Countryman, who wrote to Zinn in 1989 to point out the error. Zinn apologized, citing his "inefficiency" in referencing, and remedied the mistake in the next edition of the book. See Edward Countryman to Howard Zinn, February 24, 1989, and Zinn's response, February 28, 1989, HZP, box 10, folder 31.

80. Warren Susman, "The Historian's Task" (1952), in *History and the New Left: Madison, Wisconsin, 1950–1970*, ed. Paul Buhle (Philadelphia: Temple University Press, 1990), 284.

81. Barton J. Bernstein, introduction to *Towards a New Past: Dissenting Essays in American History* (New York: Random House, 1968), x.

82. Frances Fox Piven and Richard A. Cloward, *Poor People's Movements: Why They Succeed, How They Fail* (New York: Random House, 1977), xxi, 358–59.

83. Howard Zinn to Frances Fox Piven, March 20, 1978, FFPP, box 20, folder 8.

84. Howard Zinn to Frances Fox Piven, August 25, 1981, FFPP, box 20, folder 9.

85. Michael Kazin, "Howard Zinn's History Lessons," *Dissent* 51, no. 2 (Spring 2004), 81, 82, 85.

86. Sam Wineburg, *Why Learn History (When It's Already on Your Phone)* (Chicago: University of Chicago Press, 2018), 58–59, 73.

87. Oscar Handlin, "Arawaks," *American Scholar* 49, no. 4 (Autumn 1980): 548.

88. Howard Zinn, "Arawaks," *American Scholar* 50, no. 3 (Summer 1981): 431.

89. Eliot Marshall, "New Group Targets Political Bias on Campus," *Science*, August 20, 1985, 841.

90. Don Feder, "BU as a Police State," *Boston Herald*, May 22, 1985, clipping in HZP, box 39, folder 11.

91. "Hate America History," *Campus Report from Accuracy in Academia*, March 1986, 1, 5.

92. Howard Zinn, "War in the Classroom," speech given on December 1, 1985, Community Church of Boston, typescript in HZP, box 39, folder 11.

93. Melissa Cook, "Zinn Fends Off AIA Written Attack," *Daily Free Press*, March 14, 1986, 1.

94. Steven Mintz, *Huck's Raft: A History of American Childhood* (Cambridge, MA: Harvard University Press, 2004), 339.

95. Quoted in Mintz, 367.

96. Allan Bloom, *The Closing of the American Mind: How Higher Education Has Failed Democracy and Impoverished the Souls of Today's Students* (New York: Simon & Schuster, 1987).

97. For discussion of Zinn's relationship with Damon, see Duberman, *Howard Zinn*, 236.

98. John Patrick Diggins has provided a reading of this scene in the context of Gordon Wood's impact on popular ideas about early American history in *On Hallowed Ground: Abraham Lincoln and the Foundations of American History* (New Haven, CT: Yale University Press, 2000), 49–51.

99. A "snowballing" of sales of the book is referenced as a result of it becoming a "pop culture sensation" is mentioned in a *TimeOut* interview with Zinn from the early 2000s, although no specific figures are given. See Barbara Aria, "History in the Making," *TimeOut*, c. 2003, clipping in HZP, box 15, folder 18.

100. Andrew Hartman, "'A Trojan Horse for Social Engineering': The Curriculum Wars in Recent American History," *Journal of Policy History* 25, no. 1 (2013): 129.

101. Paul Buhle, "Howard Zinn (1922–2010): Historian as Storyteller," *History Workshop Journal* 71, no. 1 (Spring 2011): 296.

102. Bruce Triggs, *Accordion Revolution: A People's History of the Accordion in North America from the Industrial Revolution to Rock and Roll* (Vancouver: Demian & Sons, 2019); Joy Lisi Rankin, *A People's History of Computing in the United States* (Cambridge, MA: Harvard University Press, 2018); Chris Harmon, *A People's History of the World: From the Stone Age to the New Millennium* (London: Verso Books, 1999).

103. Daniels cited in Tom LoBianco, "AP Exclusive: Daniels Looked to Censor Opponents," *Associated Press State & Local Wire*, July 17, 2013.

104. Susan Curtis and Kristina Bross, Open Letter to Mitch Daniels, July 22, 2013, https://academeblog.org/2013/07/23/an-open-letter-to-mitch-daniels-from-90-purdue-professors/; "AHA Statement on the Mitch Daniels Controversy," July 19, 2013, https://www.historians.org/publications-and-directories/perspectives-on-history/september-2013/the-mitch-daniels-controversy-context-for-the-aha-statement.

105. "Mitch Daniels Was Right," *National Review*, July 29, 2013, https://www.nationalreview.com/2013/07/mitch-daniels-was-right-editors/.

106. This point is particularly well made in William Munn, "Gaming the System: Social Studies Textbook Adoption in Indiana," *Indiana Magazine of History* 110, no. 2 (June 2014): 148–52.

107. "Mitch vs. Zinn," *Weekly Standard*, August 5, 2013, 3–4.

Chapter Five

1. The previous winners were Dumas Malone (1984), C. Vann Woodward (1986), Richard B. Morris (1988), Henry Steele Commager (1990), Edmund S. Morgan (1992), John Hope Franklin (1994), Arthur Schlesinger Jr. (1996), Richard N. Current (1998), and Bernard Bailyn (2000). See "The Bruce Catton Prize," Society of American Historians, https://sah.columbia.edu/content/prizes/bruce-catton-prize.

2. Linda Kerber, "Citation: Bruce Catton Prize for Lifetime Achievement, 2002," GLP, Series MC769, box 28, folder 9.

3. Gerda Lerner, "Remarks Made on the Occasion of the Presentation by the Society of American Historians of the Bruce Catton Prize for Lifetime Achievement in the Writing of History," May 16, 2002, 4, GLP, MC769, box 28, folder 9.

4. Gerda Lerner, *The Creation of Patriarchy* (New York: Oxford University Press, 1986), 6.

5. Gerda Lerner, *The Creation of Feminist Consciousness: From the Middle Ages to Eighteen-Seventy* (New York: Oxford University Press, 1993), 12.

6. Gerda Lerner, *Fireweed: A Political Autobiography* (Philadelphia: Temple University Press, 2003), 11.

7. Lerner, 42.

8. Lerner, 71.

9. Lerner, 158–59.

10. Mary Inman, *In Woman's Defense* (Los Angeles: Committee to Organize the Advancement of Women, 1940), 149.

11. For more detail on this chapter in CPUSA history, see Kate Weigand, *Red Feminism: American Communism and the Making of Women's Liberation* (Baltimore: Johns Hopkins University Press, 2001), 29–45.

12. Gerda Lerner, interview by Nancy MacLean, transcript of video recording, September 13, 2003, Voices of Feminism Oral History Project, Sophia Smith Collection, 27, https://www.smith.edu/libraries/libs/ssc/vof/transcripts/Lerner.pdf.

13. Francisca de Hahn, "Continuing Cold War Paradigms in Western Historiography of Transnational Women's Organisations: The Case of the Women's International Democratic Federation (WIDF)," *Women's History Review* 19, no. 4 (September 2010): 548.

14. Celia Donert, "Women's Rights in Cold War Europe: Disentangling Feminist Histories," *Past & Present* 218 (2013): 184.

15. Lerner, *Fireweed*, 264–69.

16. Helen Laville, *Cold War Women: The International Activities of American Women's Organisations* (Manchester: Manchester University Press, 2002), 7.

17. Amy Swerdlow, "The Congress of American Women: Left-Feminist Peace Politics in the Cold War," in *U.S. History as Women's History: New Feminist Essay*, ed. Linda K. Kerber, Alice Kessler-Harris, and Kathryn Kish Sklar (Chapel Hill: University of North Carolina Press, 1995), 302.

18. Quoted in Swerdlow, 303.

19. *American Women in Pictures: Souvenir Journal* (New York: Congress of American Women, 1949), 4.

20. Swerdlow, "The Congress of American Women," 306.

21. Lerner, *Fireweed*, 257.

22. The best account of the CAW's demise is Weigand, *Red Feminism*, 47–64.

23. Gerda Lerner, "A Life of Learning," *American Council of Learned Societies Occasional Papers* 60 (2006): 18.

24. Lerner, *Fireweed*, 36.

25. Lerner, 11.

26. Lerner, 55.

27. Lerner, 190.

28. For an overview of the LAW's activities that emphasizes its attempts to fuse a range of political viewpoints in the service of a left-wing American culture, see Judy Kutulas, "Becoming 'More Liberal': The League of American Writers, the Communist Party, and the Literary People's Front," *Journal of American Culture* 13, no. 1 (Spring 1990): 71–80.

29. Lerner, *Fireweed*, 231.

30. Lerner, 215. Two examples of Lerner's early short stories, written while she still used the surname of her first husband, are Gerda Jensen, "Prisoners," *The Clipper!* 2 (September 1941): 19–22; and Gerda Jensen, "The Russian Campaign," *Story* 23, no. 103 (September–October 1943): 59–66.

31. This analysis builds on that provided in Marjorie Lamberti, "Blazing New Paths in Historiography: 'Refugee Effect' and American Experience in the Professional Trajectory of Gerda Lerner," in *The Second Generation: Émigrés from Nazi Germany as Historians*, ed. Andreas W. Daum, Hartmut Lehmann, and James J. Sheehan (New York: Berghahn Books, 2016), 249–50.

32. Joyce Antler, *The Journey Home: Jewish Women and the American Century* (New York: Free Press, 1997), 290–91.

33. Gerda Lerner and Eve Merriam, *Singing of Women: A Dramatic Review* (New York: New York Council of the Arts, 1951), 1, GLP, MC498, box 40, folder 1.

34. Lerner, interview by Nancy MacLean, 63.

35. Lerner and Merriam, *Singing of Women*, 13.

36. Lerner and Merriam, 13.

37. Lerner and Merriam, 16–17.

38. Betty Feldman, "*Singing of Women*: Important Achievement in People's Theater," *Daily Worker*, April 5, 1951, 11.

39. An account of the founding of Associated Authors is provided in Lerner, *Fireweed*, 343–45.

40. Lillian Smith, "Out of New Creative Tensions Will Come Peace," in *The Winner Names the Age: A Collection of Writings by Lillian Smith*, ed. Michelle Cliff (New York: W. W. Norton, 1978), 129. The piece was originally published in *Saturday Review*, December 24, 1961.

41. Lillian Smith to Gerda Lerner, January 22, 1961, in *A Lillian Smith Reader*, ed. Margaret Rose Gladney and Lisa Hodgens (Athens: University of Georgia Press, 2016), 265–66.

42. Lerner, *Fireweed*, 366.

43. Lerner, "A Life of Learning," 10.

44. Rosalind Rosenberg, "Women in the Humanities: Taking Their Place," in *The Humanities and the Dynamics of Inclusion since World War II*, ed. David A. Hollinger (Baltimore: Johns Hopkins University Press, 2006), 248–49.

45. In the case of Franklin, these debts are discussed in more detail in chapter 3. In Lerner's case, it is clear that she drew on the work of women writers, archivists, and librarians who developed a range of resources for the study of American women's history between the 1880s and the 1940s. One of these was Mary Ritter Beard, whose influence on Lerner is discussed in later in this chapter. For more on this context, see Julie Des Jardins, *Women and the Historical Enterprise in America: Gender, Race, and the Politics of Memory, 1880–1945* (Chapel Hill: University of North Carolina Press, 2003).

46. Gerda Lerner to Carl Degler, November 22, 1966, GLP, MC498, box 3, folder 8.

47. Lerner, interview by Nancy MacLean, 72–73.

48. Gerda Lerner, "The Grimké Sisters and the Struggle against Race Prejudice," *Journal of Negro History* 48, no. 4 (October 1963): 291.

49. Gerda Lerner, "The Lady and the Mill Girl: Changes in the Status of Women in the Age of Jackson," *American Studies* 10, no. 1 (Spring 1969): 11.

50. Gerda Lerner, "Women's Rights and American Feminism," *American Scholar* 40, no. 2 (Spring 1971): 236.

51. Lerner, 243–44.

52. Lerner, 248.

53. Kathryn Kish Sklar, "For the Future of Women's Past," *Journal of Women's History* 26, no. 1 (Spring 2014): 14.

54. On Thompson, see Stephen Roberts, "Memories of Dottie: Dorothy Thompson (1923–2011)," *Labour History Review* 76, no. 2 (August 2011): 161–68. On Perrot, see Denise Z. Davidson, "Michelle Perrot (1928–)," in *French Historians, 1900–2000: New Historical Writing in Twentieth-Century France*, ed. Philip Daileader and Philip Whalen (Oxford: Blackwell, 2010), 475–85.

55. Gerda Lerner to Carl Degler, May 15, 1967, GLP, MC498, box 3, folder 8.

56. Gerda Lerner, *The Woman in American History* (Menlo Park, CA: Addison-Wesley, 1971), 6.

57. Lerner, 189–90.

58. On the New Left and the politics of inequality in an age of abundance, see Howard Brick, *Transcending Capitalism: Visions of a New Society in Modern American Thought* (Ithaca, NY: Cornell University Press, 2006), 186–218. On second-wave feminism and welfare rights, see Premilla Nadasen, *Welfare Warriors: The Welfare Rights Movement in the United States* (New York: Routledge, 2005); Annalise Orleck, *Storming Caesars Palace: How Black Mothers Fought Their Own War on Poverty* (Boston: Beacon Press, 2006); Marisa Chappell, *The War on Welfare: Family, Poverty, and Politics in Modern America* (Philadelphia: University of Pennsylvania Press, 2009), 21–64.

59. Gerda Lerner to Robert Keller, November 18, 1967, GLP, MC498, box 23, folder 2.

60. Lerner to Keller, November 18, 1967.

61. Gerda Lerner to Robert Keller, May 28, 1970, GLP, MC498, box 23, folder 2.

62. Alice E. Ginsberg, "Triumphs, Controversies, and Change: Women's Studies, 1970s to the Twenty-First Century," in *The Evolution of American Women's Studies: Reflections on Triumphs, Controversies, and Change* (New York: Palgrave Macmillan, 2008), 10–15.

63. Ellen Messer-Davidow, *Disciplining Feminism: From Social Activism to Academic Discourse* (Durham, NC: Duke University Press, 2002), 207.

64. Lerner, "A Life of Learning," 14–15.

65. Gerda Lerner to Larry Wilson, January 3, 1972, GLP, MC498, box 23, folder 2.

66. Gerda Lerner to John Scram, February 5, 1974, GLP, MC498 box 23 folder 3.

67. Warren Stone to Gerda Lerner, November 21, 1974, GLP, MC498, box 23, folder 3.

68. June Arnold, "Feminist Presses and Feminist Politics," *Quest* 3, no. 1 (Summer 1976): 22.

69. Arnold, 19.

70. Jennifer Gilley, "Feminist Publishing/Publishing Feminism: Experimentation in Second-Wave Book Publishing," in *This Book Is an Action: Feminist Print Culture and Activist Aesthetic*, ed. Jaime Harker and Cecilia Konchar Farr (Urbana: University of Illinois Press, 2016), 23–24.

71. All twenty-four rejection letters, which are dated between 1963 and 1966, have been diligently archived in GLP, MC498, box 22, folder 1. The variety of ways in which the editors Lerner approached found to justify their rejection of her manuscript make for revealing reading and demonstrate the deep uncertainty trade publishers had about publishing a book on women's history even as late as the mid-1960s.

72. Gerda Lerner, "Placing Women in History: Definitions and Challenges," *Feminist Studies* 3, nos. 1/2 (Autumn 1975): 8.

73. Gerda Lerner, "The Majority Finds Its Past," *Current History* 70, no. 416 (May 1976): 231.

74. Betty Anne Clarke to Sheldon Meyer, March 22, 1978, GLP, MC498 box 20, folder 1. Clarke was Lerner's literary agent at the time.

75. Sheldon Meyer to Gerda Lerner, December 5, 1979, GLP, MC498, box 20, folder 1.

76. Gerda Lerner to Sheldon Meyer, July 19, 1983, GLP, MC498, box 20, folder 1.

77. Angus Phillips, "Trade Publishing," in *The History of Oxford University Press*, vol. 4: *1970 to 2004*, ed. Keith Robbins (Oxford: Oxford University Press, 2017), 340.

78. Phillips, 333.

79. These details of the history of the OUP office in New York are drawn from Thorin Tritter, "New York," in *The History of Oxford University Press*, ed. Robbins, 4:545–47.

80. "About Gerda Lerner," OUP publicity document, c. 1993, GLP, MC498, box 19, folder 7.

81. Gerda Lerner to Sheldon Meyer, January 27, 1985, GLP, MC498, box 20, folder 1.

82. William E. Leuchtenberg, preface to *American Places: Encounters with History, a Celebration of Sheldon Meyer* (New York: Oxford University Press), x.

83. Jerrold Cooper to Sheldon Meyer, January 11, 1985, GLP, MC498, box 19, folder 12.

84. Gerda Lerner to Jerrold Cooper, February 8, 1985, GLP, MC498, box 19, folder 12.

85. Sheldon Meyer to Gerda Lerner, c. early 1984, GLP, MC498, box 19, folder 16.

86. Sheldon Meyer to Edith Margolis, November 3, 1966, GLP, MC498, box 22, folder 1.

87. Gerda Lerner to Sheldon Meyer, March 27, 1992, GLP, MC498, box 19, folder 3.

88. Lerner, *The Creation of Patriarchy*, 3.

89. Lerner, 19.

90. Betty Friedan, *The Feminine Mystique* (1963; repr., London: Penguin, 2010), 98.

91. Kate Millett, *Sexual Politics* (1970; repr., Urbana: University of Illinois Press, 2000), 178.

92. Nathan G. Hale Jr., *The Rise and Crisis of Psychoanalysis in the United States: Freud and the Americans, 1917–1985* (New York: Oxford University Press, 1995), 9, 345–46. See also Eli Zaretsky, *Political Freud: A History* (New York: Columbia University Press, 2015), 170–78.

93. Glenn Collins, "Patriarchy: Is It Invention or Inevitable?" *New York Times Style*, April 28, 1986, GLP, MC498, box 20, folder 6.

94. Friedrich Engels, *The Origin of the Family, Private Property and the State* (1884; repr., London: Penguin, 2010), 95, 199.

95. Lerner, *The Creation of Patriarchy*, 22–24.

96. Judith Finlayson, "The Birth of Sexual Slavery," *Toronto Globe & Mail*, July 11, 1986, GLP, MC769, box F+D.3v; Julia Adams, "Engels Reconsidered: New Look at Patriarchal Origins," *Guardian Book Supplement*, Fall 1986, GLP, MC769, box F+D.3v.

97. Lerner, interview by Nancy MacLean, 77.

98. Mary R. Beard, *Woman as Force in History: A Study in Traditions and Realities* (New York: Macmillan, 1946), 11.

99. Beard, 283.

100. Lerner, *The Creation of Feminist Consciousness*, 15.

101. Catharine R. Stimpson, "Gerda Lerner on the Future of Our Past," *Ms.*, September 1981, 92.

102. Lerner, *The Creation of Feminist Consciousness*, 160.

103. Lerner, 167.

104. Lerner, 198.

105. Ian Barber, "Patriarchy and the Control of Womanhood," *Sunstone*, March 1987, 36.

106. William A. Johnson, review of *The Creation of Patriarchy* by Gerda Lerner, *Christian Century*, November 5, 1986, 983.

107. Lerner, *The Creation of Feminist Consciousness*, 12.

108. For feminist Bible criticism, see Lerner, 138–66; for women's history, see 247–73.

109. Lerner, 268, 261.

110. Lerner, 283.

111. John Patrick Hunter, "UW Prof Writes, Speaks Out for Women," *Capitol Times*, April 15, 1993, GLP, MC498, box 19, folder 8.

112. Lerner, *The Creation of Feminist Consciousness*, 8.

113. "Books for Vacation Reading," *New York Times Book Review*, June 6, 1993, 34.

114. "For the Sake of Humanity, Patriarchy Is Dead," *Milwaukee Journal Sentinel*, June 10, 1993, GLP, MC769, box 37, folder 17.

115. Mary McLaughlin, "In Search of a Usable Past," *Women's Review of Books*, October 1993, 20.

116. Louise Hamilton to Gerda Lerner, August 17, 1986; and Patricia Robinson to Gerda Lerner, March 28, 1987, GLP, MC498, box 20, folder 2.

117. Gabriella Bueno to Gerda Lerner, March 6, 1992, GLP, MC498, box 20, folder 2.

118. Alison Andron to Gerda Lerner, May 27, 1994, GLP, MC498, box 19, folder 5.

119. Lynne Pearce, *Feminism and the Politics of Reading* (London: Arnold, 1997), 2–7.

120. Fay Honey Knopp to Gerda Lerner, May 16, 1986, GLP, MC498, box 20, folder 2.

121. Feminist Issue Group to Gerda Lerner, August 12, 1994, GLP, MC498, box 19, folder 5.

122. Daphne Spain, *Constructive Feminism: Women's Spaces and Women's Rights in the American City* (Ithaca, NY: Cornell University Press, 2016), 88.

123. Nora Frenkiel, "Five Rooms of Their Own: Feminist Community Makes Bookstore a Part of Themselves," *Baltimore Sun*, August 20, 1987.

124. "University Press Ordering," *Feminist Bookstore News*, January–February 1987, 35.

125. "From the University Presses," *Feminist Bookstore News*, March–April 1993, 101.

126. Steven Feierman to Gerda Lerner, December 10, 1991, GLP, MC498, box 19, folder 6.

127. Jean Bethke Elshtain, "In the Grand Manner," *Women's Review of Books*, January 1987, 13.

128. Joan W. Scott, "Gender: A Useful Category of Historical Analysis," *American Historical Review* 91, no. 5 (December 1986): 1054.

129. Scott, 1075.

130. Scott, 1055.

131. Lerner, *The Creation of Patriarchy*, 77.

132. Lerner, 80.

133. Lerner, 100.

134. Lerner, *The Creation of Feminist Consciousness*, 16.

135. Gerda Lerner, "Black and White Women in Interaction and Confrontation," *Prospects* 2 (October 1977): 207.

136. Martha Irvine, "Consciousness Raising," *Minnesota Women's Press*, March 24, 1993, 11.

137. Kristin Hogan, *The Feminist Bookstore Movement: Lesbian Antiracism and Feminist Accountability* (Durham, NC: Duke University Press, 2016), 109.

138. For an important overview of these divisions, see Benita Roth, *Separate Roads to Feminism: Black, Chicana, and White Feminist Movements in America's Second Wave* (New York: Cambridge University Press, 2004).

139. Lerner, interview by Nancy MacLean, 84.

140. Lerner, interview by Nancy MacLean, 85–86.

141. Judith Butler, *Gender Trouble: Feminism and the Subversion of Identity* (1990; repr., New York: Routledge, 2002), 181.

142. For an early report on how this process impacted women's bookstores, see Judith Rosen, "Women's Bookstores: Surviving in a Chain-Gang Retail Climate," *Publishers Weekly*, April 28, 1997, 23–25.

143. For a compelling overview of these processes, see Schiffren, *The Business of Books*.

Conclusion

1. For a critical overview of research funding in UK higher education, see Roger Brown and Helen Carasso, *Everything for Sale? The Marketisation of UK Higher Education* (London: Routledge, 2013), 41–70.

2. Jessica Pressman, *Bookishness: Loving Books in a Digital Age* (New York: Columbia University Press, 2020).

3. In January 2021, the AHA reported that amid the COVID-19 pandemic, the historical profession was seeing "historically low levels of academic hiring." See Dylan Ruediger, "The 2021 AHA Jobs Report," *Perspectives on History*, January 20, 2021, https://www.historians.org/ahajobsreport2021.

4. For the original publication of the project, see Nikole Hannah-Jones et al., "The 1619 Project," *New York Times Magazine*, August 18, 2019, 1–93. More recently, the project has been published as a book: Nikole Hannah-Jones, *The 1619 Project: A New Origin Story* (New York: One World, 2021). For a useful scholarly overview of the controversies within the historical profession that the project first met, see Alex Lichtenstein, "1619 and All That," *American Historical Review* 125, no. 1 (February 2020): xv–xxi. The conservative backlash against the project has been significant. For a useful journalistic overview, see Jelani Cobb, "The Republican Party, Racial Hypocrisy, and the 1619 Project," *New Yorker*, May 29, 2021, https://www.newyorker.com/news/daily-comment/the-republican-party-racial-hypocrisy-and-the-1619-project.

5. Jill Lepore, "A New Americanism," *Foreign Affairs* 98, no. 2 (March/April 2019): 11.

6. Jill Lepore quoted in Evan Goldstein, "The Academy Is Largely Itself Responsible for Its Own Peril," *Chronicle of Higher Education*, November 13, 2018.

7. Jill Lepore, *These Truths: A History of the United States* (New York: W. W. Norton, 2018), xix.

8. Goldstein, "The Academy Is Largely Itself Responsible for Its Own Peril."

9. Lepore, *These Truths*, 788.

10. Goldstein, "The Academy Is Largely Itself Responsible for Its Own Peril."

11. Reinhold Niebuhr quoted in Lepore, *These Truths*, 783.

12. Lepore, *These Truths*, 788.

13. Jennifer Szalai, "A Reckoning for the Republic," *New York Times*, September 12, 2018; H. W. Brands, "How Did America Get Here?" *Washington Post*, September 21, 2018.

14. Richard White, "New Yorker Nation," *Reviews in American History* 47, no. 2 (June 2019): 165–67.

15. For critiques of the book from the perspective of Indigenous history, see Christine DeLucia, "The Vanishing Indians of *These Truths*," *Los Angeles Review of Books*, January 10, 2019, https://lareviewofbooks.org/article/the-vanishing-indians-of-these-truths/; and Ned Blackhawk, "The Iron Cage of Erasure: American Indian Sovereignty in Jill Lepore's *These Truths*," *American Historical Review* 125, no. 5 (December 2020): 1752–63. From the Latinx history perspective, see Matt Garcia, "Lepore's America, 'Our America'?" *American Historical Review* 125, no. 5 (December 2020): 1768–72; and Paul Ortiz, "A Civics Primer for American History," *American Historical Review* 125, no. 5 (December 2020): 1773–77.

16. Daniel Immerwahr, "The Center Does Not Hold," *The Nation*, November 11, 2019, https://www.thenation.com/article/archive/jill-lepore-these-truths-this-america-review/. Immerwahr has recently published his own popular national history that builds on transnational perspectives to tell the story of US empire. See Daniel Immerwahr, *How to Hide an Empire: A History of the Greater United States* (New York: Picador, 2019).

17. Keisha Blain and Ibram X. Kendi, "How to Avoid a Post-Scholar America," *Chronicle of Higher Education*, June 18, 2017.

18. Ibram X. Kendi, *Stamped from the Beginning: The Definitive History of Racist Ideas in America* (New York: Nation Books, 2016), 1.

19. Kendi, 11.

20. Kendi, 510.

21. Kendi, 352–53.

22. See Ibram X. Kendi, *Antiracist Baby* (New York: Penguin Random House, 2020); "Netflix to Animate Ibram X. Kendi's Antiracist Baby," *Animation Xpress*, January 18, 2021, https://www.animationxpress.com/animation/netflix-to-animate-ibram-x-kendis-antiracist-baby/.

23. Carlos Lozada, "The Racism of Good Intention," *Washington Post*, April 17, 2016.

24. For a generally positive account of *Stamped from the Beginning* in an academic journal, see Matthew Frye Jacobson, review of *Stamped from the Beginning*, by Ibram X. Kendi, *Journal of American History* 104, no. 1 (June 2017): 165–66. For a significantly more critical review, see Richard King, review of *Stamped from the Beginning*, by Ibram X. Kendi, *Reviews in History* 2165 (September 2017), https://reviews.history.ac.uk/review/2165.

25. Rich Lowry, "The Incredible Lightness of Ibram X. Kendi's 'Anti-Racism,'" *NR Plus*, July 25, 2021, https://www.nationalreview.com/2021/07/the-incredible-lightness-of-ibram-x-kendis-anti-racism/.

26. Christopher Caldwell, "Ibram X. Kendi, Prophet of Anti-Racism," *National Review*, August 10, 2020, 24.

Index

Aaron, Daniel, 34
academic publishing, 147
Accuracy in Academia (AIA), 126
Accuracy in Media (AIM), 126
activist-historians, 170
activist readers, 3, 10, 74, 78, 90, 94, 101–2, 114, 134, 161, 165, 172
Adams, Abigail, 139, 155
Adams, Herbert Baxter, 6
Adams, John Truslow, 6; American Dream, 34; *The Epic of America*, 34
Addison-Wesley, 143–46, 150
Africa, 81, 84, 96, 101
African American history, 2, 83, 91, 93, 134; Amistad slave revolt, 90; ancient civilizations, 95; Black diaspora, 84, 92; Egyptian and Ethiopian culture, 95–96; historical writing, 80–82
African Americans, 4, 79–83, 86, 88, 97, 108–9; Afrocentrism, 96, 101; Black Arts movement, 91; Black cultural nationalism, 89, 94, 101; Black diaspora, 84, 92; Black freedom struggle, 38, 65, 78, 89, 99, 102–3, 120; Black nationalism, 70; on college campuses, expansion of, 91; cultural identity, 91; cultural identity, and jazz music, 98; double consciousness of, 53; "names controversy," 99; "Negro," linked with slavery, 99; protest of, as "inherently American," 111; racial individualism, 87. *See also* Black intellectuals; Black Power movement
African American studies, 78, 94–95, 101; Black cultural nationalism, 91–92, 99
age of fracture, 10–11
Age of Jackson, The (Schlesinger), 24, 35
Age of Reform, The (Hofstadter), 44
Agnew, Spiro, 72
Alexander, Sally, 143

Alfred A. Knopf, 16, 25, 28, 30, 33–34, 41, 61–62, 77–78, 86–88, 103, 113–15, 119, 148–49, 200n42; Knopf Fellowship, 29; race thinking, influence by, 85; racial liberalism, espousal of, 85; Vintage Books, 32, 42
Alperovitz, Gar, 122–23
Amazon Bookstore, 157
America at 1750: A Social Portrait (Hofstadter), 41
American Century, 7
American Dilemma, An (Myrdal), 85
American Historical Association (AHA), 5–6, 40, 44, 132, 208n3
American Indian Movement, 118
American Judaism (Glazer), 54
American Left, 4, 18, 20
American Negro Slave Revolts (Aptheker), 120
American Political Tradition and the Men Who Made It, The (Hofstadter), 15, 17, 19–20, 24–25, 27–29, 37, 41–42, 45, 48–49, 60, 73, 109, 167; accessibility of, 34; American democracy, discussion of, 21–22; commissioning of, 16; critique of, 39–40; general readers, 55; individualism, critique of, 38; irony and tragedy, themes of, 23; paperback revolution, effect on, 32; political critique, as form of, 38; as popular history, 16, 23, 33–35; promotion of, 30–31; prose style, praise of, 26; reviews of, 34–36, 38; sales of, 32
American Revolution, 69, 129–30
Americans, The (Boorstin), 52, 55, 67; audience of, and timeliness, 57; Bancroft Prize, 64; as celebratory, 45, 70; foundations of, 54; "Getting There First," 62; New Left, criticism of, 70; popularity of, 66; praise for, 69; Relm Foundation award, 56; themes of, 62; as three-volume trilogy, 45, 60, 66, 68, 71–73; volume 1, 50, 64; volume 2, 58, 60–62; volume 3, 58, 60, 70